AURORA'S
EAST-WEST
FOOTBALL RIVALRY

CONTENTS

ACKNOWLEDGEMENTS

S o many people helped make this book a reality—it's hard to know whom to thank first.

I'll start with Randy Konstans, former West Aurora athletic director, who gave me the idea for this book fifteen years ago. Sorry I took so long. Thanks, too, to my neighbor Neal Ormond, the fifty-year "Voice of the Blackhawks," who could have written much of this content from memory and was always willing to share his recollections. Thanks to my friends at the Aurora Historical Society, John Jaros and Jennifer Putzier, and to Matt Hanley, East Aurora's assistant director of community relations and fellow History Press author, who helped in any way they could, whenever I asked. Thanks to east-siders Steve "Benny" Kenyon and Bob Burnell for introducing me to the guys at the East Aurora Football Old-Timers Association, who were all so willing to reminisce. What an amazing organization. Gracias to Robert Winder and the staff at the Aurora Public Library, where I've spent countless hours with the microfilm readers over these past few years. Special thanks go to Batavia Public Library director and fellow high school football enthusiast George H. Scheetz for reading my drafts and gently correcting my writing. To the good folks at The History Press who took a chance on an unproven author, and to everyone who offered the stories and pictures that went into this book, please accept my heartfelt gratitude. I've made so many new friends.

Of course, I have to thank my family, including my parents, Gil and Mary, and my son Adam, the former Blackhawk who listened while I regaled him with stories—whether he wanted to or not. And last but not least, thanks to my wife, Janet, for supporting me while I took the "career break" I needed to finish this project. I love you all.

CHAPTER 1

THE *BEACON*

The *Aurora Beacon* of Aurora, Illinois, was established as a weekly paper in 1846 and, in one form or another, has been diligently chronicling the city's business, social and sporting events ever since. By the time boys from Aurora's two rival high schools first began meeting at Hurd's Island to play football, the paper had evolved into the *Aurora Daily Beacon*, one of a handful of papers covering the town. The *Beacon*'s coverage of the first East-West game in 1893 may have consisted of just a few lines buried in the middle of the issue, but the paper's editors must have realized they were on to something because the next autumn, the *Beacon* began dutifully covering both local school teams. Within a few years, the *Beacon* became the first Midwest paper outside of Chicago to regularly devote a full section to sports.

Although East and West did not schedule a game in 1894, the *Beacon* covered the activities of both teams throughout the football season, published several articles lobbying for a Thanksgiving Day game and provided readers with daily reports describing the negotiations between the schools that ultimately broke down, leading both East and West to invite teams from Cook County to celebrate Thanksgiving in Aurora. When the two schools agreed to meet on Thanksgiving in 1895, the *Beacon* offered multiple pre-game reports followed by an in-depth description of the game itself, beginning an annual tradition that evolved to include game-week reports of the comings and goings of both teams, ticket sale announcements, directions to the field, weather and field condition reports, team photos, rosters, season recaps and series summaries before the game, with a detailed play-by-play account of the action published the following day. The attention given by the *Beacon* to East-West games represented an early, localized version of a media-created event, not unlike the hype that surrounds today's Super Bowl.

Over time, Aurora's other newspapers either went out of business or merged with one another until the *Beacon* merged with the *Aurora Daily News* in 1912 to become the city's last daily paper, the *Aurora Beacon-News*. The paper's long-standing commitment to local high school sports coverage, which continues in 2014, has left a comprehensive account of Aurora's East-West football rivalry. With few exceptions, the results and specifics of games referenced in this book were taken from *Beacon* reports, although it was occasionally necessary to fill in gaps or confirm details with information from other sources.

CHAPTER 2

A RIVALRY IS BORN

In 1834, twenty-five-year-old Joseph McCarty, along with his apprentice Jeffry Beardslee and guide Robert Faracre, were paddling their canoe along Illinois' Fox River in search of a location suitable for a sawmill when they arrived at the Pottowatomie village of Chief Waubonsie, in what is now the city of Aurora, Illinois. The party stopped to explore the surroundings, and after finding the area to his liking, McCarty staked a 360-acre claim to a heavily wooded area on the east side of the river, about a mile south of the village, near the present-day intersection of New York and Broadway Streets in downtown Aurora. McCarty also staked a second 400-acre claim to the south for his brother, Samuel, who arrived in November of the same year. During that first year, the McCartys built a cabin, sawmill and dam and secured uninterrupted water rights by purchasing an additional 100 acres on the west side of the river. Over the next few years, the brothers opened a gristmill next to the original sawmill and were joined by about forty settlers. The village had no official name, but locals called it McCarty Mills.

Shortly after settling in, the McCartys sold their land on the river's west side to brothers Zaphna and Theodore Lake, founders of West Aurora, and laid out a plan for a village on their east-side property. When local citizens petitioned the federal government to establish a post office in the area in 1837, a town name was needed, and the McCarty clan chose "Aurora."

Unfortunately, Joseph McCarty left the area for health reasons in 1838 and died the following year, but Samuel stayed to help settle the town and remained until his death in 1899. By the end of 1838, the area had its post office, as well as a bridge spanning the river, sawmills on either side, a gristmill, a hotel and about one hundred residents. The island situated between the east and west villages was owned by Joseph Stolp, who established Aurora Woolen Mills there in about 1837. The east bank's village of Aurora incorporated in 1845, and the smaller West Aurora followed suit nine years later. Meanwhile, by 1849, Stolp had significantly expanded Aurora Woolen Mills into the area's first significant industry.

Aurora established the state's first free public school district (now East Aurora District 131) in 1851. Not to be outdone, West Aurora established its own district (now West Aurora District 129) one year later, and the need for separate districts has been open to discussion ever since. The 1857 agreement to unite the two villages into the City of Aurora was approved only after the draft of the city charter was amended to include a provision requiring that city hall be built on Stolp Island, which was considered neutral territory. Over the years, this attitude influenced decisions to build most public buildings—including city hall, the library, the post office and GAR the building—on Stolp Island. For many years, the four east–west streets that traversed the river changed names at Stolp Avenue, which marked both the center of the island and the figurative center of town. It was there that the east side's New York, Main, Fox and Benton Streets became Walnut, Galena, Downer and Holbrook Streets as they crossed the island and headed west. Although terribly confusing for travelers, 108 years passed before the street names were unified in 1965.

Indeed, the seeds of competition between Aurora's east and west sides had been sown and were well established long before boys began competing on ball fields. In retrospect, it seems only natural that high school sports would provide a vessel for locals to channel their inherent geography-based antagonism. The rivalry's intensity, fueled primarily by adults, was so palpable from the very beginning that Daniel Martin Kagay, a 1898 East graduate who played football for the Red and Black, drew on his experiences in writing his 1909 novel, *East Side Boys*, which is loosely based on life as an Aurora teenager around 1900.

Since the very beginning, the East-West rivalry has featured arguments, fisticuffs, accusations, shenanigans and traditions. Disagreements in two of the series' first four years caused games to be cancelled. It was not uncommon for hooligans to decorate their wagons with the colors of their schools and parade around the other side of town looking for a fight. A favorite activity at games on Hurd's Island was to throw snowballs at opponents' wagons in an effort to spook the horses into the Fox River. A boy who sought the company of a girl from the other side of the river did so at the risk of physical harm. Even visitors who innocently wore the colors of one school or the other were threatened with harm if they were caught downtown or, God forbid, on the wrong side of the river during East-West week. Post-game fights, which more often than not involved more adults than students, were a tradition until school administrators began promoting sportsmanship while the police cracked down on the off-field violence. In 1906, people were elated that "only" three fights were reported.

Despite the off-field violence, East-West week was a festive time in town, especially after 1902, the year the Thanksgiving game became a firmly entrenched tradition. Shopkeepers decorated their windows in support of their favorite school. People camped out overnight to purchase tickets. Ticket scalpers and bookies did a brisk business. On the Wednesday night before the big game, both schools organized pep rallies featuring cheers led by coaches, team captains and returning alumni. The east side's Rally Night was centered on a huge bonfire, and in the early days, it wasn't uncommon for ne'er-do-wells to steal an outhouse or two from the west side for use as firewood. Pranks like these led police to close the bridges that spanned the Fox River each night in an attempt to keep fans separated during Thanksgiving week. According to legend, that did not prevent a group of mischievous and enterprising east-siders from walking across a shallow section of river with an outhouse that was deposited next to the flagpole at old West High.

Although somewhat tamer, Thanksgiving week in Aurora during the 1940s and '50s continued to be an odd combination of festivities and fisticuffs. In addition to window decorations, local merchants demonstrated their school allegiance by purchasing ads of encouragement that appeared in the *Beacon*. To curtail fighting, players were sent into the local grade schools and junior high schools to encourage younger students to behave—and to ask them to tell their parents to stay home. Administrators asked student leaders to help keep their classmates on their own side of the river.

Of course, these efforts to prevent hostilities were only marginally effective. East-West weeks during the '40s and '50s often featured rumbles between groups of students from both sides of town who met on neutral Stolp Island in the center of the city. One year, just as police arrived to break up a fight, someone threw a fully dressed dummy off a bridge and into the Fox River. When officers raced down to the water to rescue the "victim," the fight continued on the bridge above. Over time, the violence turned to mere mischief involving toilet-papering school grounds or hanging derogatory signs from flagpoles. Once, a prankster painted "Beat East" (or was it West?)

on the soles of coach John Wrenn's shoes, which went unobserved until he knelt at the altar during his wedding ceremony.

Through it all, regardless of how the season went, the on-field action during an East-West game was always intense, and the game itself took on a special meaning, especially for the participants. This book is written for past and future participants.

CHAPTER 3

1893–1915: AURORA FOOTBALL'S FORMATIVE YEARS

The evolution of high school football in the United States closely parallels and sometimes overlaps the development of college football. The earliest primitive games played by teams representing colleges, preparatory schools and high schools took place in the Northeast between the mid-1860s and about 1880. Later in the nineteenth century, high schools tended to follow the lead of college football pioneers like Walter Camp, Amos Alonzo Stagg and John Heisman, who were working to refine and standardize rules as the high school game spread from New England and New York south along the Atlantic seaboard, to the Midwest and beyond.

Although few details about the earliest days of prep football in Illinois are known, the beginnings can be traced to Chicago and its nearby suburbs, where a handful of schools began to create football clubs in the late 1870s. The game's violent nature, which caused frequent injuries and even occasional deaths, made it controversial among educators and parents from the start, and growth to regions beyond Cook County took place gradually from the late 1880s to the 1890s.

Football of the 1890s was far different from the game we know today. To begin with, the game was commonly referred to as "foot ball," not football. Officially, an 1890s football field measured 110 yards from goal line to goal line, as opposed to the 100-yard gridiron we know today. Unofficially, high schools at that time often played on unkempt grounds roughly laid out to fit the space available. Goalposts were located directly on the goal line.

Games were not played in standard twelve-minute quarters but rather in two equal halves of varying lengths determined in advance by the participants. Ideally, two officials—one referee and one umpire—organized play and enforced the rules.

Players in the earliest days did not wear helmets or protective equipment, although light padding sewn into jerseys and quilted canvas or moleskin pants slowly appeared on the field. The football itself resembled a lopsided leather medicine ball filled with air, and it was difficult to throw—not that throwing mattered much; prior to 1906, forward passes were illegal. A first down was earned by gaining five yards (not ten) or, alternatively, retreating twenty yards. A set of downs consisted of three plays, not four.

Without benefit of the forward pass, offenses and defenses were bunched so tightly that advancing even five yards in three plays was a challenge. Skilled punters who could help control field position were invaluable. Goal kicks were "drop-kicked" through the goal by letting the ball fall from the hands and kicking it at the very instant it bounced off the ground; holders and tees would come later. A "touch-down" (advancing the ball over the goal line) in 1893 scored four points, and a goal (kick through the uprights) following a touch-down scored two points. Goals kicked from the field (known as a field goal today) scored five points. For example, a game that ended with a score of 6–5 most likely meant that the winning team scored one 4-point touch-down followed by one successfully kicked 2-point goal following the touch-down, while the losing team kicked a 5-point field goal. Being tackled behind one's own goal line was a safety, which scored two points for the defense.

Just as the game on the field was far different in the 1890s, so, too, was its organization. High school football clubs were typically formed by students, with a faculty member or other adult working in the background to schedule and organize practices, arrange for officials, serve as publicity agents, collect gate receipts and manage expenses. Coaches, if present at all, tended to work anonymously in the background, and in-game coaching was prohibited by rule. Team rosters were generally drawn from the school's student population, but occasionally alumni or other "ringers" found their way onto the field. Players supplied their own "uniforms." Leagues or conferences did not exist, except in Cook County.

Once assembled, clubs would issue challenges to other teams representing high schools, colleges, neighborhood athletic associations, small towns or even teams sponsored by businesses. Because clubs were few and far between, any organized team willing to accept a challenge was fair game. Of course, the challenge system was not always reliable, making scheduling a very fluid proposition. Games were often scheduled just a week or two in advance and were canceled just as quickly. Sometimes cancellations were due to transportation issues or weather. Other times injuries would leave a team too decimated to field an "eleven." Or a school might cancel a game simply because it received a more attractive challenge that offered a better chance of winning, larger gate receipts or greater prestige. Within just a few years, written contracts came into use, but teams still retained open dates late into the season so that the schools with the best records or reputations could square off with one another in a sort of unofficial round robin at season's end.

***

By 1890, Aurora was a growing railroad town of about twenty thousand. The city's two high schools, formally named East Aurora and West Aurora but generally known to locals as East High and West High, drew students from rural communities throughout the area. It was an urban community and the region's financial and transportation center.

The earliest documented game between students from East High and West High took place on October 8, 1887, when a game was organized to raise money for the Aurora City Hospital, which had begun operating in rented quarters a year earlier. The *Beacon* reported that nearly four hundred tickets were sold at $0.25 each, but far fewer actually witnessed the game. Although no score was reported, the east-siders were declared the victors, and both sides were commended for adding $100 to the hospital fund's coffers. In 1888, the new Aurora City Hospital facility, which would later change its name to Copley Hospital, opened on Lincoln Avenue on the city's east side.

Although boys from both sides of the Fox River were undoubtedly playing football before and after the 1887 game, it would be another six years before information about student-organized football clubs began to appear regularly in local newspapers. Thus, 1893 is widely recognized as the genesis of school-sanctioned football at both East Aurora and West Aurora, which places both schools among Illinois high schools' earliest football pioneers, especially beyond the borders of Cook County.

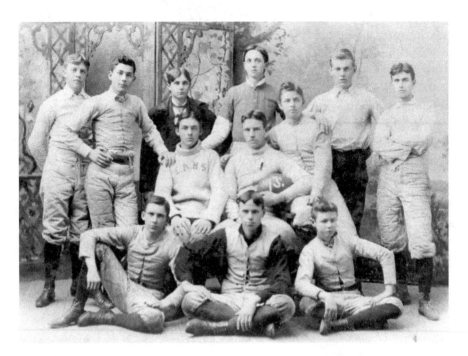

This 1893 photo of the East Aurora team is the earliest known Aurora high school team photo. *Courtesy of the Aurora Historical Society.*

West Aurora team photo, 1894. Professor A.V. Greenman, namesake of Aurora's Greenman School, stands at the far left. *Courtesy of the Aurora Historical Society.*

Howard Felver, *West Class of 1894*. Like many students at the time, Felver was a Batavian who attended West Aurora. Nothing is known about Felver's high school career, as West did not officially organize its first football club until his senior year, and detailed news coverage of that first season was scant. But based on his later accomplishments, it seems likely that Felver played on unofficial sandlot teams West students might have organized prior to 1893, as well as the inaugural East-West game. After graduating high school, Felver attended the University of Michigan, where he played quarterback for the great Blue and Maize teams of 1896 and 1897 that went 15-2-1 over two years. After graduating with a degree in engineering, Felver coached football at Rockford (Illinois) High School for two years before entering the business world as a structural engineer.

Local papers reported the results of just two games in 1893, as attempts by both schools to schedule additional games either fell through or went unreported and are lost to time. On November 11, East's boys traveled to Elgin to take on Elgin High School and returned with a resounding 20–12 victory. The following week, in a game likely intended to be a tune-up for a scheduled return game with Elgin that never materialized, the *Beacon* reported that the east-siders had whitewashed West Aurora 28–0 in a match played on Hurd's Island.

Hurd's Island, located in the middle of the Fox River and just south of Stolp Island and downtown Aurora, was the site of all East-West football games prior to 1920. That first game took place with no pre-game fanfare and just a four-line article reporting the results. It was an inauspicious beginning for what would quickly become the city's annual must-see event, but it was a beginning, nonetheless.

Newspaper reports from that early period suggest that east-side officials embraced football first and remained generally more supportive than West's administration throughout the 1890s. Although he later became "something of an enthusiast," West Aurora superintendent A.V. Greenman was initially opposed to football but concluded that "it was bound to come in" and grudgingly supported the west-side team. Thus, the east side's football program often seemed to be a year or two ahead of its west-side

1894: The Rivalry Is Off to a Rough Start

Although both East and West enjoyed greater success with scheduling in 1894 than they had in the inaugural 1893 season, crosstown bickering prevented the two schools from cultivating the seeds of rivalry that were unknowingly sowed one year earlier.

By the opening of the 1894–95 school year, football was big news on both sides of Aurora. The *Beacon* carried a weekly feature called "School Notes" or "Notes of the Schools," which was written by administrators from each high school to report on day-to-day activities, brag about academic and extracurricular accomplishments and, on occasion, publicly ridicule the football team from across the river. Indeed, the rivalry's competitive nature started quite early.

In mid-September, East announced that an early-season game with West had been scheduled for September 29, only to report a week later that the game had been cancelled, snidely adding, "From all appearances, the west side team is afraid of our team."

Then, after school on Friday, October 5, the clubs met at Hurd's Island for what West believed to be a friendly pre-season scrimmage. One can imagine the west-siders' surprise upon reading a brief article that appeared on page four of the following day's paper reporting that the two schools had played at Hurd's Island the evening before and that East had come away with a 6–0 victory. Imagine further West's outrage when East boasted of the victory in the weekly installment of "School Notes" the following Saturday. Throughout the rest of the season, West used every opportunity to remind people that the October 5 meeting was not an actual game, going out of its way to announce later in October that its "first regular game" was scheduled for October 24 and reminding people again in late November that the Red and Blue "had never been vanquished."

Despite this ongoing animosity, the two teams did agree to meet on Thanksgiving Day. However, East called the game off after learning that Archie Sylvester, the twenty-year-old star of the Aurora YMCA team, which had been challenging (and beating) high school and town teams throughout the fall, had enrolled at West and would, of course, be playing football. (At the time, players were eligible until their twenty-first birthday.)

This led to a series of letters to the *Beacon* from both sides of town debating Sylvester's eligibility. East questioned Archie's intentions, claiming it was not in the spirit of the game to enroll students for the sole purpose of playing in a football game and suggesting that the famous University of Chicago coach and football pioneer Amos Alonzo Stagg be asked to arbitrate the case. West countered that Archie was, in fact, a serious student who had every intention of completing his studies, that there were no rules governing the situation and that East's primary objection was that Sylvester had spurned East's offer in favor of West's. When the west-siders refused arbitration, East relented, suggesting Sylvester could play if East received two-thirds of the gate rather than the usual fifty-fifty split. West declined, declared victory by forfeit due to breach of contract and went about finding another opponent for Thanksgiving. East followed suit.

On Thanksgiving morning, West hosted a game with the Armour Institute of Chicago at the Driving Park, winning 10–6 in a well-played, friendly game. Following the game, both teams banqueted at a local restaurant, after which the visitors boarded a train to return home to Chicago.

That afternoon East played Evanston at Hurd's Island in an ugly game that was marred by violence and fighting and that saw players from both clubs sidelined by injuries. The game ended in dispute, with East claiming a 10–10 tie while the referee ruled that East's game tying 2-point kick had failed, leaving Evanston ahead 10–8. The arguments continued at the post-game banquet, which ended when police were summoned to break up the fight and escort the Evanston boys to the train station.

And what became of Archie Sylvester? No one knows whether he actually attended classes at West that semester, but he did go on to become a decorated hero of the Spanish-American War; a foreman for the Chicago, Burlington and Quincy Railroad; a member of the Aurora City Council; and a local army recruiting officer during World War I before moving to California, where he died in 1968.

East Aurora High School on Root Street, circa 1900. *Courtesy of the Aurora Historical Society.*

rivals. Whereas East's 1893 team initiated a concerted effort to field a team to compete against high schools from other communities, West's was seemingly hastily assembled for the sole purpose of scrimmaging East on that snowy November Saturday. From 1893 to 1895, East was first to form a team, first to consistently promote games in local papers, first to pose for a team picture, first to identify and promote Hurd's Island as a desirable football destination and to invite formidable opponents from Elgin and Chicago to play in Aurora and first to embrace the concept that a competitive football team could lift a school's spirit and enhance its reputation outside the city. Meanwhile, in these earliest years, West seemingly approached football with indifference, generally playing fewer games with less fanfare against inferior competition—and losing to East.

One exception was 1896, when, under the leadership of Walter Garrey, who played at the University of Chicago, West rose to East's level by moving its home games from Driving Park to the more desirable Hurd's Island and replacing small-fry opponents from St. Charles, Geneva and Joliet with a challenging nine-game schedule

1896: Did East and West Really Meet Twice?

Ever since the *Beacon* published its first historical summary of the East-West series on the eve of the 1906 Thanksgiving game, Aurorans have been secure in their knowledge that two East-West games were played in 1896. Early summaries said that East won the first game by a score of 6–0 and that the second game ended in a 10–10 tie. Later, both games were listed as ties. What really happened?

The year 1896 was the fourth in which both schools fielded football teams and the first year that West competed on East's level by playing a full schedule against established competition. Leading up to a Thanksgiving showdown, East lost only to Elgin, a team that West defeated. Meanwhile, West's only loss came at the hands of Hyde Park, which East had beaten. Local interest in the comings and goings on both sides of the river was high, as this marked the first time both schools simultaneously fielded outstanding teams.

The *Beacon*, recognizing an opportunity to boost circulation, made football news a regular front-page feature and delivered consistent coverage of both schools throughout the season. On the Friday after Thanksgiving, the paper's front page reported that East and West had played to a 10–10 tie on Hurd's Island the preceding day. The game marked the second time the schools met on Thanksgiving, and it was the first East-West match that East did not win. It was also the only East-West game reported by the *Beacon* in 1896.

In a season of such high interest and consistent newspaper coverage, it is difficult to accept that an East-West game went totally unreported at the time it allegedly happened, only to become part of the historical record ten years later and widely accepted as truth for more than one hundred years since.

The legend began on November 28, 1906, when the *Beacon*'s first historical recap of the East-West series listed two games in 1896. The accuracy of that first summary is certainly questionable, as no game was listed for 1893, a year in which a game was played, while East was credited with a 12–0 victory in 1894, a year in which no game was played.

In fact, the *Beacon*'s annual summaries did not include that inaugural 28–0 East victory of 1893 until 1917, while the reported score of the 1894 game vacillated between 12–0 and 10–4 before the game disappeared from the record in 1923. In the early years, the score of East's 1895 victory was reported as 10–4, 16–6 and 12–6 before the correct count of 12–0 became part of the official record. Even the mysterious second game of 1896 was originally shown as a 6–0 East victory, changed to a 0–0 tie (1909–20), changed back to a 6–0 East win in 1922 and finally accepted as a 0–0 tie. Regardless of which score was reported in after-the-fact series reviews, the fact remains that no report of a second game was published at the time the game allegedly took place.

It is possible the *Beacon* simply did not cover that second game. Given that coverage of both schools was very complete that year, and that readers' interest levels were very high, it seems unimaginable that a game would have gone unreported, which leaves room for speculation.

Perhaps an unofficial sandlot game organized by a group of students to settle the Thanksgiving Day tie somehow made its way into that first series summary. Or maybe East's 6–0 "victory" in the disputed 1894 pre-season scrimmage incorrectly worked its way into the first annual East-West summary and was later changed to a tie game.

It's unlikely that we will ever know the truth. However, in keeping with the sage advice of the fictitious newspaper reporter in the movie *The Man Who Shot Liberty Valance* ("When the legend becomes fact, print the legend."), the Aurora community maintains that East and West played two tie games in 1896.

that included early powerhouses from Elgin, Hyde Park, Oak Park and Amos Alonzo Stagg's University of Chicago Second Team. The 1896 Red and Blue lost only to Hyde Park and then posted six consecutive victories over formidable opponents before playing East to a 10–10 tie on Thanksgiving and, according to legend, to a second tie (0–0) at some other point in that season (see sidebar). Despite this outstanding success, West's teachers joyfully celebrated the end of the season, not for its glory but simply because it was over. By 1897, Coach Garrey had left town to continue his medical studies, and the Red and Blue fell back into a three-year period of indifference during which just a handful of

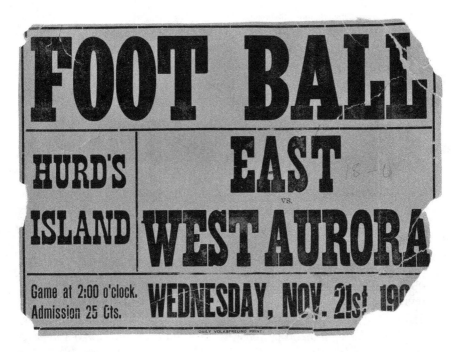

A placard promoting the East-West game played November 21, 1900. The date was moved up so the winner could accept challenges to play the state's other top teams vying for the "state championship." After disposing of a tough West squad, the Red and Black went on to beat Hyde Park and Urbana to claim the school's first mythical state championship. *Courtesy of the Aurora Historical Society.*

games against weak competition were played each year. The west side's apathy toward football became so strong that officials proposed that the two schools merge teams. When the east-siders ignored that suggestion, West disappointed the entire community by canceling the East-West game for 1897. It would be 1900 before West competed seriously again.

Meanwhile, from 1897 to 1901, East Aurora developed a reputation as an Illinois football powerhouse, amassing a five-year record of thirty-seven wins, six losses and six ties against competition that included the best schools from Cook County and throughout the state.

In 1897, the east-siders' only loss was by two points to Chicago's Austin in the season opener. Along the way, the Red and Black defeated two teams from Chicago's south side, including a 6–4 win over perennial powerhouse Englewood and a 60–0 annihilation of Calumet High School. The fact that the *Chicago Tribune* reported both games solidified East's reputation in Cook County.

Frank Slaker, *West Class of 1898.* Captain of West's undefeated 1897 team, Slaker went on to attend the University of Chicago, where he played two seasons at halfback under legendary Maroons coach Amos Alonzo Stagg. He was one of three all-Americans on Chicago's great 1899 team that finished 16-0-2 and won the Western Conference (now Big Ten) title. With much fanfare, Slaker transferred to Stanford University prior to the 1900 season and helped revive a sagging program. His last game as a collegian was the very first Rose Bowl game, on January 1, 1902. Slaker served as an assistant coach at Stanford for a few years before beginning a career as a fire insurance underwriter in Arizona and California. He died in 1957.

After posting a 4-2-2 record in 1898, the Red and Black began the 1899 season by giving up just two points in winning its first eight games before traveling to Indiana, where Midwest power Culver Academy spanked the Red and Black in the season finale, 35–5.

The end of the century saw a continuation of East's brilliance and resurgence on the west side. Under new coach George Wilbert, the Red and Blue started the 1900 season with eight consecutive shutouts and a 7-0-1 record, while the Red and Black shut out its first five challengers, avenged the prior season's only loss with an 11–5 win over Culver and then shut out Chicago's Marshall High to run its record to 5-0-2. With both East and West having championship aspirations, the scheduled Thanksgiving Day clash was moved up to Wednesday, November 21, to enable the winner to compete against the state's other championship contenders. With much fanfare, East cruised past the west-siders on Hurd's Island, 17–0, and then rolled past two of Chicago's best, Hyde Park and West Division, to set up a meeting with downstate's Urbana High School to play for the unofficial "state championship." In a hotly contested game played on the campus of the University of Illinois, the Red and Black claimed its first mythical Illinois state championship with a 10–6 victory.

***

The twentieth century began with heightened concerns for player safety. Protective leather head harnesses, nose guards, mouth guards and improved padding began to appear, but they were crude and worn at the discretion of individual players. Newspapers routinely reported and tracked deaths that occurred on football fields nationwide. Locally, several papers reported that in a game between East Aurora and Batavia on October 20, 1900, Batavian William Jaber was knocked unconscious and thought to be near death, although reports of Jaber's actual death did not appear and are presumed unfounded. Nonetheless, reports like these led college football officials to tweak the rules and introduce new equipment almost annually in an effort to make the game both safer and more exciting. High schools always followed suit, but results were mixed.

West Aurora High School, circa 1905. *Courtesy of the Aurora Historical Society.*

Mark Catlin, *West Class of 1902*. An outstanding football and track athlete and two-time football captain at West, Catlin followed Slaker to the University of Chicago, where he served as captain of the Maroons' 1905 national championship team and earned second team all-American honors as an end. After receiving his undergraduate degree from Chicago, Catlin attended law school at the University of Iowa, where he simultaneously served as head football coach. Law degree in hand, Catlin moved to Appleton, Wisconsin, where he coached at Lawrence College on and off for thirteen seasons from 1909 to 1927 and established a law practice. A man of many talents, Catlin served in Wisconsin's state legislature, on the State Conservation Commission and wrote *Fly Fishing for Trout*, which was published in 1930. He passed away in Appleton, Wisconsin, in 1956.

On the gridiron, both East and West continued to play well, winning more than 60 percent of games played from 1901 to 1910. The tradition of a Thanksgiving Day game, which had been on again, off again during the rivalry's first decade, solidified in 1902 and would continue unbroken for fifty years. That year, West beat the Red and Black for the first time, 22–0.

West surprised East again in 1903, scoring the game's only touchdown when an East punt returner's fumble was picked up by West's Kelley, who then fumbled himself while racing toward the goal. West's Snell scooped up the second fumble and carried it in for a touchdown. The subsequent goal kick was good, and the Red and Blue held on for a 6–5 victory. The next day, the *Beacon*'s game summary accurately reported that West had scored on a "fluke" play, that the east-siders had out-gained West by a two-to-one margin and that East had missed what would have been a tying goal kick by a mere six inches, all of which led the reader to conclude that East was the better team but that West was luckier. The report incensed several west-siders, who accused the *Beacon* of biased reporting. The *Beacon*, wanting to retain the appearance of being neutral, made peace by printing a west-sider's interpretation of the facts a day or so later.

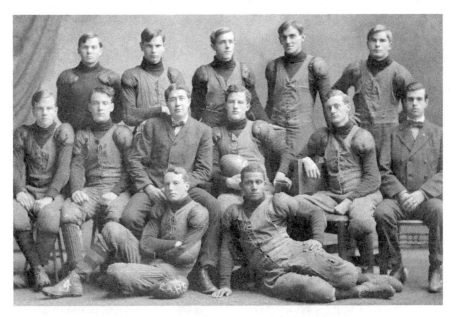

East Aurora team photo, 1906. Twelve years later, quarterback Henry Boger (seated on the ground at right) died in action during World War I. *Courtesy of the Aurora Historical Society.*

East Aurora players and fans prior to the 1909 Thanksgiving Day clash, which ended in a 5–5 tie. *Courtesy of East Aurora High School Speculum and the Aurora Historical Society.*

East's Gale Brothers. From 1892 until 1902, Henry, Eli and Burton Gale went from playing football on the east side to academic and athletic acclaim at the University of Chicago.

Henry Gordon Gale, East Class of 1892, passed through East before football was organized at the school but nonetheless went on to become Aurora's first noteworthy college player during his days at Chicago. Henry played from 1892 until 1895 and was the Maroons' team captain as a senior. Later, while working on his PhD in physics, Henry was an assistant coach for Amos Alonzo Stagg's championship teams of the late 1890s. After receiving his doctorate in 1899, Henry went on to become a renowned astrophysicist who published numerous articles and books on the subject. Professor Gale was a University of Chicago faculty member for twenty-five years, serving as instructor, department chair and dean. He retired in 1940 and passed away in 1942.

Eli Pike Gale, East Class of 1900, played on the Red and Black's great 1899 team and went on to become an outstanding track athlete in college. He later entered the business world as a sales manager in Iowa and during World War II worked as a chemist at an ordnance plant in Indiana.

Burton Gale, East Class of 1902, played center on the Maroons' 1905 national championship squad and went on to become a successful stockbroker in the Chicago area. He passed away in Evanston, Illinois, in 1939.

The best and most controversial rivalry game of the decade came in 1906, when once-beaten West Aurora took on an undefeated East squad that was vying for a second state championship. In a seesaw game, the Red and Black twice lost leads and missed several opportunities to score. West's captain, Al Lytle, disrupted one East goal try by throwing his head gear at the kicker. He was penalized, of course, but West later held on downs, and East missed a scoring opportunity. Finally, with West pinned deep in its own territory and time running out, the Red and Black burst through the line and scored what appeared to be a game-tying safety, only to learn that the referee had ruled East to be offside and that the safety was

The East High School Foot Ball Squad - 1914 - Aurora, Illinois

STEWART STAMM RISLEY PRITCHARD PIKE MERCER COOK BARDWELL CROMER DAVIS (Athletic Director)
STEPHENSON HANNEY REILY SCHULTZ (Captain) TOMLINSON BETZ YOUNG MATHEWS WILLIAMS
BABCOCK SLATER GUMZ RAMMER GROMETER
NIBLACK MARX

Postcards of the team photos printed in the *Aurora Beacon-News* on the eve of the 1914 "state championship" game. *Postcards from author's private collection.*

The West High School Foot Ball Squad - 1914 - Aurora, Illinois

MacDONALD BANBURY LONG BENNETT CHAP__ (Coach) COOPER STEPHENS HIGGINS
BUCKNER YALE HICKEY DAVEY CIGRAND (Captain) OLESON BROCKWAY WRIGHT WHEELOCK MERCER
SANDERSON SADARO DODGE KRAMER HOLMBERG HARRINGTON SCHODER
NEILL O'HARA

film the game so that it could later be shown at a downtown theater. Amid the pomp and circumstance, the game itself was a defensive struggle. East scored first and effectively held Cigrand in check until he broke a long punt return to tie the game in the second half. Then, in the final quarter, the Red and Black blocked a punt, recovered the ball at West's one-yard line and

Fans gather at Hurd's Island on Thanksgiving, 1914. East claimed the state championship with a 14–7 victory over their crosstown rivals. *Courtesy of East Aurora High School Speculum and the Aurora Historical Society.*

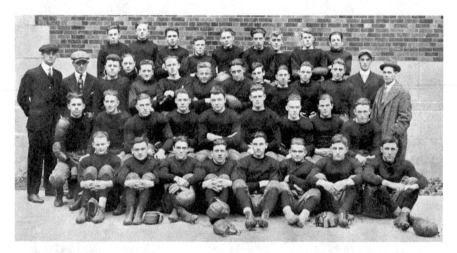

East Aurora's 1915 "state champions" featured five all-staters and lost only to New York's Hamilton Institute in a highly publicized intersectional contest. *Courtesy of East Aurora High School Speculum and the Aurora Historical Society.*

punched in the go-ahead touchdown one play later. As it had done all game long, East's defense, led by the sure tackling of Albert Pike, stymied the west-siders the rest of the way to win 14–7 and claim the state championship for the first time since 1900. The following week, East's Pike and Raymond Schultz, together with West's Cigrand, Bennett and Brockaway, were named to the *Rockford Morning Star*'s all-state team.

Honey Stuart left Aurora in 1915 to play semipro football on the West Coast, and Martin Shale took over as East's coach. Shale drove the Red and

Frank "Duke" Hanny, Albert Pike and Elliott Risley, *East Class of 1916*. These three all-staters from East's 1914 and '15 state championship teams made names for themselves after high school.

Hanny (sometimes spelled Hanney), a splendid two-way end and punter, was the target of an intense recruiting war that ended when he selected Indiana University. After playing with Risley on the Cream and Crimson's freshman team in 1916, he entered the Army Ambulance Corps. Hanny served in Italy during World War I and was highly decorated for his service. He resumed his career at Indiana in 1920 and played three years for the Hoosiers, serving as team captain in 1922. After college, Hanny had an eight-year NFL career, including stops with the Chicago Bears, Providence Steamrollers, Green Bay Packers and Portsmouth Spartans. When his playing days were over, Hanny returned to Aurora to work for the WPA, Illinois Cleaners and Dryers and Aurora Pump until his untimely death in 1946.

Pike, a two-year all-stater, was captain and spiritual leader of East's 1915 state championship team. The six-foot-two, 180-pound fullback was a bruising runner on offense and a devastating tackler on defense. After graduating from East, Pike attended the University of Illinois and served in World War I but did not continue with football. He returned to Aurora to join Pike Dairy, the family business founded by his father, which operated just a few blocks from present East High at the corner of Smith Boulevard and Second Avenue, until 1965. Pike served as company president from 1920 until his death in 1964. He was a director of the Illinois Milk Dealer's Association and throughout his adult life was an active member of the Aurora community, serving as a director on several local boards and as a member of local Elks and Moose clubs, the Aurora Country Club, the Union League Club and Holy Angels Catholic Church.

Risley, a resident of tiny Compton, Illinois, attended East and went on to play both football and baseball at Indiana University. After playing for Indiana's freshman team in 1916 and for the varsity in '17, Riz missed the 1918 season while serving in the navy. He returned to Indiana in 1919 and played two more seasons at tackle, while also serving as the team's placekicker and, as a senior, captain.

> After receiving his degree, Riz played parts of three seasons with the Hammond Pros of the APFA and NFL, while at the same time serving four years as sheriff of Lee County, Illinois. As sheriff, he was wounded in a gun battle with moonshiners in 1923. Three years later, Risley left law enforcement to operate a sand and gravel contracting business in Dixon, Illinois. He died in 1942 at age forty-six.

Black to new heights, as East averaged 45 points a game while giving up just 12 total points in winning its first nine games. East's victories that year included an 83–0 thrashing of Rochelle, a 71–0 win over Waukegan and a 65–0 thumping of Peoria, regarded as the best team in downstate Illinois. Finally, the Red and Black steamrolled West 25–0 before another enormous Thanksgiving Day crowd on Hurd's Island.

Proclaimed by some as "champions of the West" (the United States in 1915 remained very East Coast–centric), East Aurora was invited to travel to New York to take on Brooklyn's Hamilton Institute in an intersectional game on December 4. An estimated eight thousand people saw the sixteen players and a contingent of dignitaries that included Principal K.D. Waldo, Athletic Director Roy E. Davis, Coach Shale and sixteen prominent community leaders leave Aurora on a train bound for New York, with a stop to sightsee at Niagara Falls along the way.

On a chilly afternoon, about three thousand spectators gathered at Brooklyn's Washington Park to watch East fall to the New Yorkers, 13–12. The nervous visitors fell behind early after two fumbled kickoffs led to Hamilton touchdowns in the game's first four minutes. From then on, the Red and Black dominated play, only to have a potential game-winning field goal blocked in the game's final minute. Despite the loss, newspapers in both New York and Chicago proclaimed East Aurora the better team. After a post-game banquet at the home of New York financier and Aurora native Frank Vanderlip, the boys returned home to a hero's welcome.

East placed five players on the United Press all-state team for 1915, including first-teamers Albert Pike, George Stamm and Frank Hanny and second-teamers Elliott Risley and Mark Mercer. West quarterback Allen Davey was also named to the first team.

Allen Davey, *West Class of 1916.* The diminutive all-state quarterback who resided in St. Charles but attended West Aurora was an exceptional open-field runner. As a college freshman in the fall of 1916, Davey made the University of Wisconsin team as a reserve running back but had his career interrupted by military service in 1917. Davey returned to Wisconsin after fulfilling his one-year military commitment overseas and carved out a remarkable three-year career as a quarterback, kick returner and placekicker for the Badgers. His fourth-quarter heroics almost single-handedly won several games for the Badgers, and his all-around play earned him a spot on Walter Camp's 1920 all-American team. An outstanding student-athlete and citizen, Davey also played baseball for the Badgers and was elected president of both the junior class and the Wisconsin Athletic Board. In 1921, he was awarded Wisconsin's Big 10 Medal of Honor, which is presented annually to the one graduating student-athlete from each conference university who "attained the greatest proficiency in athletics and scholastic work." When his college days were over, Davey went to work for the Wisconsin Public Service Corporation and settled in Oshkosh, where he also spent twenty years as a high school football and basketball referee. In 1944, Davey took a job as sales manager in Chicago and relocated to Downers Grove. He passed away in 1965 at the age of sixty-seven.

Note: Aurora's main local newspaper, the *Aurora Beacon-News,* and its predecessor, the *Aurora Daily Beacon,* were used as the primary sources for game results shown here. However, prior to about 1900, results of road games were often self-reported, and since it appears that some road losses did not always find their way to the editing desk, a few of the results listed were found in out-of-town papers. When discrepancies between newspaper accounts were identified, the *Beacon* score was used unless it was clearly incorrect.

EAST AURORA　　　　　　　　　　WEST AURORA

1893

	W	L	T	Coach		W	L	T	Coach
Overall Record:	2	0	0	Frank Darby	Overall Record:	0	1	0	Unknown

Date	Opponent		EA	Opp	Date	Opponent		WA	Opp
11.11	Elgin	W	20	12	11.18	East Aurora	L	0	28
11.18	West Aurora	W	28	0					

1894

	W	L	T	Coach		W	L	T	Coach
Overall Record:	3	0	1	Frank Darby	Overall Record:	5	0	0	Unknown

Date	Opponent		EA	Opp	Date	Opponent		WA	Opp
10.10	LaGrange	W	8	0	10.20	Geneva (town team)	W	8	0
10.20	Elgin	W	18	0	10.26	Geneva (town team)	W	42	0
11.03	Elgin	W	14	0	11.03	Joliet	W	34	4
11.29	Evanston	T	10	10	11.17	Joliet	W	16	4
					11.29	Armour Institute	W	10	6

1895

	W	L	T	Coach		W	L	T	Coach
Overall Record:	3	2	4	Tom Reid	Overall Record:	2	3	0	George Nichols

Date	Opponent		EA	Opp	Date	Opponent		WA	Opp
09.28	St. Charles	W	16	0	10.12	St. Charles (town team)	L	0	12
10.02	LaGrange	T	0	0	10.26	Joliet	W	12	0
10.05	Hinsdale	T	0	0	11.02	Joliet	W	16	0
10.19	Hinsdale	L	0	12	11.08	LaGrange	L	0	12
11.02	LaGrange	T	0	0	11.28	East Aurora	L	6	12
11.05	Aurora YMCA	T	0	0					
11.15	LaGrange	W	12	8					
11.23	Englewood	L	0	4					
11.28	West Aurora	W	12	0					

Key: W = Win, L = Loss, T = Tie, WF = Win by forfeit, LF = Loss by forfeit, **Bold** = Conference game, *Italics* = state playoff game

EAST AURORA

WEST AURORA

1896

East Aurora

	W	L	T	Coach
Overall Record:	5	2	2	T. Darby/H. Willard

Date	Opponent		EA	Opp
UNK*	West Aurora	T	0	0
09.19	St. Charles	L	0	10
10.03	Hyde Park	W	6	0
10.10	Epworth Cadets	W	26	0
10.24	Lake Forest Academy	W	12	0
10.31	Elgin Academy	W	36	6
11.07	Elgin	L	0	10
11.14	JV Fawell Athletic Club	W	30	0
11.26	West Aurora	T	10	10

*Legendary second game; details unknown

West Aurora

	W	L	T	Coach
Overall Record:	6	1	2	Walter Garrey

Date	Opponent		WA	Opp
UNK*	East Aurora	T	0	0
09.23	Hyde Park	L	0	4
10.07	Oak Park	W	18	4
10.10	Wheaton	W	4	0
10.17	Elgin	W	6	0
10.24	LaGrange	W	22	0
11.11	U of Chicago (2nd team)	W	14	6
11.14	LaGrange	W	14	12
11.26	East Aurora	T	10	10

1897

East Aurora

	W	L	T	Coach
Overall Record:	7	1	1	Unknown

Date	Opponent		EA	Opp
09.25	Austin	L	6	8
10.02	Englewood	W	6	4
10.09	Elgin Academy	W	26	0
10.16	LaGrange	T	0	0
10.23	Calumet	W	60	0
10.30	Yorkville (town team)	W	14	4
11.06	Elgin	W	10	0
11.12	Aurora Modern College	W	16	0
11.20	Batavia	W	40	0

West Aurora

	W	L	T	Coach
Overall Record:	4	0	1	Unknown

Date	Opponent		WA	Opp
10.16	Yorkville (town team)	T	0	0
10.23	Marshall	W	26	0
10.30	LaGrange	W	12	6
11.06	Joliet	W	40	0
11.17	Elgin	W	24	6

1898

East Aurora

	W	L	T	Coach
Overall Record:	4	3	1	Bill Hazard

Date	Opponent		EA	Opp
10.01	Hyde Park	L	0	6
10.08	Austin	W	33	5
10.15	West Aurora	T	6	6
10.22	Englewood	L	6	8
10.29	Bloomington	L	17	23
11.05	West Aurora	W	34	0
11.12	Northwestern College	W	24	0
11.19	U of Chicago (2nd team)	W	18	11

West Aurora

	W	L	T	Coach
Overall Record:	0	3	2	Unknown

Date	Opponent		WA	Opp
10.08	Elgin	L	0	2
10.15	East Aurora	T	6	6
10.27	Elgin	L	5	12
10.29	Riverside	T	0	0
11.05	East Aurora	L	0	34

EAST AURORA   WEST AURORA

1899

	W	L	T	Coach			W	L	T	Coach
Overall Record:	8	1	0	Coach Harris		Overall Record:	4	3	0	Unknown

Date	Opponent		EA	Opp		Date	Opponent		WA	Opp
09.30	Naperville (town team)	W	32	2		10.14	Elgin	L	6	17
10.07	Northwestern College	W	6	0		10.31	Yorkville	W	NA	NA
10.14	Ottawa	W	12	0		11.4	Elgin	L	0	16
10.21	Ottawa	W	22	0		11.11	Elgin Academy	W	12	0
10.28	Naperville	W	5	0		11.15	Northwestern College	W	5	0
11.04	Marshall Field Team	W	6	0		11.18	St. Charles	W	6	5
11.11	Lake Forest Academy	W	11	0		11.25	East Aurora	L	0	33
11.25	West Aurora	W	33	0						
12.01	Culver Military Academy	L	5	35						

1900

	W	L	T	Coach			W	L	T	Coach
Overall Record:	9	0	2	Coach Stewart		Overall Record:	7	1	1	George Wilbert

Date	Opponent		EA	Opp		Date	Opponent		WA	Opp
09.29	Northwestern College	W	12	0		09.15	Geneva (town team)	W	11	0
10.06	St. Charles	T	0	0		09.22	Marshall	W	17	0
10.11	Armour Institute	T	0	0		09.29	Rockford	W	12	0
10.18	Mendota	W	6	0		10.06	Northwestern College	W	12	0
10.20	Batavia	W	23	0		10.13	Elgin Academy	W	29	0
11.10	Culver Military Academy	W	11	5		10.19	Elgin	T	0	0
11.17	Marshall	W	6	0		10.27	DeKalb	W	12	0
11.21	West Aurora	W	17	0		11.10	St. Charles	W	6	0
11.24	Hyde Park	W	16	5		11.21	East Aurora	L	0	17
11.29	West Division	W	21	0						
12.08	Urbana	W	10	6						

Mythical State Champions

Key: W = Win, L = Loss, T = Tie, WF = Win by forfeit, LF = Loss by forfeit, **Bold** = Conference game, *Italics* = state playoff game

EAST AURORA   WEST AURORA

1901

	W	L	T	Coach		W	L	T	Coach
Overall Record:	10	2	1	Billy Lindsey	Overall Record: 7	2	0		Claude Briggs

Date	Opponent		EA	Opp	Date	Opponent		WA	Opp
09.21	Englewood	W	5	0	09.28	Elgin Academy	W	6	0
09.28	Hyde Park	T	0	0	10.12	St. Charles	W	10	0
10.05	North Division	W	27	5	10.19	Rockford	W	5	0
10.12	U of Chicago (2nd team)	W	6	5	10.23	Plano	W	NA	NA
10.19	Ottawa	W	15	0	10.26	U of C Preparatory School	W	40	0
10.26	Morgan Park Academy	L	0	11	11.02	Geneva (town team)	W	10	6
11.02	Culver Military Academy	W	17	0	11.09	Elgin	L	5	18
11.09	English	W	22	0	11.28	Rockford	W	6	5
11.16	Austin Titan Athletic Assn.	W	51	5	12.04	East Aurora	L	0	6
11.20	Armour Institute	W	34	0					
11.28	Chicago All-stars	W	23	0					
11.30	Urbana	L	0	22					
12.04	West Aurora	W	6	0					

1902

	W	L	T	Coach		W	L	T	Coach
Overall Record:	7	4	0	Billy Lindsey	Overall Record: 4	5	0		Claude Briggs

Date	Opponent		EA	Opp	Date	Opponent		WA	Opp
09.20	Englewood	L	0	10	09.13	Geneva (town team)	L	0	10
09.27	Geneva (town team)	W	5	0	09.27	Joliet	L	0	11
09.30	Aurora Modern College	W	50	0	10.11	Ottawa	W	12	5
10.08	Austin	W	48	0	10.18	Rockford	L	0	12
10.11	Culver Military Academy	L	0	39	10.25	Elgin Academy	W	17	0
10.18	Armour Institute	W	28	5	11.01	Ottawa	W	6	0
10.25	Marshall Field Team	L	0	11	11.08	Rockford	L	0	17
11.01	Joliet	W	24	6	11.15	Joliet	L	0	17
11.04	West Division	W	23	5	11.27	East Aurora	W	22	0
11.08	Elgin	W	12	6					
11.27	West Aurora	L	0	22					

East Aurora

West Aurora

1903

	W	L	T	Coach			W	L	T	Coach
Overall Record:	3	5	0	Coach Johnson	Overall Record:		5	3	1	Claude Briggs

Date	Opponent		EA	Opp	Date	Opponent		WA	Opp
09.26	North Division	L	0	24	09.26	Geneva (town team)	W	NA	NA
10.03	Englewood	L	0	22	10.03	Joliet	L	0	17
10.17	West Division	W	39	0	10.10	Rockford	W	6	5
10.24	LaGrange	W	27	0	10.17	Elgin	T	5	5
10.31	Elgin	L	0	12	10.24	Princeton	W	6	0
11.07	Elgin Academy	W	6	0	10.31	Rockford	L	0	29
11.14	Joliet	L	0	37	11.07	Joliet	L	5	18
11.26	West Aurora	L	5	6	11.14	DeKalb	W	11	5
					11.26	East Aurora	W	6	5

1904

	W	L	T	Coach			W	L	T	Coach
Overall Record:	6	3	0	O.A. Rawlings	Overall Record:		7	3	1	Claude Briggs

Date	Opponent		EA	Opp	Date	Opponent		WA	Opp
09.24	Austin	W	6	5	09.10	Geneva (town team)	W	8	0
10.01	Plano	W	35	6	09.17	St. Charles	W	12	0
10.08	Englewood	L	0	16	09.24	DeKalb	W	27	0
10.15	Rockford	L	0	6	10.01	Joliet	W	12	0
10.22	Elgin	W	17	5	10.08	Elgin	L	0	10
10.29	Oak Park	W	6	0	10.15	Plano	W	10	4
11.05	Culver Military Academy	L	0	23	10.22	Kewanee	L	0	11
11.12	Joliet	W	6	5	10.29	Joliet	W	6	0
11.24	West Aurora	W	4	0	11.05	Chicago Latin School	W	11	6
					11.12	DeKalb	T	0	0
					11.24	East Aurora	L	0	4

Key: W = Win, L = Loss, T = Tie, WF = Win by forfeit, LF = Loss by forfeit, **Bold** = Conference game, *Italics* = state playoff game

EAST AURORA

WEST AURORA

1905

Overall Record:	W	L	T	Coach		Overall Record:	W	L	T	Coach
	4	4	1	O.A. Rawlings			8	1	1	Claude Briggs

Date	Opponent		EA	Opp		Date	Opponent		WA	Opp
09.23	Joliet	W	21	0		09.16	Batavia	W	22	0
09.30	Plano	W	31	0		09.23	St. Charles	W	51	0
10.07	Oak Park	L	0	24		09.30	Elgin	W	45	0
10.14	Englewood	W	16	0		10.07	Joliet	W	11	0
10.21	DeKalb	T	0	0		10.14	DeKalb	T	0	0
10.28	Rockford	L	0	22		10.21	Crane Tech	W	10	0
11.11	Wheaton College	W	20	12		10.28	Rochelle	W	13	0
11.18	Elgin	L	0	5		11.04	Rockford	L	0	12
11.30	West Aurora	L	5	6		11.18	Joliet	W	6	0
						11.30	East Aurora	W	6	5

1906

Overall Record:	W	L	T	Coach		Overall Record:	W	L	T	Coach
	6	1	0	O.A. Rawlings			6	1	2	Claude Briggs

Date	Opponent		EA	Opp		Date	Opponent		WA	Opp
09.29	Englewood	W	5	0		09.22	St. Charles School for Boys	W	18	0
10.13	Plano	W	6	0		10.06	Sandwich	W	16	0
10.20	Elgin	W	18	4		10.13	Englewood	W	12	0
10.27	Rockford	W	11	0		10.20	Oak Park	T	0	0
11.03	DeKalb	W	6	0		10.27	Plano	L	0	12
11.10	Oak Park	W	7	0		11.03	Elgin	W	15	5
11.29	West Aurora	L	10	12		11.10	Rockford	T	0	0
						11.17	DeKalb	W	11	0
						11.29	East Aurora	W	12	10

EAST AURORA

WEST AURORA

1907

Overall Record:	W	L	T	Coach		Overall Record:	W	L	T	Coach
	5	3	1	W.F. Shirley			4	4	1	Claude Briggs

Date	Opponent		EA	Opp		Date	Opponent		WA	Opp
09.28	Englewood	W	9	4		09.21	St. Charles School for Boys	W	50	6
10.05	Rochelle	L	0	5		09.28	Sandwich	W	27	0
10.12	Elgin	L	0	7		10.05	Phillips	W	12	0
10.19	Sandwich	T	0	0		10.12	Crane Tech	T	0	0
10.26	DeKalb	W	33	0		10.19	Oak Park	L	4	12
11.02	Oak Park	L	0	18		10.26	Elgin	W	12	0
11.09	Streator	W	30	6		11.02	Rockford	L	0	41
11.16	Streator	W	12	0		11.09	Rochelle	L	6	12
11.28	West Aurora	W	13	4		11.28	East Aurora	L	4	13

1908

Overall Record:	W	L	T	Coach		Overall Record:	W	L	T	Coach
	3	4	2	W.F. Shirley			4	2	4	J.L. Stevenson

Date	Opponent		EA	Opp		Date	Opponent		WA	Opp
09.26	St. Charles	W	18	0		9.19	St. Charles School for Boys	W	42	0
10.03	Oak Park	W	11	10		9.26	Sandwich	T	5	5
10.10	Elgin	L	0	9		10.3	Phillips	W	12	5
10.17	St. Charles	T	0	0		10.10	St Charles	W	14	0
10.24	Rockford	L	0	14		10.17	Rochelle	W	5	0
10.31	DeKalb Normal School	W	12	5		10.24	Sandwich	T	0	0
11.7	Elgin	L	0	5		10.31	Rockford	L	6	11
11.14	DeKalb	L	0	25		11.7	Thornton	L	0	10
11.26	West Aurora	T	6	6		11.14	Elgin	T	0	0
						11.27	East Aurora	T	6	6

Key: W = Win, L = Loss, T = Tie, WF = Win by forfeit, LF = Loss by forfeit, **Bold** = Conference game, *Italics* = state playoff game

EAST AURORA   WEST AURORA

1909

Overall Record:	W	L	T	Coach		Overall Record:	W	L	T	Coach
	3	2	3	W.F. Shirley			2	3	2	J.L. Stevenson

Date	Opponent		EA	Opp		Date	Opponent		WA	Opp
09.25	Batavia	W	25	0		10.02	Batavia	T	0	0
10.02	Waukegan	W	15	0		10.16	DeKalb	L	0	35
10.16	Rochelle	T	0	0		10.23	Elgin	W	2	0
10.23	DeKalb	W	11	5		10.30	Rockford	L	0	75
10.30	Elgin	T	0	0		11.06	Sandwich	W	6	0
11.06	Rockford	L	0	15		11.13	Oak Park	L	0	22
11.13	Urbana	L	0	13		11.25	East Aurora	T	5	5
11.25	West Aurora	T	5	5						

1910

Overall Record:	W	L	T	Coach		Overall Record:	W	L	T	Coach
	3	2	1	Boyd Lehman			6	2	1	Harry Smith

Date	Opponent		EA	Opp		Date	Opponent		WA	Opp
10.08	Rockford	L	0	30		09.24	Sandwich	W	51	0
10.15	Evanston	W	6	0		10.01	Rockford	L	0	34
10.22	Rochelle	W	11	8		10.08	Phillips	L	0	16
10.29	DeKalb Normal School	W	16	0		10.15	Lockport	W	18	11
11.12	DeKalb	L	2	23		10.22	DeKalb	W	11	6
11.24	West Aurora	T	0	0		10.29	Elgin	W	6	0
						11.05	Thornton	W	29	0
						11.12	Crane Tech	W	11	5
						11.24	East Aurora	T	0	0

EAST AURORA   WEST AURORA

1911

	W	L	T	Coach			W	L	T	Coach
Overall Record:	5	2	1	Boyd Lehman		Overall Record:	5	2	3	Elvin Berkheiser

Date	Opponent		EA	Opp		Date	Opponent		WA	Opp
09.23	Crane Tech	W	6	0		09.23	St. Charles School for Boys	W	10	0
09.30	DeKalb	W	18	0		09.30	Evanston Academy	L	0	17
10.14	Rockford	W	11	5		10.07	Sycamore	W	71	0
10.28	Elgin	W	21	0		10.14	Thornton	W	8	6
11.04	Princeton	L	0	8		10.21	Elgin	T	0	0
11.11	Rochelle	W	27	0		10.28	Lake Forest Academy	L	3	32
11.18	DeKalb Normal School	L	0	10		11.04	DeKalb Normal School	T	0	0
11.30	West Aurora	T	0	0		11.11	DeKalb	W	20	0
						11.18	Joliet	W	21	0
						11.30	East Aurora	T	0	0

1912

	W	L	T	Coach			W	L	T	Coach
Overall Record:	2	7	0	Boyd Lehman		Overall Record:	10	0	0	Elvin Berkheiser

Date	Opponent		EA	Opp		Date	Opponent		WA	Opp
09.21	St. Charles	W	7	0		09.21	Batavia	W	42	0
10.05	Kewanee	L	0	18		09.28	Rochelle	W	15	0
10.12	Elgin	L	0	16		10.05	Rockford	W	31	19
10.19	Moline	L	0	34		10.19	Lane Tech	W	24	7
10.26	Joliet	W	14	6		10.26	Thornton	W	20	2
11.02	Rockford	L	0	37		11.02	DeKalb	W	71	0
11.09	DeKalb Normal School	L	10	33		11.09	Sandwich	W	51	0
11.16	Rochelle	L	0	18		11.16	Elgin	W	10	9
11.28	West Aurora	L	0	37		11.23	Kewanee	W	16	3
						11.28	East Aurora	W	37	0

Mythical State Champions

Key: W = Win, L = Loss, T = Tie, WF = Win by forfeit, LF = Loss by forfeit, **Bold** = Conference game, *Italics* = state playoff game

EAST AURORA

WEST AURORA

1913

Overall Record:	W	L	T	Coach		Overall Record:	W	L	T	Coach
	4	6	0	Walter Dyer			9	0	0	Byron Chappel

Date	Opponent		EA	Opp		Date	Opponent		WA	Opp
09.27	Geneva	W	12	6		09.20	Batavia	W	34	0
10.04	Batavia	W	7	6		09.27	Lane Tech	W	7	6
10.11	Rockford	L	6	20		10.04	Elgin	W	19	3
10.18	Moline	L	0	48		10.11	Rochelle	W	51	0
10.25	Joliet	L	0	17		10.18	Kewanee	W	10	6
11.01	Kewanee	W	12	0		10.25	DeKalb	W	99	6
11.08	Elgin	L	0	16		11.01	Rockford	W	14	2
11.15	Rochelle	W	43	0		11.15	Thornton	W	14	7
11.22	Naperville	L	3	10		11.27	East Aurora	W	13	3
11.27	West Aurora	L	3	13						

Mythical State Champions

1914

Overall Record:	W	L	T	Coach		Overall Record:	W	L	T	Coach
	8	0	0	George Stuart			6	2	0	Byron Chappel

Date	Opponent		EA	Opp		Date	Opponent		WA	Opp
09.26	Batavia	W	10	0		09.26	Thornton	W	73	0
10.03	Joliet	W	29	0		10.03	Batavia	W	53	0
10.17	Rockford	W	19	7		10.10	Clinton (Clinton, IA)	L	0	14
10.24	DeKalb	W	97	0		10.17	Kewanee	W	36	0
10.31	Kewanee	W	41	3		10.31	Rockford	W	44	0
11.07	Elgin	W	6	0		11.07	Naperville	W	126	6
11.14	Ottawa	W	46	0		11.14	Champaign	W	13	0
11.26	West Aurora	W	14	7		11.26	East Aurora	L	7	14

Mythical State Champions

EAST AURORA   WEST AURORA

1915

	W	L	T	Coach			W	L	T	Coach
Overall Record:	9	1	0	Martin Shale		Overall Record:	5	3	1	J.D. Fletcher

Date	Opponent		EA	Opp		Date	Opponent		WA	Opp
09.25	Woodstock	W	58	0		09.25	Morris	W	16	0
10.02	Rochelle	W	83	0		10.02	DeKalb Normal School	W	17	0
10.09	Waukegan	W	71	0		10.09	Elgin	W	12	6
10.16	Freeport	W	39	3		10.16	DeKalb	W	12	0
10.23	Joliet	W	9	6		10.23	Kewanee	L	7	13
10.30	Peoria Central	W	65	0		10.30	Proviso	W	19	0
11.06	Elgin	W	40	3		11.06	Joliet	L	12	18
11.13	Kewanee	W	16	3		11.13	Rockford	T	7	7
11.25	West Aurora	W	25	0		11.25	East Aurora	L	0	25
12.04	Hamilton (New York)	L	12	14						

Mythical State Champions

Key: W = Win, L = Loss, T = Tie, WF = Win by forfeit, LF = Loss by forfeit, **Bold** = Conference game, *Italics* = state playoff game

This drawing depicts the enlistment of several West Aurora athletes into the army just prior to graduation in 1917. *Courtesy of West Aurora High School Eos and the Aurora Historical Society.*

The epidemic quickly spread to town, and by the first week of October, 234 were dead, and Rockford was under quarantine. On October 10 alone, 218 soldiers and Rockfordians died. When Rockford's epidemic passed a few weeks later, the death toll stood at 323 in town and more than 1,400 at Camp Grant.

Meanwhile, at Mooseheart Camp in Kane County, a local soldier named Remner Schroeder became the first Auroran to die from the flu on October 2. Two weeks later, the *Beacon* reported one thousand cases and thirty-three local deaths. On October 14, the Aurora City Council imposed a quarantine that indefinitely closed schools, theaters, places of amusement, churches, social gatherings and public meetings, which included football practices and games.

With no end to the quarantine in sight, and assuming the season lost, West Aurora coach John McGough enlisted in the military. He left for duty on October 31, leaving Billy Robinson in charge of the team while administrators scrambled to find a permanent replacement. As it happened, the epidemic subsided within a week, and on November 2, the quarantine ended.

Although football was allowed to resume, so many games were missed that the league schedule was cancelled, and schools were left to piece together the remainder of the season. East Aurora quickly scheduled a match with Mooseheart for the day the quarantine lifted, losing the contest 6–0. West, under new coach R.E. Valentine, an alumnus who had recently been coaching in Nebraska, resumed play with a victory over Freeport one week later. During the following weeks, the end of the war ignited Armistice Day celebrations across the country, and football more or less resumed its ordinary November cadence. For Aurorans, that meant gathering on Hurd's Island for the annual East-West Thanksgiving Day clash, which the Red and Blue won 6–0.

With the war over, life returned to normal in 1919. DeKalb rejoined the NIHSC, which was now commonly known as the Big 7. The Burlington railroad, which had purchased Hurd's Island, precipitated the eventual relocation of the city's football venue by beginning construction of the tracks that bisect the island and remain in use today. West Aurora, led by future college football Hall of Famer Andy Gustafson, fielded an outstanding team that year and came into Thanksgiving with just one loss. East, meanwhile, was winless in non-conference play but undefeated in league games, meaning that an East win or a tie in the season finale would give the Red and Black the undisputed conference championship. A West victory would mean the schools would share the title. It seemed only fitting that the final game ever played on Hurd's

Henry Boger, *East Class of 1907*. The son of a local African American minister and community leader, the diminutive Boger quarterbacked East Aurora at a time when African Americans were not often placed in leadership positions. His 1906 East squad was undefeated until Thanksgiving Day, when West concentrated its defense on stopping him and came away with a two-point victory that prevented East from claiming the state championship. Twelve years later, Lieutenant Boger served in the U.S. Army's 365th Infantry Regiment of the all-black 92nd Division and fought alongside the French in the last major offensive of World War I, the Meuse-Argonne Offensive. Tragically, Boger was killed in action on November 11, 1918, the day the war ended.

Andy Gustafson, *West Class of 1921*. Red and Blue captain in 1920, Gustafson was a hard-running fullback who went on to the University of Pittsburgh, where he played for three years under Hall of Fame coaches Pop Warner and Jock Sutherland, and is credited with scoring the first-ever touchdown in old Pitt Stadium in 1925. After graduating from Pitt, Gustafson served as head football coach at Virginia Polytechnic Institute (now Virginia Tech). From 1926 to 1929, his teams crafted a four-year record of 22-13-1. For eighteen years beginning in 1930, "Gus" held roles as backfield coach at Pitt, Dartmouth and finally at Army, where he coached back-to-back Heisman Trophy winners Doc Blanchard and Glenn Davis. While at Army, Gustafson is crediting with developing the drive series belly option, considered the forerunner of today's veer and wishbone offenses. In 1948, Gus became head coach at the University of Miami, where, over sixteen seasons, he led the Hurricanes to a 93-65-3 record and four bowl appearances. Gustafson is a member of the College Football Hall of Fame as well as the Hurricane and Blackhawk Halls of Fame. He passed away in Coral Gables, Florida, in 1979.

would defeat the west-siders in nine of Thompson's first eleven years. One legendary exception took place on Thanksgiving Day in 1926, the first crosstown game played at West Aurora's new home field. Hampered by persistent rain and fog and a field that was ankle deep in mud, both teams had trouble moving the ball. The game was scoreless until the second half. East's Ed Schindel, punting from his own end zone, kicked the ball straight up, and when it landed, West's Leo Grass fell on it for the only score of the Red and Blue's 6–0 victory.

The Red and Black went undefeated in 1927, winning the conference title and finishing 8-0-1, including a 30–0 whitewashing of West. Ralph Fletcher left West after the 1927–28 school year to take the head coaching job at Waukegan High School. He would return two years later.

Prior to the 1929 season, the Big 7 Conference was reduced to the Big 6 when DeKalb once again withdrew. More significantly, East helped create the state's "Friday Night Lights" phenomenon by following Vermillion County's Westville High School as the second school in the state—and the

East Aurora coach Glen Thompson, ready to mix it up in practice. *Courtesy of East Aurora High School Speculum and the Aurora Historical Society.*

first in northern Illinois—to install permanent lights for night football.

Experiments with night games in all sports date back to the 1800s, but in 1929, technology, economics and social acceptance were still evolving. Lights had only begun to appear in minor-league baseball parks a few years earlier and would not reach the major leagues until the Cincinnati Reds installed them at old Crosley Field in 1935. College and high school football remained a Saturday afternoon tradition, leaving Sunday afternoons to professional and semipro teams.

East athletic director Roy Davis was the visionary behind East's venture into night football. Six-day workweeks were still common in 1929, making it difficult for many working fans to attend Saturday games. It was Davis who recognized the boon night football would be to attendance and then convinced the East High Athletic Association to raise the $3,000 needed to install lights. Once the money was raised, it was Davis who supervised construction. The original system consisted of fourteen giant reflectors mounted on fifty-five-foot poles, each with three one-thousand-watt bulbs. Students marveled at how well the action could be seen, with no noticeable shadows.

Program from the 1927 East-West game, which East won 30–0. *Courtesy of East Aurora High School.*

On September 21, 1929, East Aurora hosted the first high school game played under lights, defeating Downers Grove High School 43–0. *Courtesy of the Aurora Historical Society.*

Slade Cutter, East Class of 1928. Discouraged from participating in sports by his father, who had been injured while playing in college, the six-foot-two, 190-pound Cutter did not play football at East; he was a flutist in the band. As a senior, Cutter finished first in the flute in a national competition for high school musicians, which led him to enroll at Severn School, at the time a Maryland prep school for U.S. Naval Academy aspirants. While at Severn, Cutter met future Hall of Fame football coach Paul Brown and was persuaded to play football. Cutter then entered the Academy, where he earned three football letters and became an all-American tackle. He also earned two letters in lacrosse and three in boxing, and he won the collegiate heavyweight boxing championship. Cutter earned national notoriety when, on December 1, 1934, his twenty-yard field goal propelled Navy to a 3–0 victory over Army. It was the Midshipmen's first win over the Cadets in thirteen years.

As a submarine commander in World War II, Cutter was credited with sinking nineteen enemy ships, and for his service, he was a four-time Navy Cross, two-time Silver Star and one-time Bronze Star recipient. Cutter later served as the Naval Academy's director of athletics and as curator of the Naval War College Museum before his retirement in 1965. Captain Cutter was elected to the College Football Hall of Fame in 1967. He passed away in Annapolis, Maryland, in 2005.

The first game under the new lights was the 1929 season opener on Saturday, September 21, against Downers Grove High School. Approximately six thousand people, including representatives from several Chicago-area schools that were contemplating installing lights of their own, saw East crush their guests 43–0. From there, the Red and Black went on to a fine 8-1-0 record, with the only blemish being a 1-point loss to Elgin that cost them the 1929 conference championship.

Increased attendance brought on by night football during that first season enabled East to recoup its investment in just one year and continued to pay dividends for years. Before lighted fields became common, the Red and Black took full advantage of the novelty by inviting schools from across the state to experience night football. The grandstands were expanded, as twenty-two of East's twenty-five non-conference games played from 1929 through 1934 were home games, including twenty played at night. Early on, night football created a huge home-field advantage that enabled the Red and Black to win eighteen of those twenty games.

***

Coach Thompson's legacy continued to grow throughout the 1930s. "Tommy," as his players affectionately called him, was the inspiration behind East's Tomcat nickname, which first appeared in 1931. According to legend, the name came about when the school newspaper, the *East High Auroran*, ran a headline referring to "Tom's Cats," which quickly evolved into Tomcats. Whether it actually happened that way or not, in 1931, the *Beacon* picked up the story, and the name stuck.

Meanwhile, on the west side, Ralph Fletcher returned to once again lead West's football and basketball programs. After a 3-6-0 campaign in 1930, Fletcher's squad won the 1931 Big 6 championship with a 2-0-3 league record and ended a four-game losing streak to East with a 13–0 victory.

Both schools fielded mediocre teams in 1932, '33 and '34, but the east-siders at least took solace in the fact that Glen Thompson continued his mastery over West as the Tomcats won three consecutive shutouts.

This Turkey Day cartoon appeared in the November 25, 1931 edition of West Aurora's school newspaper, *The Red and Blue. Courtesy of the Aurora Historical Society.*

Marger Apsit, WA 1927

Marger "Migs" Apsit was born in Aurora on June 9, 1909, to Latvian immigrants Rhinart and Bertha Apsit, who arrived in the United States in 1903 and settled in what is now Aurora's Tanner Historic District shortly thereafter.

Growing up in the shadows of the old West High building on Blackhawk Street, one can imagine young Migs and the other neighborhood boys watching the Red and Blue practice during the week and then trekking over to Hurd's Island to take in the big game on Saturday.

Although Apsit played on some unremarkable West teams from 1924 to 1926, he was regarded as a remarkable player. The five-foot-eleven, 170-pound Apsit was a high-powered, smashing fullback who "hit the line like a thunderbolt," an outstanding blocker and a devastating tackler. After graduation, Migs found his way to the University of Southern California, where he was a three-year starter at halfback for legendary Trojan head coach Howard Jones. During his time at USC, the Trojans compiled a record of 27-4-1, were named 1928 national champions and appeared in the 1930 Rose Bowl.

Although never USC's featured back, Apsit was good enough to forge a three-year professional career as a journeyman player with the NFL's Brooklyn Dodgers, Frankford Yellow Jackets, Green Bay Packers and Boston Redskins.

After his playing days ended, Apsit returned to a hero's welcome at West Aurora, where he succeeded his high school mentor, Ralph Fletcher, as head coach in 1935. Almost immediately, Apsit breathed new life into what had become a middling program, leading the Blackhawks to a perfect 9-0-0 season and a conference championship in his second year as coach.

Although the '36 squad would be the Hawks' only conference championship during Apsit's eight years at West, his teams suffered just one losing season, and his .653 winning percentage ranks second all time among coaches with more than fifty games at West. His record against the Tomcats was 5-3-0.

Following the 1942 season, Apsit left Aurora for California, where he coached East Bakersfield High School for over twenty years. He is a member of both the Blackhawk and East Bakersfield Halls of Fame.

Throughout his life, Marger Apsit was known as a decent man who took an uncommon interest in his students and exuded good sportsmanship as a coach. He died in California in 1988 at age seventy-nine.

LaSalle-Peru High School, located in LaSalle, Illinois, sixty miles southwest of Aurora, joined the NIHSC for the 1935–36 school year. This returned the league to seven members for the first time since 1928. Earlier in the year, Ralph Fletcher resigned as football coach, although he remained as West's basketball coach and athletic director. Fletcher was replaced by Marger "Migs" Apsit.

Apsit was an Aurora native and 1927 West graduate who went on to play football at the University of Southern California before embarking on a three-year NFL career. Although his return to his hometown seemed to rejuvenate the west-siders, it did not produce immediate results, as the team posted a losing record for the sixth time in seven years while the 1935 "Thompsonmen," as East was sometimes called, tied for second in the Big 7 and shut out West for the fourth year in a row.

Things turned around for West Aurora in 1936. The players began the school year by adopting "Blackhawks" as the team nickname. The inspiration came from the school's location on Blackhawk Street, which was named to honor the great Sauk American Indian leader and warrior Black Hawk, who resided in northern Illinois and eastern Iowa from 1767 to 1838. The Blackhawk nickname seemingly gave the team newfound abilities, as West, behind the strong play of backs Vern Williamson and Ollie Hahnenstein, surrendered just 26 points in winning its first eight games of the '36 season. On the other side of town, the Tomcats and all-state end James Smith were nearly as impressive, outscoring their opponents 112–20 while going 5-0-2 before suffering a 2-point loss to Freeport in the season's next-to-last game.

The Tomcats' loss to Freeport clinched the conference championship for West and reduced the annual Thanksgiving season finale to a game for pride. The seesaw battle was tied in the fourth quarter when the

The Blackhawks' 1936 undefeated conference champions. *Top row, left to right:* Linemates Bob Peterson, Bill Murphy, John Brewer, Joe Cosentino, Melvin Sprinkel, Frank Scarpino and Bob Lage. *Bottom row, left to right:* The backfield of John Duke, Don Stephens, Oliver Hahnenstein and Vernon Williamson. *Courtesy of West Aurora High School Eos and the Aurora Historical Society.*

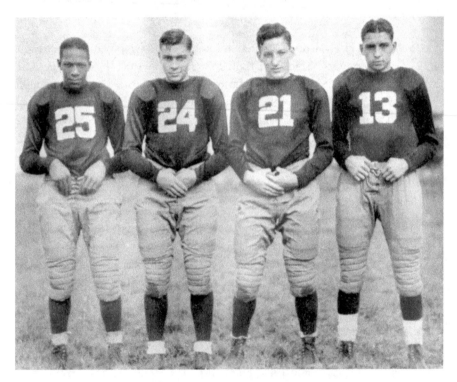

Blackhawks' Joe Constentino intercepted a pass and rumbled seventy-five yards for what would prove to be the game-winning touchdown. West's 18–12 victory capped the Blackhawks' perfect season and ended a four-game losing streak against East.

In 1937, East's innovative athletic director, Roy Davis, invited Horlick High School from Racine, Wisconsin, to play a non-conference interstate game, which the Tomcats won 24–6. The experiment proved so successful

Ralph Zilly, *East Class of 1939.* Team captain in 1938 and an all-state tackle, Zilly went on to play football at Northwestern University while studying business administration. After earning his bachelor's degree in 1943, Zilly entered the navy and served in the Philippines during World War II. At the war's end, Zilly embarked on a business career during which he was an executive in private industry before joining the administration of Brown University, from which he received an honorary master's degree in 1955. From Brown, Zilly moved to Penn State University, where he served as vice-president of financial affairs. He retired from Penn State in 1995 and passed away at his Rhode Island home in 1999.

that East would schedule out-of-state opponents in four of the next five years before the United States' entry into World War II produced gas shortages that limited travel. The '37 East-West game matched the 7-2-0 Tomcats and all-state guard Merril Heagy against the 6-2-0 Blackhawks and all-state running back Bob Peterson. An East victory would clinch a conference championship, but a safety and a thirty-yard touchdown pass from Frank Burgess to Peterson lifted West to a 9–6 victory that handed the crown to Rockford.

Many observers believe that the 1938 Tomcats were East's greatest team ever. A defensive juggernaut led by dominating all-state tackle Ralph Zilly and all-conference players Floyd Houghtby, George Presbrey, Anthony Jurgelonis and Roy Holle, the Tomcats did not give up a single point through their first eight games. Only Freeport had come within two touchdowns of the Red and Black.

A Thanksgiving Day crowd of over 8,000, including an estimated 2,500 who stood along fences behind the end zone, gathered at West Athletic Field to see whether the Tomcats could complete the ultimate unbeaten, untied and unscored-on perfect season. The crowd was stunned in the first quarter when the Blackhawks' Bill Nicholson broke through to block a Holle punt deep in Tomcat territory, and Dick Mumm scooped it up at the seven-yard line and ran in for an early touchdown. The play happened right in front of grade schooler Ed Colton, who had walked to the game with his east-side buddies and who would play for East in the mid-'40s. He vividly recalled seventy-five years later that East players were so visibly angry at having been scored on that they immediately broke through the line to block the extra point. After that, East's impenetrable defense allowed just forty-four yards, while East's Holle, Lee Barnett and Jack Hollen scored touchdowns to preserve the team's undefeated season.

In the following weeks, East was hopeful of receiving an invitation to play in a Christmas Day game affiliated with the Orange Bowl in Miami, but the invitation instead went to a school from Pennsylvania.

After the great three-year run of 1936–38, which produced two undefeated teams, two conference championships and just eleven total losses, both East and West entered a period of mediocre results and unique challenges brought on by World War II. In the 1939 East-West game, the Blackhawks scored three fourth-quarter touchdowns to erase a 7–0 Tomcat lead and win going away.

***

In 1940, the Big 7 became the Big 8 as Rockford split into Rockford East and Rockford West. LaSalle-Peru took conference honors, while East Aurora smashed West 25–6 in a battle for second place.

Economic conditions in Rockford in 1941 caused the district to shut down completely on November 7, and games played against Rockford East and West were not counted in the league standings that year. That gave Joliet its first league crown since '35. West's two all-staters, Gordon Peterson and Mercer Barnes, put on a show on Thanksgiving, as Peterson scored on runs

Thanksgiving Day, 1943. Tomcats 12, Blackhawks 0 at West Athletic Field. *Courtesy of East Aurora High School Speculum and the Aurora Historical Society.*

Coach Glen Thompson

Glen Thompson served as East Aurora's head football coach from 1925 until 1942. His 167 games coached and 105 victories are school records, and his .662 winning percentage is highest among East coaches with more than two years at the helm.

By 1924, the fortunes of East Aurora's program had fallen precipitously from the heights of the state championships claimed a decade earlier. Whereas the Red and Black had suffered just four losing seasons during the program's first 25 years, it took just seven years to produce four more losing seasons. Worse yet, East had beaten their crosstown rivals just once since 1915 and failed to even score in six of those nine games. When Coach Johnny Sabo announced he was leaving East at the end of the 1924–25 school year to pursue an assistant coaching position at the University of Kansas, the east-siders turned to twenty-nine-year-old Michigan native Glen Thompson to lead them out of the doldrums. He was, as it turned out, just the man for the job.

Born in Rockford, Michigan, on August 12, 1896, Thompson attended Kalamazoo College, where he starred in football, basketball and track. As a senior, Thompson was named the football team's most valuable player and was captain of the track team. He received a degree in economics in 1921.

With his degree in hand, Thompson moved to Danville, Illinois, where he taught and coached the local high school's football, basketball and track teams for two school years. Danville's football squads were 11-5-3 in two seasons under Thompson. From Danville, Thompson returned to his home state of Michigan, where he led the Orange and Black of Escanaba High School to undefeated seasons in 1923 and '24.

Hired by East Aurora in 1925, Thompson arrived with a reputation as a quiet but firm leader who demanded that his players be in top physical condition. Early in his career, he was known for his willingness to demonstrate a point by "lacing up the moleskins" and joining his players in the trenches, believing that actions speak louder than words.

Whereas no previous coach had lasted more than three seasons at East, Coach Thompson became an institution by remaining at the helm for more than seventeen years. During his tenure, Thompson led the Red and Black to two conference titles, helped introduce night football to northern Illinois and provided the inspiration for the Tomcat nickname when the school newspaper referred to the team as "Tom's Cats."

"Tommy's" greatest team, the undefeated and untied 1938 squad, was not scored on until the season finale with West Aurora. Overall, Coach Thompson's teams were 11-6-0 against the west-siders.

Coach Thompson likely would have remained at East for several more years if the U.S. Coast Artillery Corps hadn't called him to active service just prior to the 1942 Thanksgiving Day tilt with West. Captain Thompson left school in mid-November to serve "for the duration."

When he returned to Aurora at the war's end, Thompson, finding no openings at East, moved across town to Marmion Military Academy and coached the Cadets for three seasons beginning in 1948. After the 1950 season, Thompson left high school coaching to pursue a business career with the Stephens-Adamson Company. He and his wife, Marion, who was a mainstay in East Aurora's library for years, eventually bought a small farm near LaSalle, Illinois, but Coach held on to his Aurora ties by coaching the Aurora Clippers semipro team and remaining active with the East High Football Old-Timers Association. Glen Thompson passed away at his farm on October 5, 1966.

of forty-three, forty-five and seventy-seven yards and threw a touchdown pass to Barnes in the Hawks' 34–6 romp.

During the war years, all NIHSC schools endured the challenges of gas rationing, supply shortages and the loss of players and coaches to the war effort. In 1942, with only the East-West finale remaining, Tomcat coach Glen Thompson was called to active duty and left to serve in the U.S. Coast Artillery Corps, ending his eighteen-year reign as East's mentor. In Joe Maze's debut at East's helm, the Blackhawks' Bob Spackman scored two touchdowns in West's 13–8 victory in what would be Marger Apsit's last

Charles Mercer Barnes, *West Class of 1942*. An outstanding three-sport high school athlete, "Merc" Barnes earned all-state honors as a running back in 1941. He went on to play freshman football at the University of Illinois before enlisting in the navy, where he served as a pilot and flight instructor for the duration of World War II. When the fighting ended, Merc resumed his college football career as a center at the University of Southern California and also appeared in several "B" movies, including *Saturday's Hero, The Frogmen, Pride of St. Louis* and *The Stratton Story*. Barnes ultimately entered the business world and was co-founder and president of the Bay Seal Company in Hayward, California, which, as of 2014, is still in operation. Merc Barnes passed away at his home in Austin, Texas, in 2005.

game at West. Apsit was replaced by Leo Tilly, who would resign after just one season. Tilly was succeeded by Ken Zimmerman.

Coach Maze's 1944 Tomcats, led by all-state John O'Neil, compiled a 7-1-1 overall record and won the Big 8 crown with a 5-1-1 conference record. Meanwhile, on the west side, Ken Zimmerman's tenure as the Blackhawks' head coach got off to an inauspicious start, as West, despite the presence of all-state back Bill Gustafson, finished last in the league and lost to East, 14–13, when Rollin Tesch blocked West's attempt at a game-tying extra point.

Although the war ended in the summer of 1945, and soldiers and sailors began returning home, things on the home front did not immediately return to normal. A polio outbreak in Winnebago County caused the two Rockford schools and Freeport to cancel football that season. Both East and West were also-rans in the five-team league; the championship was won by LaSalle-Peru. For the second year in a row, Tesch was a Thanksgiving Day hero, as he returned a blocked punt forty-five yards for the only points in East's 6–0 victory. At that point, the Tomcats led the crosstown series 25-19-9.

Paul Patterson, *East Class of 1944*. A member of Aurora's Patterson clan that produced several outstanding athletes, Paul Patterson was an exceptional football, basketball and track athlete for the Tomcats. He entered the University of Illinois with future pro football star Buddy Young, and together they formed one of the most dynamic backfields in Illini history. After playing on the Illini freshman team in 1944, Patterson and Young entered the navy together and starred on one of the most famous base teams of the World War II era. The pair returned to lead the Illini to the 1946 Big Ten championship and a Rose Bowl victory. Patterson played professionally with the Chicago Hornets of the All-American Football Conference in 1949 and later worked for the Chicago Bears as scout, director of player relations and traveling secretary. He was chairman of the Illinois State Athletic Board, a member of the University of Illinois Athletic Board and a director of the United Negro College Fund. Paul Patterson passed away in 1982 at age fifty-five.

John O'Neil, *East Class of 1945*. East's co-captain (with Ed Coffee) and an all-state fullback as a senior, O'Neil, like so many young men at the time, enlisted in the marines a few weeks prior to graduation. As it turned out, the war ended as O'Neil was on his way to Japan, and he was mustered out after serving for one year. O'Neil then attended the University of Notre Dame, where he played for legendary Irish coach Frank Leahy and was a member of Notre Dame's undefeated 1949 national championship team. Upon his 1951 graduation, O'Neil returned to Aurora to join R.J. O'Neil Inc., the mechanical contracting firm his father founded in 1926. He retired as company president in 1992. John O'Neil passed away in Aurora in 2002.

Bill Gustafson, *West Class of 1945.* A cousin of West Hall of Famer Andy Gustafson, Bill was an all-state halfback and Blackhawk captain as a senior. He attended Northwestern University for one year before receiving an appointment to West Point, where he was a member of the Cadets' 1946 national championship team and a two-year letter winner. After completing his military service in 1953, Gustafson embarked on a thirty-year career with U.S. Steel, eventually rising to president of U.S. Steel International in Pittsburgh. He passed away in Pasadena, California, in 2004.

The year 1945 marked the end of an era in which the country endured a worldwide flu pandemic, fought two world wars and survived both the Great Depression and a polio scare. During this period, Aurora's high school sports teams soldiered on, and the annual Thanksgiving Day football game continued to be a local highlight each and every November. But the world was changing, and soon Aurora and its high schools would change as well.

EAST AURORA

WEST AURORA

1916

	W	L	T	Coach
Overall Record:	5	2	0	Telford Mead
Conference Record:	4	2	0	

Date	Opponent		EA	Opp
09.30	DeKalb Normal School	W	13	3
10.07	**DeKalb**	W	33	0
10.21	**Joliet**	W	40	0
11.04	**Rockford**	W	13	6
11.11	**Elgin**	W	3	0
11.18	**Freeport**	L	13	14
11.30	**West Aurora**	L	7	20

	W	L	T	Coach
Overall Record:	7	2	0	Carl Breneman
Conference Record:	3	1	1	

Date	Opponent		WA	Opp
09.23	Morris	W	13	0
09.30	Glen Ellyn	W	68	0
10.07	Mt. Morris College	W	33	0
10.14	**Freeport***	L	7	10
10.28	**Rockford**	L	0	7
11.04	**Joliet**	W	13	0
11.11	**DeKalb**	W	35	0
11.18	**Elgin***	W	6	0
11.30	**East Aurora**	W	20	7

*Results not included in conference record.

1917

	W	L	T	Coach
Overall Record:	5	1	2	Telford Mead
Conference Record:	2	1	2	

Date	Opponent		EA	Opp
09.29	Schurz	W	32	0
10.13	Galesburg	W	13	0
10.20	**Joliet**	T	0	0
10.27	LaGrange	W	31	0
11.03	**Rockford**	W	3	0
11.10	**Elgin**	W	13	0
11.17	**Freeport**	L	13	14
11.29	**West Aurora**	T	0	0

	W	L	T	Coach
Overall Record:	3	4	1	George Bogard
Conference Record:	1	3	1	

Date	Opponent		WA	Opp
09.22	Wheaton	W	7	0
10.06	**Freeport**	L	0	27
10.13	Champaign	L	0	20
10.20	Kewanee	W	29	0
10.27	**Rockford**	L	0	26
11.03	**Joliet**	W	14	6
11.17	**Elgin**	L	6	13
11.29	**East Aurora**	T	0	0

Key: W = Win, L = Loss, T = Tie, WF = Win by forfeit, LF = Loss by forfeit, **Bold** = Conference game, *Italics* = state playoff game

East Aurora   West Aurora

1918

	W	L	T	Coach				W	L	T	Coach
Overall Record:	2	5	0	Tracey Cone		Overall Record:		4	2	2	J. McGough (1-1-1)
Conference Record:	Season cancelled					Conference Record:		Season cancelled			R. Valentine (3-1-1)

Date	Opponent		EA	Opp		Date	Opponent		WA	Opp
09.28	Streator	W	12	0		09.28	Wheaton	W	45	0
10.05	Freeport	W	25	0		10.05	Elgin	T	7	7
10.10	Northwestern College	L	13	20		10.12	Oak Park	L	0	33
11.02	Mooseheart	L	0	6		11.09	Freeport	W	20	13
11.09	Culver Military Academy	L	0	61		11.16	LaGrange	W	29	14
11.16	Elgin	L	0	26		11.20	Northwestern College	L	7	14
11.28	West Aurora	L	0	6		11.28	East Aurora	W	6	0
						11.30	DeKalb	T	0	0

1919

	W	L	T	Coach				W	L	T	Coach
Overall Record:	5	4	0	David Glascock		Overall Record:	7	2	0	George Bogard
Conference Record:	5	1	0			Conference Record:	5	1	0	

Date	Opponent		EA	Opp		Date	Opponent		WA	Opp
09.27	LaGrange	L	7	27		09.26	Naperville	W	39	0
10.04	**Freeport**	W	13	6		10.04	Proviso	W	7	0
10.11	**DeKalb**	W	12	0		10.11	**Elgin**	W	13	6
10.18	**Rockford**	W	7	6		10.18	**Joliet**	W	53	0
10.25	Streator	L	13	28		10.25	**Rockford**	L	0	6
11.01	**Joliet**	W	33	12		11.08	**Freeport**	W	20	0
11.08	Mooseheart	L	0	3		11.15	**DeKalb**	W	16	0
11.15	**Elgin**	W	13	6		11.27	**East Aurora**	W	13	0
11.27	**West Aurora**	L	8	13		12.06	Flushing (New York)	L	0	27

Conference Co-champions   *Conference Co-champions*

EAST AURORA

WEST AURORA

1920

	W	L	T	Coach		W	L	T	Coach
Overall Record:	2	6	1	Billy Robinson	Overall Record:	3	5	1	R. Courtwright
Conference Record:	2	3	1		Conference Record:	3	4	0	

Date	Opponent		EA	Opp	Date	Opponent		WA	Opp
09.25	LaGrange	L	0	7	09.25	Dundee	T	7	7
10.02	**Freeport**	L	12	20	10.02	Mooseheart	L	0	51
10.09	**DeKalb**	T	7	7	10.09	**Elgin**	L	6	13
10.16	**Rockford**	L	6	26	10.16	**Joliet**	W	13	0
10.23	Streator	L	7	28	10.23	**Rockford**	L	0	2
10.30	**Joliet**	W	28	0	10.30	Streator	L	0	42
11.06	Mooseheart	L	0	31	11.06	**Freeport**	W	40	6
11.13	**Elgin**	L	7	34	11.13	**DeKalb**	W	14	0
11.25	**West Aurora**	W	14	6	11.25	**East Aurora**	L	6	14

1921

	W	L	T	Coach		W	L	T	Coach
Overall Record:	6	4	0	Billy Robinson	Overall Record:	4	4	0	Ralph Fletcher
Conference Record:	3	3	0		Conference Record:	4	2	0	

Date	Opponent		EA	Opp	Date	Opponent		WA	Opp
09.24	LaGrange	W	13	7	09.24	Mooseheart	L	0	6
09.30	DeKalb Normal School	W	13	3	10.01	Oak Park	L	0	50
10.01	**Freeport**	W	28	6	10.08	**Elgin**	L	7	10
10.08	**DeKalb**	W	16	6	10.15	**Joliet**	W	20	0
10.15	**Rockford**	L	7	13	10.22	**Rockford**	L	0	20
10.22	Streator	W	10	0	11.05	**Freeport**	W	30	0
10.29	**Joliet**	W	14	0	11.12	**DeKalb**	W	16	0
11.05	Mooseheart	L	7	14	11.24	**East Aurora**	W	7	0
11.12	**Elgin**	L	0	7					
11.24	**West Aurora**	L	0	7					

Key: W = Win, L = Loss, T = Tie, WF = Win by forfeit, LF = Loss by forfeit, **Bold** = Conference game, *Italics* = state playoff game

EAST AURORA

WEST AURORA

1922

	W	L	T	Coach		W	L	T	Coach
Overall Record:	4	4	0	Billy Robinson	Overall Record:	10	0	1	Ralph Fletcher
Conference Record:	3	3	0		Conference Record:	6	0	0	

Date	Opponent		EA	Opp	Date	Opponent		WA	Opp
09.30	**Freeport**	L	6	12	09.23	Batavia	W	13	7
10.07	**DeKalb**	W	6	0	09.30	Ottawa	W	33	0
10.14	**Rockford**	L	0	12	10.07	**Elgin**	W	13	0
10.28	**Joliet**	W	7	6	10.14	**Joliet**	W	33	0
11.04	Mooseheart	L	0	7	10.21	**Rockford**	W	32	13
11.11	**Elgin**	W	6	0	10.28	Mooseheart	T	0	0
11.18	Ottawa	W	20	0	11.04	**Freeport**	W	26	0
11.30	**West Aurora**	L	0	6	11.11	**DeKalb**	W	20	0
					11.18	Morris	W	54	12
					11.30	**East Aurora**	W	6	0
					12.09	Findlay (Findlay, OH)	W	20	6

Conference Champions

1923

	W	L	T	Coach		W	L	T	Coach
Overall Record:	2	3	3	Johnny Sabo	Overall Record:	5	1	1	Ralph Fletcher
Conference Record:	1	2	3		Conference Record:	5	0	1	

Date	Opponent		EA	Opp	Date	Opponent		WA	Opp
09.29	St. Charles	W	19	7	09.29	Mooseheart	L	0	16
10.06	**Freeport**	W	19	0	10.13	**Elgin**	W	7	3
10.13	**DeKalb**	T	0	0	10.20	**Joliet**	W	25	7
10.20	**Rockford**	L	13	14	10.27	**Rockford**	W	3	2
11.02	**Joliet**	T	0	0	11.10	**Freeport**	W	3	0
11.10	Mooseheart	L	0	10	11.17	**DeKalb**	W	6	0
11.17	**Elgin**	L	0	9	11.29	**East Aurora**	T	3	3
11.29	**West Aurora**	T	3	3					

Conference Champions

EAST AURORA

WEST AURORA

1924

	W	L	T	Coach			W	L	T	Coach
Overall Record:	3	7	0	Johnny Sabo	Overall Record:		5	3	0	Ralph Fletcher
Conference Record:	0	6	0		Conference Record:		3	3	0	

Date	Opponent		EA	Opp	Date	Opponent		WA	Opp
09.20	St. Charles	W	16	0	09.27	Sandwich	W	26	0
09.27	St. Ignatius	W	32	6	10.04	Naperville	W	10	0
10.04	**Freeport**	L	6	31	10.11	**Elgin**	L	0	16
10.11	**DeKalb**	L	6	9	10.18	**Joliet**	W	13	7
10.18	**Rockford**	L	7	27	10.25	**Rockford**	L	0	13
10.25	Mooseheart	L	0	20	11.08	**Freeport**	L	6	20
11.01	**Joliet**	L	13	20	11.15	**DeKalb**	W	26	0
11.08	Glenbard	W	14	13	11.27	**East Aurora**	W	28	0
11.15	**Elgin**	L	14	16					
11.27	**West Aurora**	L	0	28					

1925

	W	L	T	Coach			W	L	T	Coach
Overall Record:	6	4	0	Glen Thompson	Overall Record:		2	5	1	Ralph Fletcher
Conference Record:	3	3	0		Conference Record:		2	3	1	

Date	Opponent		EA	Opp	Date	Opponent		WA	Opp
09.19	Mendota	W	17	0	09.26	Glenbard	L	0	31
09.26	Bloom	W	7	6	10.03	**DeKalb**	T	7	7
10.03	**Elgin**	L	0	7	10.17	**Elgin**	L	0	7
10.10	**Freeport**	L	0	27	10.24	**Joliet**	W	24	7
10.17	**DeKalb**	W	9	0	10.31	**Rockford**	W	7	0
10.24	**Rockford**	W	14	0	11.07	Morton	L	2	6
10.31	Mooseheart	L	0	42	11.14	**Freeport**	L	0	44
11.07	**Joliet**	L	0	6	11.26	**East Aurora**	L	0	3
11.14	Austin	W	2	0					
11.26	**West Aurora**	W	3	0					

Key: W = Win, L = Loss, T = Tie, WF = Win by forfeit, LF = Loss by forfeit, **Bold** = Conference game, *Italics* = state playoff game

EAST AURORA   WEST AURORA

1926

	W	L	T	Coach		W	L	T	Coach
Overall Record:	5	4	1	Glen Thompson	Overall Record:	5	3	0	Ralph Fletcher
Conference Record:	1	4	1		Conference Record:	4	2	0	

Date	Opponent		EA	Opp	Date	Opponent		WA	Opp
09.18	Downers Grove	W	27	0	09.25	Naperville	W	21	0
09.25	Geneva	W	51	0	10.02	**Freeport**	W	13	0
10.02	**DeKalb**	L	3	7	10.09	**Rockford**	L	0	20
10.09	Normal Community	W	29	0	10.23	**Elgin**	L	0	6
10.16	**Joliet**	W	14	6	10.30	**Joliet**	W	22	0
10.23	**Freeport**	T	7	7	11.06	**DeKalb**	W	7	6
10.30	Fenger	W	48	0	11.13	Morton	L	0	2
11.06	**Elgin**	L	0	6	11.25	**East Aurora**	W	6	0
11.13	**Rockford**	L	0	3					
11.25	**West Aurora**	L	0	6					

1927

	W	L	T	Coach		W	L	T	Coach
Overall Record:	8	0	1	Glen Thompson	Overall Record:	1	2	5	Ralph Fletcher
Conference Record:	5	0	1		Conference Record:	0	2	4	

Date	Opponent		EA	Opp	Date	Opponent		WA	Opp
09.17	Downers Grove	W	37	0	09.24	Crane Tech	W	19	6
09.24	Morgan Park	W	53	0	10.01	Morton	T	0	0
10.01	**Rockford**	W	13	0	10.08	**Freeport**	T	6	6
10.08	**DeKalb**	W	55	0	10.15	**Rockford**	L	2	9
10.22	**Joliet**	W	12	3	10.29	**Elgin**	T	0	0
10.29	**Freeport**	W	19	6	11.05	**Joliet**	T	0	0
11.05	Sterling	W	13	0	11.12	**DeKalb**	T	6	6
11.12	**Elgin**	T	6	6	11.24	**East Aurora**	L	0	30
11.24	**West Aurora**	W	30	0					

Conference Champions

81

EAST AURORA   WEST AURORA

1928

	W	L	T	Coach			W	L	T	Coach
Overall Record:	4	4	2	Glen Thompson		Overall Record:	5	3	0	Emil Schultz
Conference Record:	2	3	1			Conference Record:	3	3	0	

Date	Opponent		EA	Opp	Date	Opponent		WA	Opp
09.22	Downers Grove	W	18	6	09.29	Naperville	W	32	0
09.29	Glenbard	L	12	13	10.06	**DeKalb**	W	13	0
10.06	**Elgin**	L	7	38	10.13	Morton	W	6	0
10.13	**Rockford**	L	0	6	10.20	**Freeport**	W	13	0
10.20	**DeKalb**	T	0	0	10.27	**Rockford**	W	7	0
10.27	Sandwich	W	25	0	11.10	**Elgin**	L	6	40
11.03	**Joliet**	L	6	13	11.17	**Joliet**	L	0	20
11.10	**Freeport**	W	21	0	11.29	**East Aurora**	L	6	12
11.17	Bloom	T	0	0					
11.29	**West Aurora**	W	12	6					

1929

	W	L	T	Coach			W	L	T	Coach
Overall Record:	8	1	0	Glen Thompson		Overall Record:	2	5	2	Emil Schultz
Conference Record:	4	1	0			Conference Record:	0	3	2	

Date	Opponent		EA	Opp	Date	Opponent		WA	Opp
09.21	Downers Grove	W	43	0	09.21	Sandwich	W	25	0
09.27	Glenbard	W	18	0	09.28	Riverside	W	23	0
10.04	Hall	W	18	6	10.05	**Joliet**	L	12	13
10.12	**Elgin**	L	6	7	10.19	Elgin	L	6	18
10.19	**Rockford**	W	27	0	10.26	**Freeport**	T	13	13
10.25	Parker	W	21	6	11.02	**Rockford**	T	13	13
11.09	**Joliet**	W	12	0	11.09	Wheaton	L	7	39
11.16	**Freeport**	W	54	0	11.16	**Elgin**	L	0	21
11.28	**West Aurora**	W	28	0	11.28	**East Aurora**	L	0	28

Key: W = Win, L = Loss, T = Tie, WF = Win by forfeit, LF = Loss by forfeit, **Bold** = Conference game, *Italics* = state playoff game

EAST AURORA

WEST AURORA

1930

	W	L	T	Coach		W	L	T	Coach
Overall Record:	8	1	0	Glen Thompson	Overall Record:	3	6	0	Ralph Fletcher
Conference Record:	4	1	0		Conference Record:	1	4	0	

Date	Opponent		EA	Opp	Date	Opponent		WA	Opp
09.19	Hyde Park	W	26	6	09.20	York	L	0	2
09.26	Wheaton	W	53	0	09.27	Sandwich	W	7	6
10.03	**Freeport**	W	47	7	10.04	**Elgin**	L	12	20
10.10	Belvidere	W	63	7	10.10	**Joliet**	L	0	12
10.17	**Elgin**	W	14	7	10.18	**Freeport**	W	26	12
10.24	**Rockford**	L	0	21	10.31	Wheaton	W	13	6
10.31	Bowen	W	50	0	11.08	**Rockford**	L	0	40
11.15	**Joliet**	W	41	2	11.15	**DeKalb**	L	6	13
11.27	**West Aurora**	W	13	0	11.27	**East Aurora**	L	0	13

1931

	W	L	T	Coach		W	L	T	Coach
Overall Record:	5	4	0	Glen Thompson	Overall Record:	6	0	3	Ralph Fletcher
Conference Record:	3	2	0		Conference Record:	2	0	3	

Date	Opponent		EA	Opp	Date	Opponent		WA	Opp
09.18	Urbana	W	19	0	09.26	York	W	13	6
09.25	Parker	L	7	20	10.03	Sandwich	W	26	6
10.02	Thornton	W	12	7	10.10	**Rockford**	W	13	7
10.09	**Joliet**	L	6	7	10.16	**Elgin**	T	14	14
10.16	**Freeport**	W	8	6	10.23	**Freeport**	T	0	0
10.23	**Elgin**	W	19	0	10.31	**Joliet**	T	6	6
10.31	**Rockford**	W	14	7	11.07	DeKalb	W	25	13
11.14	Moline	L	6	7	11.14	Lockport	W	20	13
11.26	**West Aurora**	L	0	13	11.26	**East Aurora**	W	13	0

Conference Champions

EAST AURORA   WEST AURORA

1932

	W	L	T	Coach		W	L	T	Coach
Overall Record:	5	3	1	Glen Thompson	Overall Record:	2	4	3	Ralph Fletcher
Conference Record:	2	2	1		Conference Record:	0	3	2	

Date	Opponent		EA	Opp	Date	Opponent		WA	Opp
09.16	Parker	W	3	0	09.24	York	L	0	7
09.23	St. Charles	W	13	7	10.01	Glenbard	W	14	0
09.30	Urbana	W	7	0	10.08	Lockport	W	27	6
10.14	**Joliet**	L	0	13	10.15	**Rockford**	L	0	13
10.21	**Freeport**	W	2	0	10.22	**Elgin**	T	0	0
10.28	**Elgin**	L	0	6	10.29	**Freeport**	T	0	0
11.05	**Rockford**	T	0	0	11.05	**Joliet**	L	13	18
11.12	Moline	L	0	6	11.12	DeKalb	T	6	6
11.24	**West Aurora**	W	31	0	11.24	**East Aurora**	L	0	31

1933

	W	L	T	Coach		W	L	T	Coach
Overall Record:	7	1	1	Glen Thompson	Overall Record:	3	6	0	Ralph Fletcher
Conference Record:	3	1	1		Conference Record:	0	5	0	

Date	Opponent		EA	Opp	Date	Opponent		WA	Opp
09.22	St. Charles	W	32	0	09.23	York	L	0	7
09.29	York	W	18	0	09.30	Glenbard	W	13	0
10.06	Morton	W	32	0	10.06	DeKalb	W	19	0
10.20	**Joliet**	T	0	0	10.21	**Rockford**	L	0	6
10.27	**Freeport**	W	19	0	10.27	**Elgin**	L	7	10
11.04	**Elgin**	W	7	6	11.04	**Freeport**	L	7	13
11.11	**Rockford**	L	0	3	11.11	**Joliet**	L	8	20
11.18	Parker	W	14	6	11.18	Belvidere	W	32	0
11.30	**West Aurora**	W	13	0	11.30	**East Aurora**	L	0	13

Key: W = Win, L = Loss, T = Tie, WF = Win by forfeit, LF = Loss by forfeit, **Bold** = Conference game, *Italics* = state playoff game

EAST AURORA

WEST AURORA

1934

	W	L	T	Coach
Overall Record:	5	5	0	Glen Thompson
Conference Record:	2	3	0	

Date	Opponent		EA	Opp
09.14	St. Charles	W	13	0
09.21	Naperville	W	7	0
09.28	York	W	13	0
10.05	**Rockford**	L	6	7
10.12	Parker	L	6	12
10.26	**Joliet**	L	0	14
11.03	**Freeport**	L	0	6
11.10	**Elgin**	W	19	7
11.17	Evanston	L	0	34
11.29	**West Aurora**	W	7	0

	W	L	T	Coach
Overall Record:	3	4	2	Ralph Fletcher
Conference Record:	1	3	1	

Date	Opponent		WA	Opp
09.22	York	W	20	0
09.29	Glenbard	L	0	7
10.05	**Joliet**	L	7	12
10.13	DeKalb	W	19	12
10.26	**Rockford**	L	0	19
11.03	**Elgin**	W	6	0
11.10	**Freeport**	T	13	13
11.17	Lyons Township	T	13	13
11.29	**East Aurora**	L	0	7

1935

	W	L	T	Coach
Overall Record:	6	3	0	Glen Thompson
Conference Record:	4	2	0	

Date	Opponent		EA	Opp
09.20	St. Charles	W	19	6
09.27	Marmion Military Academy	W	24	0
10.04	**Elgin**	W	25	0
10.12	**Rockford**	W	12	7
10.18	**LaSalle-Peru**	L	6	18
11.02	**Joliet**	L	0	13
11.09	**Freeport**	W	14	0
11.15	Kankakee	L	12	19
11.28	**West Aurora**	W	20	0

	W	L	T	Coach
Overall Record:	4	6	0	Marger Apsit
Conference Record:	2	4	0	

Date	Opponent		WA	Opp
09.21	York	L	0	7
09.28	Glenbard	L	0	6
10.04	**Freeport**	W	13	0
10.12	**Joliet**	L	6	20
10.19	DeKalb	W	18	0
10.26	**LaSalle-Peru**	L	0	6
11.02	**Rockford**	L	6	20
11.09	**Elgin**	W	14	13
11.16	Marmion Military Academy	W	12	6
11.28	**East Aurora**	L	0	20

EAST AURORA

WEST AURORA

1936

	W	L	T	Coach
Overall Record:	5	2	2	Glen Thompson
Conference Record:	3	2	1	

Date	Opponent		EA	Opp
09.18	Naperville	W	14	0
09.25	Marmion Military Academy	W	53	0
10.02	Thornton	T	0	0
10.09	**Elgin**	T	0	0
10.16	**Rockford**	W	13	7
10.23	**LaSalle-Peru**	W	12	6
11.06	**Joliet**	W	20	7
11.14	**Freeport**	L	12	14
11.26	**West Aurora**	L	12	18

	W	L	T	Coach
Overall Record:	9	0	0	Marger Apsit
Conference Record:	6	0	0	

Date	Opponent		WA	Opp
09.18	York	W	7	0
09.25	Glenbard	W	12	6
10.02	Marmion Military Academy	W	18	0
10.09	**Freeport**	W	27	0
10.16	**Joliet**	W	7	0
10.30	**LaSalle-Peru**	W	7	0
11.07	**Rockford**	W	14	13
11.14	**Elgin**	W	34	7
11.26	**East Aurora**	W	18	12

Conference Champions

1937

	W	L	T	Coach
Overall Record:	7	3	0	Glen Thompson
Conference Record:	4	2	0	

Date	Opponent		EA	Opp
09.10	Naperville	W	19	2
09.17	Horlick (Racine, WI)	W	24	6
09.24	Bloom	W	12	0
10.01	**Freeport**	W	33	14
10.08	Thornton	L	12	13
10.15	**Elgin**	W	19	0
10.22	**Rockford**	L	7	19
10.29	**LaSalle-Peru**	W	15	6
11.13	**Joliet**	W	27	12
11.25	**West Aurora**	L	6	9

	W	L	T	Coach
Overall Record:	7	2	0	Marger Apsit
Conference Record:	4	2	0	

Date	Opponent		WA	Opp
09.17	Naperville	W	18	0
09.24	Morton	W	19	0
10.01	Marmion Military Academy	W	24	0
10.08	**Elgin**	W	14	0
10.15	**Freeport**	L	7	13
10.22	**Joliet**	W	18	6
11.05	**LaSalle-Peru**	L	7	13
11.11	**Rockford**	W	20	0
11.25	**East Aurora**	W	9	6

Key: W = Win, L = Loss, T = Tie, WF = Win by forfeit, LF = Loss by forfeit, **Bold** = Conference game, *Italics* = state playoff game

CHAPTER 5

1946–73: AURORA FOOTBALL DURING THE POSTWAR, BABY BOOM AND PSYCHEDELIC ERAS

L ike the rest of the country, postwar Aurora navigated through a period of unprecedented economic prosperity followed by the turmoil of social change that extended into the early 1970s. Record birth rates associated with baby boomers, together with a general migration from Chicago's city limits to its suburbs and an influx of Hispanic immigrants seeking work in local factories, drove Aurora's population to increase more than 50 percent, from 48,000 to 74,000, from 1946 to 1970.

During these years, the Aurora area was a decidedly blue-collar industrial center offering good-paying manufacturing jobs at companies that were primarily locally owned. Companies in the materials handling equipment industries included Barber-Green, Austin-Western and Stephens-Adamson. Richards-Wilcox and McKee Door made residential and commercial garage doors. All-Steel and Lyon Metal manufactured metal cabinets and storage units. Stoner Manufacturing made vending machines, while Pines Engineering, National Brush, Love Brothers, Thor Tools, Equipto, Aurora Pump and others offered jobs in other industries. The Burlington Northern Railroad continued to maintain a significant presence throughout most of this period, as did Western Electric, which had a major plant in nearby Montgomery.

Downtown Aurora circa 1950 was a bustling commerce center. The presence of Aurora National, Old Second National and Merchants National banks naturally made downtown a banking center, but the district is also fondly remembered for its shopping and entertainment options. For shoppers, downtown offered national retailers, including Sears Roebuck, Montgomery Wards, Carson Pirie Scott and Woolworth's; successful local retail stores like Block and Kuhl, Sencenbaugh's, and Ginsberg's; and a host of specialty shops. For those interested in a night on the town, the area was home to movie theaters and a variety of restaurants, including the Leland Hotel's trendy Sky Club and Plantation Room, Welches' Steak House, Paradise Inn, Strand Restaurant and the Swedish Tea Room, among others. In addition to the Leland, travelers could stay at the Aurora hotel or one of several smaller inns. A collection of ten to twenty seedy bars within a couple blocks of one another on North Broadway, near the railroad yards, and the streetwalkers of nearby LaSalle Street were also prominent features not so frequently discussed.

The economic conditions of the Great Depression and the labor and material shortages brought on by the war effort meant that very few new homes were built in Aurora from 1931 to 1945, and as was the case nationally, the new economic prosperity of the 1950s and '60s, coupled with the baby boom, created local housing shortages that led to the building of thousands of typical 1950s-style tract homes—one-thousand-square-foot homes with two or three bedrooms, one bath and an optional detached one-car garage—in previously undeveloped areas on both sides of town. Aurora's own population explosion also necessitated the construction of the present-day West Aurora High School and East Aurora High School, which opened in 1953 and 1957, respectively.

On local football fields, the Blackhawks and Tomcats provided their followers with a lot to cheer about, and the rivalry remained as intense as ever.

***

In the years immediately following the end of World War II, the Big 8 Conference, together with the Chicago Public League and the Catholic League, were among Illinois' top football conferences. And from 1946 to 1949, Ken Zimmerman's West Aurora teams ranked with Illinois' best.

The Blackhawks' dominant '46 squad, which posted a perfect 10-0-0 record and is often cited as West's greatest team, featured first-team all-staters Don Laz, Brad Quackenbush and Dick Olson, as well as all-conference honorees Ray Williams, Jack Marzuki, Owen Jaffke and John Auther. Equally dominant on offense and defense, the Hawks averaged twenty-four points per game while giving up just six en route to becoming the third West squad to

Athletic Director Roy E. Davis

From the day he arrived in Aurora as a twenty-three-year-old science teacher until his death some sixty-six years later, Roy Davis was a reserved, beloved and respected educator whose dedication to his job and devotion to East's students made him a pillar of the east-side community.

Born on September 18, 1889, Davis grew up in central Wisconsin. After graduating from Ripon College around 1910, he taught science at Eastern Illinois State Normal School in Charleston, Illinois, and State Agricultural College in East Lansing, Michigan (now Michigan State University), before arriving at East Aurora at the start of the 1913–14 school year. Hired to teach science, Davis quickly added the unpaid, part-time role of athletic director to his teaching responsibilities. He would continue in both roles for forty-three years.

As athletic director, Davis spearheaded many of East's most significant accomplishments, changes and innovations during the first half of the twentieth century. Basketball was in it's infancy when Davis arrived in 1913, and he organized all of the behind-the-scenes activities, from scheduling to supplying equipment to selling tickets. When the 1915 football team capped off a second consecutive undefeated state championship season with a 25–0 victory over West Aurora, it was Davis who organized the Red and Black's subsequent trip to New York City, where the boys played Hamilton Institute in a nationally followed intersectional game. Of course, he was part of the entourage of local dignitaries who accompanied the team, serving as chaperone, press agent, tour guide and biggest fan.

In 1916, Davis was instrumental in forming the original Northern Illinois High School Conference, subsequently referred to as the Big 8 Conference. When the railroad's takeover of Hurd's Island forced East to find a new place to play, Davis was the man who orchestrated the purchase of the property at South State Street and Fifth Avenue and managed the construction project. Nine years later, it was his vision that brought night football to northern Illinois and created the state's version of "Friday Night Lights."

Although the demands of being athletic director increased over the years, Davis remained committed to the classroom and was a popular science teacher. He somehow found time to collaborate with his brother, Ira, to write the textbook *A Combined Laboratory Manual and Workbook in Biology*, which was first published in 1937. Through it all, Davis always wanted the best for East and it's athletes, and he could often be seen on the athletic fields, personally adding a new piece of fencing, doing some painting or watering the grass.

Never one to sit idly on the sidelines, Davis was also an active leader of several local professional organizations, and his activities included terms as president of the East Aurora Teachers' Association, the Northwest Division of the Illinois Athletic Association and the Fox Valley Coaches' Association. He was a member of the Illinois Basketball Rules Committee and president and secretary-treasurer of the Illinois Coaches' Association.

At halftime of the opening game of the 1947 season, Superintendent K.D. Waldo, representatives from every other Big 8 Conference school and a capacity crowd publicly thanked Davis for his contributions by christening the football stadium Roy E. Davis Field. Seven years later, Davis announced that the 1954–55 school year would be his last, and at the '54 homecoming game, East students presented him with the keys to a new car, courtesy of a fundraising drive they themselves had organized. The *Beacon* estimated that during his forty-three years at East, Davis had taught science to some ten thousand students and awarded 4,500 letters as athletic director.

After retiring from teaching, Davis represented Knox College as a local admissions counselor. He also served on the board of directors of the Edna Smith Home and the local American Red Cross chapter, and he continued to be an active member of Aurora's Elks and Kiwanis clubs. He passed away in January 1979 at the age of eighty-nine.

stalled when John Mouis was tackled at West's 1-yard line, preserving the scoreless tie and earning West the conference title. The Blackhawks ended the season at 9-0-1, while the Cats finished 7-1-2. West's Don McGuire and East's John Hollis earned all-state honors.

The high-scoring '49 Blackhawks and all-state end Frank Smith averaged twenty-eight points per game on their way to a 9-1-0 season and their third Big 8 title in four years. The Red and Blue won their first seven games to run their unbeaten streak to 21 before dropping a 39–31 decision to Elgin in November. In the season finale, East had a chance to drop the west-siders into a three-way tie for first place with Elgin and LaSalle-Peru, but the Blackhawks won the crown outright with a 20–13 victory. East's Melvin Parker joined West's Smith on the all-state team, as the Tomcats posted a 6-3-1 overall record and finished fifth in the Big 8.

***

Don Griffin replaced Joe Maze as East's coach in 1950 and led the Cats to an overall record of 5-5-0 and a league record of 4-3-0. Meanwhile, West and all-state halfback Dean Guzman finished third in the Big 8 with a 5-2-0 record that included a 19–13 come-from-behind win over the Tomcats on Thanksgiving. Dave Ochsenschlager's four-yard touchdown with four minutes left in the fourth quarter clinched the Blackhawk victory.

Griffin's 1951 East squad finished with a better overall record than the west-siders for the first time since 1944. The entire town was embroiled in controversy by the west side's mid-season announcement that the 1952 East-West meeting, scheduled to be played at West, would not take place on Thanksgiving.

Since the early 1930s, most Illinois high schools ended their football seasons on the first or second weekend of November, but Aurora had continued to hold on to a Thanksgiving tradition that began in 1895 and had been uninterrupted since 1902. Although the decision was unpopular in many circles, West officials noted that late November weather was often uncooperative and that extending the season added two to three weeks of additional practice on cold, dark afternoons. Furthermore, since the NIHSC schedule makers did not automatically arrange for East and West to play in the season's final week, accommodating the Thanksgiving tradition often meant that the two schools had a mid-season bye week. Finally, the fact that a Thanksgiving game conflicted with the start of the increasingly popular basketball season was a primary driver of the change. East-side officials, however, were not quite convinced.

Whatever the future might bring, 1951 marked the fiftieth consecutive year Aurora's two public high schools met on the gridiron for a friendly game of football, and the seven thousand people who showed up saw West's all-state halfback Ron Smith score touchdowns on offense, defense and

Roy E. Davis Field, November 26, 1953. East defeated West 19–7 in the last Thanksgiving Day game. *Courtesy of West Aurora High School Eos and the Aurora Historical Society.*

special teams to lead West to a 32–18 victory that left the two teams tied for second in the Big 8.

Both East and West anticipated lean seasons in 1952, but Coach Griffin's Tomcats surprised prognosticators by finishing third in the Big 8, while West finished seventh. On November 14, a capacity crowd saw Jim McCue's two touchdowns propel the Cats past West, 29–7, in the first night game in series history.

In 1953, West Aurora moved from the old building on Blackhawk Street to a modern facility built on property immediately adjacent to the athletic fields at the corner of Walnut Street (now New York Street) and Commonwealth Avenue. Although it has been expanded many times over the years, the building remains in use today.

Although neither school had much to cheer about on the football field in '53, the season ended in grand style, as East hosted one last Turkey Day game. That Thanksgiving, young Bobby Burnell's family watched from the roof of their home on the north side of Fifth Avenue, directly across from Roy E. Davis Field, as East topped West 19–7. Bob later attended East and, as an adult, worked as part of the Tomcat broadcast team.

***

From 1954 to 1957, East Aurora won three Big 8 championships and finished second once, compiling a sterling four-year record of 27-6-3 overall and 23-3-2 in league play.

East Aurora's 1956 Big 8 Conference champions. *Courtesy of East Aurora High School Speculum and the Aurora Historical Society.*

All-stater Dave Timok led the Tomcats to the 1954 Big 8 championship and an 8-1-0 overall record. The only blemish was a 19–13 upset at the hands of West Aurora and Preston Hundley, who scored on two long touchdown runs, in the first mid-season clash between the crosstown rivals since the schools entered the NIHSC in 1916.

The 1954–55 school year ended with Roy Davis's retirement after forty-three years at East, and Griffin was promoted to athletic director. Art Court, who had been a Tomcat assistant coach for twenty years, took the reigns of the football program. The '54 Tomcats, led by future Tomcat Hall of Famer Bob McCue's two touchdowns, shut out West 26–0 and finished the season with a fine 7-1-1 overall record, but a late-season loss to Elgin cost them the conference title. Meanwhile, Ken Zimmerman's west-siders posted a losing record for the fourth consecutive year.

The '56 Cats started slowly, tying a tough Proviso squad and losing 13–6 to Bloom Township in non-conference action before riding all-state fullback Don Schultz to an undefeated Big 8 season. In winning their second league title in three years, East dominated opponents by an average score of 28–6, including a 25–6 blowout of the Blackhawks, who had regained their winning form to finish 6-3-0 overall and fourth in the Big 8.

East Aurora moved from the old Jackson Street building to its present campus at the corner of Fifth Avenue and Smith Boulevard in time to start the 1957–58 school year. Not all of the facilities were complete, but the classrooms and other fundamental buildings were operational. After forty years of shuttling back and forth between the old school and the practice fields, which were a mile apart, having all facilities located on the same grounds must have seemed like a luxury to players and coaches alike.

As everyone at the new school settled into a routine and the football season began, the Tomcats again started slowly, losing both non-conference games and splitting the first two league games before turning it around to post a league mark of 4-1-1 after six games. The tie was a 19-all draw with West Aurora in which East's Lee Brown prevented a loss by picking up a fumbled snap on the game-tying extra point attempt and running around the right end for the tying point (two point conversions would come later). Heading into the season's final weekend, the two rivals were tied atop the Big 8 standings. On the final Friday, the Blackhawks lost at LaSalle-Peru, 13–7, while a Tomcat touchdown in the final minute of their game with Freeport doomed the Pretzels and vaulted East to the 1957 Big 8 title, their third in four years.

***

Just as the Tomcats' run of championship seasons came to an end, Ken Zimmerman's Blackhawks embarked on a three-year revival that featured the running of all-state back Ken Zimmerman Jr. in 1958 and culminated with an undefeated Big 8 championship in 1960.

West's 1960 championship season began with Joliet leaving the Big 8 Conference, while newly built Rockford Auburn took the Steelmen's place. West Aurora and all-stater Gary Munn opened the '60 season by tying DeKalb and losing to Joliet in non-conference action, but once the Big 8 schedule kicked off, the Blackhawk defense turned stingy, and the Red and Blue swept through the Big 8 schedule, including a 12–6 victory earned in the final minutes of the finale with East Aurora. This was West's fourth conference championship under Zimmerman, and the school's ninth. Meanwhile, Art Court's Tomcats rebounded from back-to-back losing seasons to finish the year with a record of 6-2-1.

Court resigned for health reasons after the 1960 season, and Del Dufrain arrived as his replacement. Both East and West had losing seasons in '61, and the year ended with East beating the west-siders 14–6 in what would be the first of many Dufrain-led victories over the Blackhawks.

Ed Washington, East Class of 1960. After earning all-conference honors as a tackle in 1959, Washington played three years at the University of Illinois, where he was a starter on the offensive line for the Illini's 1963 Big Ten championship team that defeated the Washington Huskies in the Rose Bowl and ended the season ranked third in the nation. After his playing days ended, Washington became a teacher and coach at Larkin High School in Elgin. His memory lives on in the Ed Washington Sportsmanship Award, given annually to the Upstate 8 Conference wrestler who demonstrates outstanding character and sportsmanship throughout the wrestling season.

Pre-game hijinks struck the 1962 East-West game, which was played in September that year, when a group of East students snuck over to the west side and, depending on who you believe, either placed a box with the words "GO EAST!" or hung women's undergarments atop West Aurora's flag pole. Fifty years later, the details of the story vary, but the bottom line was that the group included at least three Tomcat players who, despite the fact that they were "merely observing," received suspensions nonetheless. East won the game anyway, 13–0, and went on to tie Auburn for the '62 Big 8 crown. It was the eighth and final Big 8 conference championship for East Aurora, as next year the Tomcats and Blackhawks would join the Upstate 8 Conference.

***

The suburbs' postwar population explosion necessitated the building of a plethora of new high schools that began sprouting up across the suburban Chicago landscape in the mid-1950s and did not slow until the 1970s. The northwest suburbs' District 214, which had been served only by Arlington High School for fifty years, opened Prospect High School in Mount Prospect in 1957. Within fifteen years, District 214 would operate eight secondary schools. Also in 1957, the south suburbs welcomed Thornton Fractional South in Lansing, Illinois. Maywood's historic Proviso High, a frequent Tomcat non-conference foe at the time, split into Proviso East and Proviso West in 1958. Maine West in Des Plaines, Homewood-Flossmoor in Flossmoor, Villa Park's Willowbrook, Northlake's West Leyden, Lombard's

Glenbard East, Niles West in Skokie and Deerfield High all opened in 1959. By 1965, Thornridge High School in Dolton, Tinley Park, Joliet West, Amos Alonzo Stagg in Palos Hills, Palatine's William Fremd, James B. Conant High in Hoffman Estates, Darien's Hinsdale South, Elgin's Larkin, Wheaton North and Guilford and Auburn High Schools in Rockford would all open their doors. To accommodate these newly opened centers of learning, a league of new schools aptly named the Interim Conference operated while the dust settled.

The opening of so many new schools in relatively close proximity to one another, together with the natural growth of existing community high schools that had previously been too small to compete regularly with the larger Big 8 schools (such as Naperville, Wheaton and St. Charles), resulted in an area-wide conference realignment intended to reduce travel time and transportation costs while cultivating new natural rivalries. Long-standing leagues like the West Suburban Conference, the Southwest Suburban Conference and the Big 8 reorganized, and new conferences were created to accommodate the growing number of schools. It was during this period that the Upstate 8 Conference (1963), the Mid-Suburban Conference (1963) and the Central Suburban League (1965)—traditional suburban leagues today—were founded.

After competing in the Big 8 conference for forty-six years, East Aurora, West Aurora and Elgin joined DeKalb, Glenbard East, Larkin, Naperville and Wheaton as charter members of the Upstate 8 Conference, which began competition in the 1963–64 school year. The Big 8, meanwhile, shifted its focus to northern Illinois' Winnebago County, as Harlem, Belvidere and Guilford High Schools replaced the three defectors in 1963, with Rockford's Boylan High School replacing LaSalle County's LaSalle-Peru High School to complete the transition in 1964. Today's Northern Illinois Conference (also known as the NIC-10) traces its history back to the old Northern Illinois High School (or Big 6, 7 or 8) Conference, with Freeport as the lone remaining original member.

***

East Aurora dominated Upstate 8 football in the early years, as the Tomcats went unbeaten in their first nineteen league games and earned league titles in 1963, '64 and '66. The '63 Cats compiled a perfect 9-0-0 season that culminated with a 27–0 win over West. A defensive juggernaut, the Cats shut out five opponents and yielded fewer than five points per game and

East assistant coach Art Court is carried off the field after the Tomcats' 21–6 victory over West in 1964. *Courtesy of East Aurora High School Speculum and the Aurora Historical Society.*

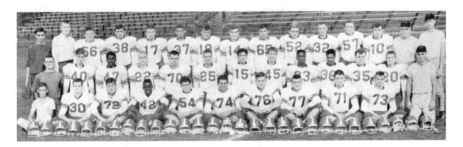

East Aurora's 1963 Upstate 8 Conference champions. *Courtesy of East Aurora High School Speculum and the Aurora Historical Society.*

Ralph Galloway, East Class of '64. A two-way lineman for East's undefeated, untied 1963 team, Galloway played offensive guard for three seasons at Southern Illinois University before embarking on an eleven-year career with the Saskatchewan Roughriders of the Canadian Football League. During his playing days with the Roughriders, Galloway appeared in three Grey Cup championship games and was a five-time CFL all-star guard. He was inducted into the Roughriders' Plaza of Honor in 1996. When his playing days were over, Galloway coached high school football in Washington State until his retirement.

placed seven players on the *Chicago Tribune*'s all-conference team, including quarterback Mike Murphy, tackles Bill Schindel and Ralph Galloway, halfback Jim Davis, linebackers Bob Court and Jack Hughes and middle-guard Michael Leonard.

Despite returning only one regular from the previous year's team, East's '64 squad featured another strong defensive unit that shut out five opponents and held two others to six points each. The Tomcats' only loss of the season was a 21–17 non-conference decision to Rockford West that ended their eleven-game win streak in the season's second week. From there, the Cats went on to post a 6-0-1 league record to claim their second Upstate 8 title and third straight conference title spanning two leagues. Their 21–6 victory over the Blackhawks was the Tomcat's fourth in a row against the west-siders.

As the new schools continued to open, conference alignments remained somewhat unstable in the mid-1960s, and Glenbard East left the Upstate 8 for the Des Plaines Valley League prior to the 1965–66 school year. St. Charles High School took the Rams' spot.

The '65 Tomcats opened the season with two non-conference shutouts and were still undefeated after six weeks. In week seven, East narrowly avoided losing to DeKalb when an errant snap on a potential game-tying extra point was tracked down by placekicker Dick Schindel, lateraled to Dan Schwartz and then passed to Tommy Jones in the end zone for a one-point conversion that tied the game at 14 and ended the scoring. The tie extended East's unbeaten streak to nineteen conference games, but lopsided losses to eventual conference champ Wheaton Central and West Aurora in the season's last two weeks left the Tomcats in fourth place in the final standings. Meanwhile, Coach Zimmerman's Blackhawks received contributions from four sets of brothers—Butch and Steve Ethington, Steve and Chuck Fuller, twins Jim and Jack Lutz and Duane and Ron Keenan—to record their best season in five years with a 6-3-0 overall record, a second-place Upstate 8 finish and a 26–13 victory over the East in the season finale that broke a string of four straight losses to their crosstown rivals.

In 1966, the Blackhawks and Tomcats found themselves embroiled in a wild four-way battle with DeKalb and Larkin for the loop title that came down to the season's final weekend. The Cats controlled their own fate, needing only to beat West Aurora to earn the championship outright, while a Larkin victory over winless Elgin coupled with an East Aurora loss would vault the Royals into first place. The Hawks needed a win over the east-siders, together with a Larkin loss to tie East, and possibly DeKalb, for the title.

On the season's final weekend, West Aurora's Steve Ethington threw three touchdown passes and scored on an interception return to lead the Hawks to a 34–7 romp over the east-siders, while DeKalb's win over St. Charles and Elgin's stunning 13–12 upset of Larkin left the Blackhawks, Tomcats and Barbs tied atop the league with 5-2-0 records. This marked the first time since 1919 the Aurora rivals shared a conference title. At season's end, West's Steve Fuller and East's Tom Jones earned all-state honors.

Aurora football fans had little to be excited about from 1967 to 1969, as East Aurora produced a string of middle-of-the pack teams, at best, while the west-siders struggled to keep up. Meanwhile, the entire community was confronted on all fronts by the same issues of social unrest that embroiled the rest of the country.

In September 1967, Friday night games at both East and West were postponed to Saturday afternoon after racially motivated disturbances led Aurora city officials to impose a curfew. Local African Americans, upset that the city council had not passed an open housing ordinance, staged a march on downtown that disintegrated into rock throwing and gunfire. Fifteen arrests were made. West's game with Marmion Military Academy and East's game with Rockford West were both moved to Saturday afternoon, which turned out to be a prudent decision, as more disturbances took place that night. Order was eventually restored, and the rest of the season went as scheduled, but neither team displayed much fight as the Blackhawks and Tomcats won just five games between them. Nonetheless, the East-West game was a barnburner settled by John Witte's late touchdown, which helped turn what had been a 13-point fourth-quarter deficit into a 14–13 Tomcat victory.

The years 1968 and '69 provided two more malaise-filled seasons, as both ended with the Tomcats taking the annual rivalry game from the Hawks with little trouble. In '68, the Blackhawks dominated the game statistically, but turnovers led to a 27–6 East rout. The following year, East's Tom Boatright returned a kickoff ninety yards for a touchdown in the Tomcats' 25–14 victory. It marked the seventh time in Dufrain's first nine years at East that the Cats had bested West.

In different ways, the 1970 season proved to be exciting on the field and shocking off for folks on both sides of the Fox River. The season began innocently enough, albeit disappointingly, as LaSalle-Peru's Cavaliers shut out East 20–0, while Joliet Catholic High School pounded the Blackhawks 30–6 on opening night. The following Monday, Coach Zimmerman shocked the entire community by announcing that, after twenty-six years at West Aurora, he was retiring from coaching immediately. At the time, Zim declined to give a reason for his departure, but the bottom line was that he was out, and longtime assistant coach Dick Zuege was promoted to the top spot.

For whatever reason, the Blackhawks were rejuvenated under Coach Zuege, and over the next six weeks, the team played some of its best football in years, winning five in a row and six of seven heading into the season's final weekend. Meanwhile, after losing both of its non-conference games, East breezed through six Upstate 8 foes and stood 6-0-0, with only the Blackhawks standing in the way of a conference championship. A Tomcat victory or tie would mean an undisputed conference championship for the east-siders, while a Blackhawk win would result in a three-way tie between East, West and DeKalb—if the Barbs won their final game with St. Charles.

On a crisp November Friday evening, the visiting Tomcats took an early 6–0 lead when quarterback Doug Dobbins connected with Gleason James on a seventy-five-yard pass play, but the Blackhawks outplayed East throughout the rest of the half and held an 8–6 halftime lead. The second half, however, was all East as Dobbins threw a touchdown pass to Kevin Buckley and James capped the scoring with a two-yard plunge in the final quarter to propel the east-siders to a 19–8 win and the conference title. DeKalb, meanwhile, held on to beat St. Charles 19–14 to clinch second place, while the Blackhawks fell to third.

However, in January of the following year, East Aurora officials announced the discovery of an administrative error that had caused the Tomcats to unknowingly use an unnamed ineligible player throughout the season. As a result, East forfeited all its conference games and vacated the conference title to the Barbs, who reluctantly accepted it. Forty-some years later, as an Upstate 8 championship trophy collects dust in a display case at DeKalb High School, fond memories of that championship season reside in the hearts and minds of the '70 Tomcats and their fans.

Coach Ken Zimmerman

West Aurora's Ken Zimmerman Field is named in honor of the Blackhawks' longtime football coach, athletic director and teacher.

Born in Gurnee, Illinois, in 1917, Zimmerman was a backfield star at Warren Township High School before enrolling at the University of Illinois, where he played multiple positions during three seasons under fabled Illini coach Bob Zuppke.

After graduating from Illinois in 1939, Zimmerman launched his high school coaching career in Wyoming, Illinois, a small farming community about thirty-five miles northwest of Peoria. Zim took over a beleaguered Wyoming football program that had won just four games in the previous five seasons, coached the basketball team and served as athletic director. He proved to be no miracle worker, as the Indians went 0-9-0 in 1939. Nonetheless, the Wyoming community was pleased with Zim's approach to teaching and the improvement the team had shown, and it was sorely disappointed when Zim resigned after one year to take a similar role at Woodstock High School, which was closer to his boyhood home and family.

Zimmerman stayed at Woodstock for two winless seasons before returning to Illinois to pursue his master's degree and coach the Illini's 1942 freshman football team. When World War II cutbacks eliminated freshman athletics prior to the '43 season, Zim returned to the high school ranks at Marengo High School, where he coached for one year before landing at West Aurora in 1944. He would remain at West until his retirement thirty years later.

The zenith of Zim's career as a football coach took place during the Blackhawks' powerhouse years of the late 1940s, when his teams lost just five games in four seasons. The 1946 Blackhawks, called West's greatest team by some observers, capped a perfect 10-0-0 season with a 41–0 rout of East Aurora and a conference championship. After breaking even in 1947, West bounced back with Big 8 Conference championships in 1948 and '49, compiling a record of 18-1-1 during those two seasons.

West Aurora added conference championships in 1960 and 1966 before Zim shocked the Aurora community by abruptly resigning one game into the 1970 season. Although he gave no explanation at the time he stepped down, Zim later told the *Beacon* that he had retired because he felt the age gap between him and his players had caused a lack of "electricity" when he coached, feelings that were typical of the pronounced conflict between older Americans and young people during the tumultuous, groundbreaking era of the late '60s and early '70s. After stepping down as head football coach, Zim continued to serve as athletic director and as a physical education teacher until he retired following the 1973–74 school year.

Although the Zimmerman-led Blackhawks were up and down throughout the 1950s and '60s, Zim built an enviable reputation as a gentleman who combined high moral character with a tremendous work ethic, and as someone who cared deeply about each and every one of his players. The positive impact Zim had on hundreds of players who came through his program over the years is undeniable.

Zim still holds school records for games coached (239), wins (125) and losses (104), and his winning percentage at West was .544. Against East Aurora, Zim's record was 10-13-3.

Ken Zimmerman was elected to the Illinois High School Football Coaches Association Hall of Fame in 1981. He died in Aurora in 1990 at the age of seventy-two.

Although the east-siders entered the 1971 season with the high expectations associated with a good team that was returning ten regulars, the Tomcats managed just one conference victory on the year. Whether the downturn was a result of the way the previous season had ended or caused by the introduction of the open campus concept (popularized in the early 1970s but later shown to cause students to lose focus over the course of the school day) is open to conjecture, but the Tomcats did not shake the doldrums until the second half of the season finale with West. Trailing 18–0 at halftime, East rallied and scored a touchdown on a pass from Doug Dobbins to Kevin Buckley in the game's final minute to claim a 21–18 victory. The Blackhawks could at least take solace in finishing one spot ahead of last-place East in the final Upstate 8 standings.

The Red and Black improved to 5-4-0 in 1972, while West Aurora fell to 1-8-0 overall and was winless in the Upstate 8. The Tomcats' most

West Aurora's longtime coach Ken Zimmerman with Bob Kellett in 1963. *Courtesy of East Aurora High School Eos and the Aurora Historical Society.*

lopsided victory of the East-West series was the 47–6 pounding they put on West that year.

In 1973, the Illinois High School Association (IHSA) lengthened the season to ten games—a prelude to the state football playoff system that was scheduled to launch the following year. East Aurora finished a respectable 6-4-0 and in fourth place in the Upstate 8, while West was 2-7-1 with one lone conference win. The Tomcats, behind Richard Williams's 192 rushing yards, won the annual East-West clash for the sixth time in seven years, 31–16. The only Blackhawk "win" during that streak was East's 1970 forfeit. At the close of the 1973 season, the rivals had met eighty-one times, with the Tomcats holding the series edge 39-30-12.

***

The city of Aurora, with its plentiful middle-class manufacturing jobs, had prospered throughout much of the postwar period. Homes constructed in the 1950s and '60s filled in older neighborhoods in what are now considered

Joe Thorgesen, West Class of 1974. West's team captain and an all-conference player in 1973, Thorgesen continued his football career at Illinois Wesleyan University, where he earned three varsity letters and also played baseball. After graduating from Wesleyan in 1978, Thorgesen began his teaching and coaching career at Kaneland High School, where he served as head football coach for twenty-six years beginning in 1981. During his tenure as head coach, the Knights had an overall record of 150-110, qualified for the state playoffs for twelve consecutive years and won back-to-back state championships in 1997 and '98. Although he stepped away from head coaching after the 2006 season, Thorgesen has remained in the program as an assistant.

the city's near-east and near-west sides. Several new schools, including the facilities used by East and West today, opened their doors. The bustling downtown district, with its many commercial, shopping and entertainment establishments, served as a destination for residents from town and the surrounding area.

During this period, the Tomcat and Blackhawk football programs achieved great success interspersed with a few down periods. Both were competitive and respected throughout Illinois, and the local rivalry retained its intensity for students and townsfolk alike. In retrospect, however, one can now see that as this era came to a close, the Aurora community had begun to change. And while the changes might have been almost imperceptible at the time, they were nonetheless powerful enough to eventually turn the city from a thriving manufacturing center to a city in decline to a diverse bedroom community that is both a Chicago suburb and Illinois' second-largest city. And while no one knew it at the time, many of those same factors had already begun to impact the football programs at East Aurora and West Aurora, as both schools were in the early stages of what would become a long downhill slide from competitive significance to also-ran status.

East Aurora

West Aurora

1946

	W	L	T	Coach			W	L	T	Coach
Overall Record:	1	7	2	Joe Maze		Overall Record:	10	0	0	Ken Zimmerman
Conference Record:	1	5	1			Conference Record:	7	0	0	

Date	Opponent		EA	Opp	Date	Opponent		WA	Opp
09.13	Naperville	L	13	45	09.13	Downers Grove	W	21	7
09.21	New Trier	L	0	32	09.20	DeKalb	W	21	0
09.27	**Elgin**	W	6	0	09.27	**LaSalle-Peru**	W	14	7
10.04	**Freeport**	T	6	6	10.04	**Rockford West**	W	20	6
10.11	**Rockford West**	L	0	14	10.11	**Joliet**	W	13	6
10.18	**LaSalle-Peru**	L	6	17	10.18	**Rockford East**	W	19	7
10.25	Bloom	T	6	6	10.25	Argo	W	27	12
11.01	**Rockford East**	L	0	6	11.01	**Elgin**	W	34	0
11.08	**Joliet**	L	0	9	11.08	**Freeport**	W	34	19
11.28	**West Aurora**	L	0	41	11.28	**East Aurora**	W	41	0

Conference Champions

1947

	W	L	T	Coach			W	L	T	Coach
Overall Record:	3	6	1	Joe Maze		Overall Record:	4	4	2	Ken Zimmerman
Conference Record:	2	4	1			Conference Record:	2	3	2	

Date	Opponent		EA	Opp	Date	Opponent		WA	Opp
09.12	Naperville	L	7	12	09.12	Downers Grove	W	12	6
09.19	Maine Township	L	0	14	09.19	DeKalb	L	6	8
09.26	**Elgin**	W	12	6	09.26	**LaSalle-Peru**	L	0	34
10.03	**Freeport**	W	12	0	10.03	**Rockford West**	T	7	7
10.10	**Rockford West**	L	6	13	10.10	**Joliet**	L	14	19
10.17	**LaSalle-Peru**	L	0	19	10.17	**Rockford East**	L	0	12
10.24	Bloom	W	7	6	10.24	Argo	W	6	0
10.31	**Rockford East**	L	6	14	10.31	**Elgin**	W	7	6
11.07	**Joliet**	L	0	25	11.07	**Freeport**	W	7	0
11.27	**West Aurora**	T	0	0	11.27	**East Aurora**	T	0	0

Key: W = Win, L = Loss, T = Tie, WF = Win by forfeit, LF = Loss by forfeit, **Bold** = Conference game, *Italics* = state playoff game

EAST AURORA   WEST AURORA

1948

	W	L	T	Coach		W	L	T	Coach
Overall Record:	7	1	2	Joe Maze	Overall Record:	9	0	1	Ken Zimmerman
Conference Record:	5	0	2		Conference Record:	6	0	1	

Date	Opponent		EA	Opp	Date	Opponent		WA	Opp
09.10	Naperville	W	19	12	09.10	Morris	W	6	0
09.17	Maine Township	L	20	32	09.17	DeKalb	W	13	0
09.24	Argo	W	20	13	09.24	Niles Township	W	25	13
10.01	**Elgin**	T	7	7	10.01	**LaSalle-Peru**	W	7	6
10.08	**Freeport**	W	20	7	10.08	**Rockford West**	W	19	0
10.15	**Rockford West**	W	32	0	10.15	**Joliet**	W	12	7
10.22	**LaSalle-Peru**	W	32	6	10.22	**Rockford East**	W	13	12
11.05	**Rockford East**	W	18	2	11.05	**Elgin**	W	14	12
11.12	**Joliet**	W	6	0	11.12	**Freeport**	W	19	6
11.25	**West Aurora**	T	0	0	11.25	**East Aurora**	T	0	0

Conference Champions

1949

	W	L	T	Coach		W	L	T	Coach
Overall Record:	6	3	1	Joe Maze	Overall Record:	9	1	0	Ken Zimmerman
Conference Record:	3	3	1		Conference Record:	6	1	0	

Date	Opponent		EA	Opp	Date	Opponent		WA	Opp
09.16	Bloomington	W	39	6	09.16	Naperville	W	20	18
09.23	Bloom	W	19	12	09.23	DeKalb	W	25	13
09.30	Maine Township	W	20	7	09.30	Niles Township	W	27	7
10.07	**Elgin**	L	6	14	10.07	**LaSalle-Peru**	W	19	9
10.14	**Freeport**	W	37	6	10.14	**Rockford West**	W	33	14
10.21	**Rockford West**	T	12	12	10.21	**Joliet**	W	33	13
10.28	**LaSalle-Peru**	L	0	7	10.28	**Rockford East**	W	38	13
11.11	**Rockford East**	W	26	6	11.11	**Elgin**	L	31	39
11.18	**Joliet**	W	20	19	11.18	**Freeport**	W	37	14
11.24	**West Aurora**	L	13	20	11.24	**East Aurora**	W	20	13

Conference Champions

Key: W = Win, L = Loss, T = Tie, WF = Win by forfeit, LF = Loss by forfeit, **Bold** = Conference game, *Italics* = state playoff game

EAST AURORA   WEST AURORA

1950

	W	L	T	Coach		W	L	T	Coach
Overall Record:	5	5	0	Don Griffin	Overall Record:	6	2	1	Ken Zimmerman
Conference Record:	4	3	0		Conference Record:	5	2	0	

Date	Opponent		EA	Opp	Date	Opponent		WA	Opp
09.15	Hinsdale	L	6	12	09.15	Naperville	W	34	6
09.22	Bloom	W	20	13	09.22	DeKalb	T	6	6
09.29	Joliet	L	14	19	09.29	Freeport	W	31	13
10.06	Maine Township	L	13	20	10.13	LaSalle-Peru	W	40	14
10.13	Elgin	L	7	17	10.20	Rockford West	W	25	13
10.20	Freeport	W	24	0	10.27	Joliet	L	14	19
10.27	Rockford West	W	20	6	11.03	Rockford East	W	23	9
11.03	LaSalle-Peru	W	26	0	11.17	Elgin	L	13	31
11.17	Rockford East	W	19	7	11.23	East Aurora	W	19	13
11.23	West Aurora	L	13	19					

1951

	W	L	T	Coach		W	L	T	Coach
Overall Record:	7	3	0	Don Griffin	Overall Record:	5	4	0	Ken Zimmerman
Conference Record:	5	2	0		Conference Record:	5	2	0	

Date	Opponent		EA	Opp	Date	Opponent		WA	Opp
09.14	Hinsdale	W	14	6	09.14	Naperville	L	12	13
09.21	Bloom	W	12	7	09.21	DeKalb	L	7	13
09.28	Joliet	L	6	13	09.28	Freeport	L	20	25
10.05	Maine Township	L	6	26	10.12	LaSalle-Peru	W	19	0
10.12	Elgin	W	21	13	10.19	Rockford West	W	20	16
10.19	Freeport	W	23	7	10.26	Joliet	L	13	20
10.26	Rockford West	W	14	6	11.02	Rockford East	W	26	0
11.02	LaSalle-Peru	W	16	6	11.16	Elgin	W	7	6
11.16	Rockford East	W	21	13	11.22	East Aurora	W	32	18
11.22	West Aurora	L	32	18					

East Aurora   West Aurora

1952

	W	L	T	Coach			W	L	T	Coach
Overall Record:	5	3	1	Don Griffin		Overall Record:	1	8	0	Ken Zimmerman
Conference Record:	5	1	1			Conference Record:	1	6	0	

Date	Opponent		EA	Opp	Date	Opponent		WA	Opp
09.12	Downers Grove	L	7	13	09.13	York	L	0	32
09.19	Bloom	L	13	25	09.19	DeKalb	L	6	13
09.26	**Rockford East**	W	20	0	09.26	**Elgin**	L	13	49
10.03	**Joliet**	T	6	6	10.03	**Freeport**	W	14	0
10.17	**Elgin**	L	13	20	10.17	**LaSalle-Peru**	L	7	15
10.24	**Freeport**	W	12	6	10.24	**Rockford West**	L	0	20
10.31	**Rockford West**	W	26	13	10.31	**Joliet**	L	19	46
11.07	**LaSalle-Peru**	W	27	7	11.07	**Rockford East**	L	13	22
11.14	**West Aurora**	W	27	9	11.14	**East Aurora**	L	7	29

1953

	W	L	T	Coach			W	L	T	Coach
Overall Record:	4	4	1	Don Griffin		Overall Record:	3	6	0	Ken Zimmerman
Conference Record:	3	3	1			Conference Record:	1	6	0	

Date	Opponent		EA	Opp	Date	Opponent		WA	Opp
09.18	East Moline	W	6	0	09.18	Morris	W	19	0
09.25	Bloom	L	6	19	09.25	DeKalb	W	26	0
10.02	**Rockford East**	L	7	15	10.02	**Elgin**	L	7	13
10.09	**Joliet**	L	6	13	10.09	**Freeport**	W	8	0
10.23	**Elgin**	L	6	32	10.23	**LaSalle-Peru**	L	7	13
10.30	**Freeport**	W	20	0	10.30	**Rockford West**	L	7	40
11.06	**Rockford West**	W	7	0	11.06	**Joliet**	L	0	27
11.13	**LaSalle-Peru**	T	6	6	11.13	**Rockford East**	L	0	46
11.26	**West Aurora**	W	19	7	11.26	**East Aurora**	L	7	19

Key: W = Win, L = Loss, T = Tie, WF = Win by forfeit, LF = Loss by forfeit, **Bold** = Conference game, *Italics* = state playoff game

EAST AURORA

WEST AURORA

1954

	W	L	T	Coach		W	L	T	Coach
Overall Record:	8	1	0	Don Griffin	Overall Record:	3	5	1	Ken Zimmerman
Conference Record:	6	1	0		Conference Record:	3	4	0	

Date	Opponent		EA	Opp	Date	Opponent		WA	Opp
09.17	East Moline	W	13	0	09.17	Blue Island Community	L	12	27
09.24	Bloom	W	6	0	09.24	DeKalb	T	6	6
10.01	**Rockford East**	W	19	7	10.01	**Rockford West**	W	14	0
10.08	**LaSalle-Peru**	W	14	13	10.08	**Freeport**	W	20	12
10.15	**Joliet**	W	19	7	10.15	**Elgin**	L	6	20
10.22	**West Aurora**	L	13	19	10.22	**East Aurora**	W	19	13
10.29	**Elgin**	W	20	12	10.29	**Joliet**	L	7	12
11.05	**Freeport**	W	40	6	11.05	**LaSalle-Peru**	L	6	20
11.12	**Rockford West**	W	41	7	11.12	**Rockford East**	L	19	34

Conference Champions

1955

	W	L	T	Coach		W	L	T	Coach
Overall Record:	7	1	1	Art Court	Overall Record:	4	5	0	Ken Zimmerman
Conference Record:	5	1	1		Conference Record:	3	4	0	

Date	Opponent		EA	Opp	Date	Opponent		WA	Opp
09.16	East Moline	W	28	10	09.16	DeKalb	L	20	33
09.23	Bloom	W	26	12	09.23	Naperville	W	20	7
09.30	**Rockford East**	W	13	0	9.30	**Rockford West**	L	0	13
10.07	**LaSalle-Peru**	W	15	0	10.07	**Freeport**	W	18	7
10.14	**Joliet**	W	26	0	10.14	**Elgin**	L	7	33
10.21	**West Aurora**	W	26	0	10.21	**East Aurora**	L	0	26
10.28	**Elgin**	L	7	20	10.28	**Joliet**	W	19	0
11.04	**Freeport**	T	0	0	11.04	**LaSalle-Peru**	W	20	7
11.11	**Rockford West**	W	27	7	11.11	Rockford East	L	0	14

EAST AURORA   WEST AURORA

1956

	W	L	T	Coach			W	L	T	Coach
Overall Record:	7	1	1	Art Court		Overall Record:	6	3	0	Ken Zimmerman
Conference Record:	7	0	0			Conference Record:	4	3	0	

Date	Opponent		EA	Opp	Date	Opponent		WA	Opp
09.14	Proviso	T	7	7	09.14	DeKalb	W	14	13
09.21	Bloom	L	6	13	09.21	Naperville	W	20	0
09.28	**Rockford West**	W	21	6	09.28	**Rockford East**	L	6	20
10.05	**Rockford East**	W	27	6	10.05	**Rockford West**	W	20	6
10.12	**LaSalle-Peru**	W	26	6	10.12	**Freeport**	W	12	0
10.19	**Joliet**	W	35	0	10.19	**Elgin**	L	14	26
10.26	**West Aurora**	W	25	6	10.26	**East Aurora**	L	6	25
11.02	**Elgin**	W	23	13	11.02	**Joliet**	W	26	0
11.09	**Freeport**	W	40	7	11.09	**LaSalle-Peru**	W	27	19

Conference Champions

1957

	W	L	T	Coach			W	L	T	Coach
Overall Record:	5	3	1	Art Court		Overall Record:	4	4	1	Ken Zimmerman
Conference Record:	5	1	1			Conference Record:	4	2	1	

Date	Opponent		EA	Opp	Date	Opponent		WA	Opp
09.14	Proviso	L	6	25	09.13	DeKalb	L	26	27
09.20	Bloom	L	7	19	09.21	Glenbrook	L	7	27
09.27	**Rockford East**	W	27	0	09.27	**Rockford East**	W	13	12
10.04	**Rockford West**	L	0	14	10.04	**Rockford West**	W	37	19
10.11	**LaSalle-Peru**	W	25	0	10.11	**Freeport**	W	12	6
10.18	**Joliet**	W	25	0	10.18	**Elgin**	L	0	25
10.25	**West Aurora**	T	19	19	10.25	**East Aurora**	T	19	19
11.01	**Elgin**	W	25	6	11.01	**Joliet**	W	31	0
11.08	**Freeport**	W	21	14	11.08	**LaSalle-Peru**	L	7	13

Conference Champions

Key: W = Win, L = Loss, T = Tie, WF = Win by forfeit, LF = Loss by forfeit, **Bold** = Conference game, *Italics* = state playoff game

EAST AURORA   WEST AURORA

1958

	W	L	T	Coach		W	L	T	Coach
Overall Record:	3	5	1	Art Court	Overall Record:	7	2	0	Ken Zimmerman
Conference Record:	2	4	1		Conference Record:	5	2	0	

Date	Opponent		EA	Opp	Date	Opponent		WA	Opp
09.12	Proviso East	W	72	26	09.12	DeKalb	W	26	0
09.19	Bloom	L	2	25	09.19	Glenbrook	W	13	12
09.26	**Freeport**	W	21	6	09.26	**LaSalle-Peru**	L	20	26
10.03	**Rockford West**	T	6	6	10.03	**Rockford East**	W	26	19
10.10	**Rockford East**	L	7	13	10.10	**Rockford West**	W	32	20
10.17	**LaSalle-Peru**	L	6	32	10.17	**Freeport**	W	33	13
10.24	**Joliet**	W	31	0	10.24	**Elgin**	L	12	13
10.31	**West Aurora**	L	0	34	10.31	**East Aurora**	W	34	0
11.07	**Elgin**	L	13	27	11.07	**Joliet**	W	45	13

1959

	W	L	T	Coach		W	L	T	Coach
Overall Record:	1	7	1	Art Court	Overall Record:	6	2	1	Ken Zimmerman
Conference Record:	1	6	0		Conference Record:	5	2	0	

Date	Opponent		EA	Opp	Date	Opponent		WA	Opp
09.19	Proviso East	L	6	34	09.18	DeKalb	T	6	6
09.25	Bloom	T	0	0	09.25	Glenbrook	W	47	26
10.02	**Freeport**	L	0	27	10.02	**LaSalle-Peru**	L	0	19
10.09	**Rockford West**	L	0	12	10.09	**Rockford East**	WF	13	19
10.16	**Rockford East**	WF	7	20	10.16	**Rockford West**	W	30	20
10.23	**LaSalle-Peru**	L	3	19	10.23	**Freeport**	L	9	32
10.30	**Joliet**	L	12	19	10.30	**Elgin**	W	24	20
11.06	**West Aurora**	L	0	19	11.06	**East Aurora**	W	19	0
11.13	**Elgin**	L	0	20	11.13	**Joliet**	W	25	0

EAST AURORA   WEST AURORA

1960

	W	L	T	Coach			W	L	T	Coach
Overall Record:	6	2	1	Art Court	Overall Record:		7	1	1	Ken Zimmerman
Conference Record:	4	2	1		Conference Record:		7	0	0	

Date	Opponent		EA	Opp	Date	Opponent		WA	Opp
09.16	Proviso East	W	7	6	09.16	DeKalb	T	7	7
09.23	Bloom	W	20	6	09.23	Joliet	L	0	20
09.30	**Elgin**	W	14	7	09.30	**LaSalle-Peru**	W	6	0
10.07	**Freeport**	T	7	7	10.07	**Auburn**	W	39	12
10.14	**Rockford West**	W	12	0	10.14	**Rockford East**	W	18	6
10.21	**Rockford East**	W	14	13	10.21	**Rockford West**	W	31	7
10.28	**Auburn**	W	53	13	10.28	**Freeport**	W	20	12
11.04	**LaSalle-Peru**	L	6	20	11.04	**Elgin**	W	6	0
11.11	**West Aurora**	L	6	12	11.11	**East Aurora**	W	12	6

Conference Champions

1961

	W	L	T	Coach			W	L	T	Coach
Overall Record:	1	7	1	Del Dufrain	Overall Record:		6	2	1	Ken Zimmerman
Conference Record:	1	6	0		Conference Record:		5	2	0	

Date	Opponent		EA	Opp	Date	Opponent		WA	Opp
09.16	Proviso East	L	0	26	09.15	DeKalb	L	0	21
09.22	Bloom	L	0	20	09.22	Joliet	L	0	25
09.29	**Elgin**	L	0	14	09.29	**LaSalle-Peru**	L	0	12
10.07	**Freeport**	L	13	21	10.07	**Auburn**	WF	13	20
10.13	**Rockford West**	T	7	7	10.13	**Rockford East**	L	0	7
10.21	**Rockford East**	L	0	20	10.20	**Rockford West**	W	13	0
10.28	**Auburn**	WF	0	27	10.27	**Freeport**	L	6	19
11.03	**LaSalle-Peru**	L	12	34	11.03	**Elgin**	W	7	0
11.10	**West Aurora**	W	14	6	11.10	**East Aurora**	L	6	14

Key: W = Win, L = Loss, T = Tie, WF = Win by forfeit, LF = Loss by forfeit, **Bold** = Conference game, *Italics* = state playoff game

EAST AURORA   WEST AURORA

1962

	W	L	T	Coach		W	L	T	Coach
Overall Record:	6	3	0	Del Dufrain	Overall Record:	2	6	1	Ken Zimmerman
Conference Record:	5	2	0		Conference Record:	1	5	1	

Date	Opponent		EA	Opp	Date	Opponent		WA	Opp
09.14	Proviso East	L	7	26	09.14	DeKalb	W	6	0
09.21	Bloom	W	27	7	09.21	Joliet	L	6	41
09.28	**West Aurora**	W	13	0	09.28	**East Aurora**	L	0	13
10.05	**Elgin**	W	22	7	10.05	**LaSalle-Peru**	L	6	18
10.12	**Freeport**	W	7	0	10.12	**Auburn**	L	0	20
10.19	**Rockford West**	L	6	7	10.19	**Rockford East**	L	27	7
10.26	**Rockford East**	W	28	20	10.26	**Rockford West**	W	7	33
11.02	**Auburn**	L	6	12	11.02	**Freeport**	T	6	6
11.09	**LaSalle-Peru**	W	33	7	11.09	**Elgin**	L	7	21

Conference Co-champions

1963

	W	L	T	Coach		W	L	T	Coach
Overall Record:	9	0	0	Del Dufrain	Overall Record:	1	8	0	Ken Zimmerman
Conference Record:	7	0	0		Conference Record:	0	7	0	

Date	Opponent		EA	Opp	Date	Opponent		WA	Opp
09.14	Proviso East	W	31	6	09.13	St Charles	W	18	6
09.20	Bloom	W	31	0	09.20	Joliet	L	7	20
09.27	**Naperville**	W	21	15	09.27	**DeKalb**	L	18	24
10.04	**DeKalb**	W	20	0	10.04	**Naperville**	L	12	38
10.11	**Larkin**	W	26	0	10.11	**Elgin**	L	6	19
10.18	**Glenbard**	W	14	13	10.18	**Wheaton**	L	12	27
10.26	**Wheaton**	W	20	0	10.26	**Glenbard East**	L	6	14
11.01	**Elgin**	W	19	7	11.01	**Larkin**	L	0	16
11.08	**West Aurora**	W	27	0	11.08	**East Aurora**	L	0	27

Conference Champions

EAST AURORA   WEST AURORA

1964

	W	L	T	Coach		W	L	T	Coach
Overall Record:	7	1	1	Del Dufrain	Overall Record:	4	4	1	Ken Zimmerman
Conference Record:	6	0	1		Conference Record:	3	4	0	

Date	Opponent		EA	Opp	Date	Opponent		WA	Opp
09.18	Proviso East	W	13	0	09.18	St Charles	W	18	7
09.25	Rockford West	L	17	21	09.25	Marmion Military Academy	T	12	12
10.02	**Naperville**	W	9	0	10.02	**DeKalb**	W	20	7
10.09	**DeKalb**	W	20	0	10.09	**Naperville**	L	7	13
10.16	**Larkin**	W	20	12	10.16	**Elgin Central**	W	51	0
10.23	**Glenbard East**	T	0	0	10.23	**Wheaton Central**	L	6	33
10.30	**Wheaton**	W	14	6	10.30	**Glenbard East**	L	0	19
11.06	**Elgin Central**	W	18	0	11.06	**Larkin**	W	12	7
11.13	**West Aurora**	W	21	6	11.13	**East Aurora**	L	6	21

Conference Champions

1965

	W	L	T	Coach		W	L	T	Coach
Overall Record:	5	2	2	Del Dufrain	Overall Record:	6	3	0	Ken Zimmerman
Conference Record:	3	2	2		Conference Record:	5	2	0	

Date	Opponent		EA	Opp	Date	Opponent		WA	Opp
09.18	Proviso East	W	6	0	09.17	Joliet Catholic	L	6	13
09.24	Rockford West	W	14	0	09.24	Marmion Military Academy	W	13	6
10.01	**Larkin**	T	13	13	10.01	**DeKalb**	W	13	12
10.08	**St. Charles**	W	13	6	10.08	**Elgin**	W	26	12
10.15	**Naperville**	W	14	13	10.15	**Wheaton Central**	L	0	25
10.22	**Elgin Central**	W	27	6	10.22	**St Charles**	L	7	13
10.29	**DeKalb**	T	14	14	10.29	**Naperville**	W	21	13
11.05	**Wheaton**	L	7	39	11.05	**Larkin**	W	7	0
11.12	**West Aurora**	L	13	26	11.12	**East Aurora**	W	26	13

Key: W = Win, L = Loss, T = Tie, WF = Win by forfeit, LF = Loss by forfeit, **Bold** = Conference game, *Italics* = state playoff game

EAST AURORA

WEST AURORA

1966

	W	L	T	Coach		W	L	T	Coach
Overall Record:	6	3	0	Del Dufrain	Overall Record:	7	2	0	Ken Zimmerman
Conference Record:	5	2	0		Conference Record:	5	2	0	

Date	Opponent		EA	Opp	Date	Opponent		WA	Opp
09.16	Proviso East	W	20	14	09.16	Joliet	W	46	0
09.23	Rockford West	L	6	10	09.23	Marmion Military Academy	W	34	26
09.30	**Larkin**	W	33	20	09.30	**DeKalb**	L	12	14
10.08	**St. Charles**	W	34	0	10.07	**Elgin**	W	27	7
10.14	**Naperville**	W	19	6	10.14	**Wheaton Central**	W	32	20
10.21	**Elgin Central**	W	16	12	10.21	**St Charles**	W	33	14
10.28	**DeKalb**	L	7	20	10.28	**Naperville**	W	26	17
11.04	**Wheaton Central**	W	14	9	11.04	**Larkin**	L	6	14
11.11	**West Aurora**	L	7	34	11.11	**East Aurora**	W	34	7

Conference Tri-Champions

Conference Tri-Champions

1967

	W	L	T	Coach		W	L	T	Coach
Overall Record:	2	7	0	Del Dufrain	Overall Record:	3	6	0	Ken Zimmerman
Conference Record:	2	5	0		Conference Record:	2	5	0	

Date	Opponent		EA	Opp	Date	Opponent		WA	Opp
09.15	Proviso East	L	6	54	09.15	Joliet East	L	7	12
09.23	Rockford West	L	0	30	09.23	Marmion Military Academy	W	20	13
09.29	**Wheaton Central**	L	0	36	09.29	**Larkin**	L	6	28
10.06	**Larkin**	L	0	22	10.06	**DeKalb**	W	18	13
10.13	**St. Charles**	W	28	0	10.13	**Elgin Central**	W	8	0
10.20	**Naperville**	L	0	13	10.20	**Wheaton Central**	L	6	47
10.27	**Elgin Central**	L	13	24	10.27	**St Charles**	L	0	6
11.03	**DeKalb**	L	13	26	11.03	**Naperville**	L	6	12
11.10	**West Aurora**	W	14	13	11.10	**East Aurora**	L	13	14

East Aurora

West Aurora

1968

	W	L	T	Coach
Overall Record:	6	3	0	Del Dufrain
Conference Record:	4	3	0	

Date	Opponent		EA	Opp
09.13	Proviso East	W	7	0
09.21	Rockford West	W	7	6
09.27	**Wheaton Central**	L	13	19
10.04	**Larkin**	L	14	19
10.11	**St. Charles**	W	53	7
10.18	**Naperville**	W	12	0
10.25	**Elgin Central**	W	26	7
11.01	**DeKalb**	L	14	17
11.08	**West Aurora**	W	27	6

	W	L	T	Coach
Overall Record:	3	6	0	Ken Zimmerman
Conference Record:	3	4	0	

Date	Opponent		WA	Opp
09.13	Joliet West	L	6	20
09.20	Marmion Military Academy	L	12	39
09.27	**Larkin**	W	33	21
10.04	**DeKalb**	L	0	34
10.11	**Elgin Central**	W	14	12
10.18	**Wheaton Central**	L	6	41
10.25	**St. Charles**	W	41	0
11.01	**Naperville**	L	13	14
11.08	**East Aurora**	L	6	27

1969

	W	L	T	Coach
Overall Record:	5	4	0	Del Dufrain
Conference Record:	4	3	0	

Date	Opponent		EA	Opp
09.12	Proviso East	L	20	26
09.19	Rockford West	W	28	6
09.26	**DeKalb**	L	14	18
10.03	**Elgin Central**	W	14	8
10.10	**Naperville**	L	0	8
10.17	**St. Charles**	W	26	9
10.24	**Larkin**	L	19	21
10.31	**Wheaton Central**	W	27	0
11.07	**West Aurora**	W	25	14

	W	L	T	Coach
Overall Record:	3	6	0	Ken Zimmerman
Conference Record:	2	5	0	

Date	Opponent		WA	Opp
09.12	Waukegan	WF	1	0
09.20	Marmion Military Academy	L	6	21
09.26	**Naperville**	L	6	22
10.03	**St. Charles**	W	30	27
10.10	**Wheaton Central**	W	22	0
10.17	**Elgin Central**	L	6	36
10.24	**DeKalb**	L	18	32
10.31	**Larkin**	L	12	14
11.07	**East Aurora**	L	14	25

Key: W = Win, L = Loss, T = Tie, WF = Win by forfeit, LF = Loss by forfeit, **Bold** = Conference game, *Italics* = state playoff game

EAST AURORA   WEST AURORA

1970

	W	L	T	Coach		W	L	T	Coach
Overall Record:	0	9	0	Del Dufrain	Overall Record:	7	2	0	K. Zimmerman (0-1-0)
Conference Record:	0	7	0		Conference Record:	6	1	0	D. Zuege (7-1-0)

Date	Opponent		EA	Opp	Date	Opponent		WA	Opp
09.19	LaSalle-Peru	L	0	20	09.19	Joliet Central	L	6	30
09.25	Rockford West	L	12	13	09.25	Marmion Military Academy	W	14	13
10.02	**DeKalb**	LF	28	0	10.02	**Naperville**	W	40	7
10.09	**Elgin Central**	LF	27	8	10.09	**St. Charles**	W	19	14
10.16	**Naperville**	LF	26	6	10.16	**Wheaton Central**	W	19	0
10.23	**St. Charles**	LF	27	7	10.23	**Elgin Central**	W	12	8
10.30	**Larkin**	LF	42	16	10.30	**DeKalb**	L	0	44
11.06	**Wheaton Central**	LF	48	21	11.06	**Larkin**	W	38	0
11.13	**West Aurora**	LF	19	8	11.13	**East Aurora**	WF	8	19

1971

	W	L	T	Coach		W	L	T	Coach
Overall Record:	3	6	0	Del Dufrain	Overall Record:	4	5	0	Dick Zuege
Conference Record:	1	6	0		Conference Record:	2	5	0	

Date	Opponent		EA	Opp	Date	Opponent		WA	Opp
09.17	LaSalle-Peru	W	50	26	09.17	Joliet Central	W	14	8
09.24	Joliet East	W	22	0	09.25	Marmion Military Academy	W	14	6
10.01	**Elgin Central**	L	20	28	10.01	**Larkin**	L	14	34
10.08	**Wheaton Central**	L	7	12	10.08	**Naperville**	L	0	6
10.15	**DeKalb**	L	14	26	10.15	**St. Charles**	W	34	15
10.22	**Larkin**	L	13	18	10.22	**Elgin Central**	L	28	30
10.29	**Naperville**	L	7	30	10.29	**Wheaton Central**	W	8	6
11.05	**St. Charles**	L	12	35	11.05	**DeKalb**	L	24	36
11.12	**West Aurora**	W	21	18	11.12	**East Aurora**	L	18	21

EAST AURORA   WEST AURORA

1972

	W	L	T	Coach			W	L	T	Coach
Overall Record:	5	4	0	Del Dufrain	Overall Record:		1	8	0	Dick Zuege
Conference Record:	4	3	0		Conference Record:		0	7	0	

Date	Opponent		EA	Opp	Date	Opponent		WA	Opp
09.15	LaSalle-Peru	L	7	18	09.15	Joliet Central	L	13	30
09.22	Joliet East	W	36	0	09.22	Marmion Military Academy	W	14	6
09.29	**Elgin Central**	W	21	20	09.29	**Larkin**	L	0	46
10.06	**Wheaton Central**	L	0	12	10.06	**Naperville**	L	14	29
10.13	**DeKalb**	W	14	12	10.13	**St. Charles**	L	29	30
10.20	**Larkin**	W	19	14	10.20	**Elgin Central**	L	6	38
10.27	**Naperville**	L	0	13	10.27	**Wheaton Central**	L	0	10
11.03	**St. Charles**	L	10	20	11.03	**DeKalb**	L	13	20
11.10	**West Aurora**	W	47	6	11.10	**East Aurora**	L	6	47

1973

	W	L	T	Coach			W	L	T	Coach
Overall Record:	6	4	0	Del Dufrain	Overall Record:		2	7	1	Dick Zuege
Conference Record:	4	3	0		Conference Record:		1	6	0	

Date	Opponent		EA	Opp	Date	Opponent		WA	Opp
09.07	Thornton	W	27	0	09.07	Hinsdale Central	L	0	21
09.14	LaSalle-Peru	W	16	8	09.14	Joliet West	W	21	14
09.22	Joliet East	L	14	18	09.22	Marmion Military Academy	T	6	6
09.28	**Naperville**	L	0	6	09.28	**Wheaton Central**	L	13	25
10.05	**St. Charles**	W	14	6	10.05	**DeKalb**	L	13	14
10.12	**Elgin Central**	W	16	8	10.12	**Larkin**	L	6	34
10.19	**Wheaton Central**	L	14	20	10.19	**Naperville**	L	6	16
10.26	**DeKalb**	W	47	18	10.26	**St. Charles**	W	14	6
11.02	**Larkin**	L	13	14	11.02	**Elgin Central**	L	6	30
11.09	**West Aurora**	W	31	16	11.09	**East Aurora**	L	16	31

Key: W = Win, L = Loss, T = Tie, WF = Win by forfeit, LF = Loss by forfeit, **Bold** = Conference game, *Italics* = state playoff game

CHAPTER 6

1974–2013: AURORA FOOTBALL IN THE PLAYOFF ERA

By the early 1970s, Aurora's population had grown to seventy-five thousand. People in town identified with their neighborhoods and their church communities, and it was not uncommon for multiple generations of families to live within a few blocks of one another. Although the old east–west lines had blurred somewhat over time, the community as a whole tended to be very insular and seemingly unprepared for the gathering confluence of socioeconomic developments that, within thirty years, would create a new city order and have a dramatic impact on local high school football.

At this time, the Burlington Northern Railroad was in the final stages of closing the shops that had served as one of the area's largest employers for over one hundred years. And although the local economy continued to be built on manufacturing jobs that offered good, middle-class wages, old-line factories at major employers like Caterpillar, Barber-Greene, Richards-Wilcox, Austin-Western, Stephens-Adamson, Equipto, All-Steel, Lyon Metal, Henry Pratt Company, Aurora Pump and others were facing uncertain futures.

Meanwhile, retail shopping in downtown Aurora was in decline. Stores had begun to pull out of the downtown district in the late 1960s, but when builders with plans to develop the unincorporated farmland between Aurora and Naperville arrived in the early '70s, the demise of downtown as a shopping destination was sealed. It was at this time that Mayor Al McCoy and the Aurora City Council began annexing huge tracts of farmland between Aurora's traditional eastern border at the Kane-DuPage county line and Illinois Route 59, the area known today as Aurora's Far East Side. The expansion into DuPage County effectively closed the gap between Aurora as a freestanding municipality and Aurora as a Chicago suburb by extending its eastern boundary about four miles east and paving the way for the addition of fifty thousand residents within twenty years. By 1975, the Fox Valley Center shopping mall had opened, and several modern suburban housing and commercial developments were well underway. Residents of the new subdivisions were more likely to commute to Chicago or other suburbs than work in town. As new retail centers went up to serve the new residents, downtown's few remaining national retailers pulled up stakes and moved to these new centers, taking their shoppers and tax dollars with them. Ultimately, local shopkeepers closed. It was an inevitable progression.

Also during the early 1970s, the Far East Side's residential developments outgrew the small, decades-old, rural grade school districts—Wheatland, Granger and Indian Plains—that served the area. High school students from these three districts, which were situated between East Aurora District 131 and Naperville District 203, were invited to attend Naperville. Rather than annex territory under development or attempt to merge with one or more of the rural districts, East officials opted to watch the three districts consolidate into Indian Prairie District 204 in 1972, a decision that left District 131 landlocked and unable to capitalize on increasing revenues generated by the new development that was occurring right next door.

Finally, Aurorans' gravitation toward the new housing developments created a void in many of the town's older middle-class neighborhoods, which, in turn, began to attract generally lower-income Hispanic immigrants who came to town looking to improve their lot in life but who had no ties to local customs, schools or, for that matter, football. This demographic shift was most prevalent on Aurora's traditional east side.

Against this backdrop of declining tax revenues and changing demographics, East Aurora and West Aurora entered the modern era of Illinois high school football, which began with the 1974 introduction of the state football championship playoffs.

*****

Since the 1930s, Chicago's Public and Catholic Leagues had been holding an annual playoff that led to the Prep Bowl, which determined Chicago's high school city champions. Played annually in late November or early

December, the contest often drew crowds in excess of seventy-five thousand people to Soldier Field, and its popularity provided part of the impetus for suburban and downstate coaches, players and fans to dream of a statewide playoff to determine a state champion.

A proposal for a playoff consisting of three eight-team classes was rejected by the Illinois High School Association (IHSA) in 1969, but athletic directors and school administrators throughout the state immediately organized to work on a revised proposal, which was submitted in 1972 and approved in February of the following year. Beginning in 1974, the regular football season would be followed by five separate playoffs, organized according to school size, to determine five state champions. Games tied at the end of four quarters would be settled by a tiebreaking system called the Kansas Plan, which would soon be adopted for regular-season games across the state. Schools from Illinois' sixty-five conferences—not including the Chicago Public League, which had declined to participate—would take part.

Each conference champion received an automatic playoff bid. If teams tied for a league title, their conference officials selected one school to represent the conference. The remaining fifteen at-large berths were selected by the IHSA from conference co-champions, runners-up and independent schools, for a total of eighty participants. The first round was scheduled to be played on the Wednesday immediately following the close of the regular season, with round two scheduled for the following Saturday. The potential of playing three games in ten days was a source of controversy among coaches and school administrators, but the IHSA steadfastly maintained this format for twenty years.

***

In 1974, the excitement of a potential playoff appearance permeated the start of football practice across the state. At East Aurora, Coach Del Dufrain's Tomcats were encouraged by the prior year's 6-4-0 record, while at West Aurora, Dick Munn had replaced Dick Zuege as head coach in an effort to breathe some fresh air into a Blackhawk program that had stagnated. The highly heralded Munn came to West from St. Theresa High School in Decatur, Illinois, where in six seasons his teams had compiled a 42-12-3 record and were in the midst of a twenty-one-game winning streak at the time he resigned to take the Blackhawk job. Without Munn, St. Theresa would go on to extend its winning streak to forty-five games while also winning the Class 2A championship in both 1974 and '75.

As the '74 season progressed, neither Aurora school was in the playoff hunt, as East finished in a three-way tie for third place in the conference and West tied for seventh. In the season finale, Tomcat quarterback Mark Lindo's fourth-quarter touchdown, followed by David Patterson's run for a two-point conversion, led East to a 15–14 win over the Blackhawks in the rivalry's eighty-second contest.

The 1975–76 school year began with the opening of Aurora's third public high school, District 204's Waubonsie Valley, on Aurora's Far East Side. That same year, the Upstate 8 Conference was reduced to six members as Wheaton and Naperville left to help form the upstart DuPage Valley Conference. The Upstate 8 would continue with six members until Streamwood and Lake Park High Schools joined the league five years later. East finished the '75 season with a 3-6 record and fifth in the newly constituted conference, while West's lone victory was an 8–3 decision over East that ended the Tomcats' win streak over the west-siders at four.

While Coach Munn's Blackhawks struggled once again in 1976, Del Dufrain's East squad, led by Kurt Becker, Bob McCue and Cleveland West, rebounded from a string of ordinary seasons to put together a 7-2 regular season that earned the Tomcats a playoff berth. Heartbreak kids all season long, the Tomcats won three games by a total of 5 points before whitewashing West 34–0 in the final regular-season game to earn a tie with Elgin Central for the Upstate 8 title. The Tomcats traveled to Blue Island, Illinois, on Wednesday, November 10, to take on Eisenhower High School. After encountering a pre-game heckler who attempted to intimidate the visitors, the Cats' drove ninety-six yards for a touchdown on their first possession and then blew the game open in the fourth quarter to win 41–13.

Three days later, at Roy E. Davis Field, the Tomcats met Glenbard West High School, which had dispatched Burbank's Reavis High School in round one and was 9-1 on the season. After spotting the Hilltoppers a 13–0 first-quarter lead, the Cats' defense stiffened, and the offense mounted a rally that ended when East, down 13–7 with five minutes to play, fumbled the ball away deep in Glenbard territory. A meaningless Hilltopper touchdown in the game's final seconds ended the scoring and sent the visitors home with a 20–7 victory.

In 1977, Bob Quinn replaced Dick Munn at West. Quinn came from Rich South High School, where he had two winning seasons and one playoff appearance in his two years there. The Blackhawks and quarterback John McGary, who would later serve as an assistant coach at West, got off to a quick start, blowing out Joliet West and Naperville Central by a combined score of 56–0 in the season's first two weeks but were up and down the rest

The 1976 Tomcats tied Elgin for the Upstate 8 Conference championship and qualified for the state playoffs for the first time. *Courtesy of East Aurora High School Speculum.*

of the way and finished the year with a 5-4 overall record and in the middle of the Upstate 8 pack. Nonetheless, West's first winning season in seven years brought renewed optimism to the west side. East, meanwhile, was unable to maintain the magic of 1976 and fell to 3-6 overall and 1-4 in the conference. McGary's two second-half touchdown passes to Don Bennett led West to a 20–14 victory in the annual rivalry game.

While East struggled through a losing 1978 season in what would be Coach Dufrain's final year as Tomcat coach, Quinn's Blackhawks built on their success of the year before. Featuring a stifling defense that yielded just twelve points while reeling off six straight wins to start the season, the Blackhawks' streak ended in a 13–10 non-conference loss to Freeport in a battle of unbeatens. In week eight, Larkin's 22–0 victory over West left the Royals and Hawks tied for first place in the conference with just one game remaining. A Royals win over archrival Elgin Central in the season's final weekend would send Larkin to the playoffs on the strength of its victory over the Blackhawks, leaving West needing to beat East and hoping that the Maroons could upset Larkin.

The '78 season records notwithstanding, the Blackhawks had little reason to be confident heading into their must-win game with East. The Tomcats held a 12-5 series edge since Coach Dufrain arrived at East in 1961, and the east-siders wanted nothing more than to deny their rivals a shot at the playoffs. But on the night of November 3, everything broke perfectly for West, as the defense made Armando Navarro's first-quarter field goal hold up for a 3–0 victory. Meanwhile, Elgin Central stunned Larkin 22–0, giving West the Upstate 8 championship and its first playoff appearance.

Coach Del Dufrain

In 1961, after serving as both head coach and assistant coach of various sports at three high schools in east central Illinois, Delbert "Del" Dufrain was named head coach at East Aurora, where he would remain for eighteen seasons. Dufrain ranks second to Glen Thompson on East's all-time win list with eighty-five, and his five conference championships are the most by a Tomcat coach. Best of all, the Tomcats held a 12–6 advantage over West Aurora during the Dufrain era.

A native of Kankakee, Illinois, young Dufrain was a football, basketball and track athlete at Kankakee High School before entering Western Illinois University, where he played end for the Leathernecks for three seasons. After completing his degree, Dufrain began his teaching career at tiny Chebanse High School in Chebanse, Illinois, where he coached the varsity basketball team. In 1950, Chebanse merged with Ashkum-Clifton High School to form Central High School in Clifton, Illinois, and Dufrain became the Comets' first football coach. In those days, establishing a football program at a small rural high school required a coach to do anything and everything to get the program started, including laying out the field, which Dufrain and his young wife, Sue, did that first summer. Two years later, in anticipation of being drafted into the military to support the Korean War effort, Dufrain resigned and recommended Central hire former University

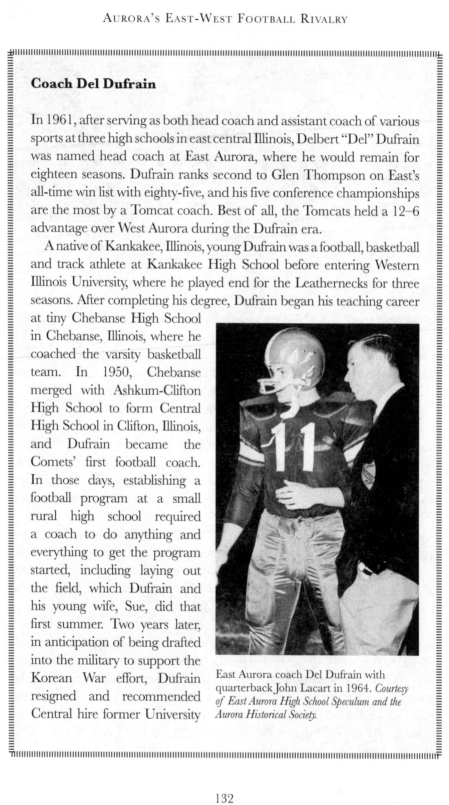

East Aurora coach Del Dufrain with quarterback John Lacart in 1964. *Courtesy of East Aurora High School Speculum and the Aurora Historical Society.*

of Illinois star Bob Cunz as his replacement. It turned out Dufrain was exempted from military service because Sue was expecting their first child, but Cunz was already on board, so Dufrain continued teaching and became Cunz's assistant. After nine years at Central, Dufrain returned to his alma mater, where he served as the Kays' sophomore coach before being offered the head coaching job at East in 1961.

Dufrain's Tomcat teams won four conference titles in a five-year period starting in 1962, and he added a fifth and final title in 1976.

Throughout his coaching career at East, Dufrain taught a full load of biology classes, and after eighteen years of doing both, he decided it was too much. Although he continued teaching until his retirement in 1986, he gave up coaching after the 1978 season. The Tomcats were 85-76-4 during his tenure.

In twenty-five years as a coach and teacher at East, Coach Dufrain was an inspiration to a generation of students, many of whom became teachers and coaches themselves. As of 2014, Coach and Mrs. Dufrain, who taught at Bardwell School in Aurora for twenty years, are retired and living in Wisconsin.

West Aurora's 1978 Upstate 8 Conference champions and first playoff team. *Courtesy of Blackhawk Jim Stone.*

On a windy Wednesday afternoon, the 7-2 Blackhawks traveled to Arlington Heights to take on 8-1 Forest View High School in the first playoff appearance for both schools. Some strong early running by West's Mike

Hildebrand led to a state playoff record forty-six-yard Navarro field goal (since broken) that gave the Blackhawks a first-quarter lead. The Falcons answered back with a touchdown and two-point conversion late in the first half to take an 8–3 lead at intermission and then extended the lead to 15–3 midway through the third quarter. Still fighting, the Blackhawks came back with a little trickery, scoring on a fifty-one-yard halfback option pass from Rob Tillman to tight end Jim Stone that trimmed the lead to 15–9. Unfortunately for the Blackhawks, the Forest View defense stiffened after that, and the game ended without further scoring.

***

In the spring of 1979, East Aurora announced the hiring of twenty-nine-year-old John Wrenn as Del Dufrain's replacement. Wrenn had spent the last two seasons as an assistant under Bob Quinn at West. That fall, Streamwood and Lake Park High Schools joined the Upstate 8 Conference, returning the league to eight schools after four years as a six-team loop.

Defending conference champ West Aurora and junior running back Alvin Ross got out of the gates quickly in '79, winning their first three games before an overtime loss to Larkin, and a 21–12 setback at St. Charles two weeks later knocked the Blackhawks out of playoff contention. The Tomcats, meanwhile, battled inconsistency early but improved over the course of the year and were at .500 heading into the finale with West. The highly anticipated game, which featured the first meeting between mentor Quinn and his protégé Wrenn, as well as the matchup of West's Ross with East's own speedy junior Darryl Hicks, lived up to the hype as Ross dazzled with 168 rushing yards and Hicks scored on an electrifying 72-yard run and later ended the series' first overtime game with a 6-yard run that put East on top 13–7. The win pushed East's record to 5-4, marking the first time in seventeen years that both schools had produced winning seasons.

In 1980, the IHSA increased the number of football classes from five to six to accommodate the Chicago Public League, which in 1979 had sent its four division champions to the state playoffs for the first time and, after a reorganization that doubled its number of divisions, would henceforth be sending eight. The size of each of the six classes remained sixteen teams, meaning that ninety-six schools would now qualify for post-season play.

Jim Czocher replaced Bob Quinn as West's head coach for the 1980–81 school year, as Quinn had left Aurora to play fast-pitch softball in Decatur, Illinois. Despite the presence of Alvin Ross, who would set several school

Future Tomcat head football and basketball coach Wendell Jeffries in 1980. *Courtesy of East Aurora High School Speculum.*

rushing records over the course of the year and be named to some high school all-American and all-state teams at season's end, the Blackhawks got off to a rough start, suffering three one-point losses in the season's first four games. West's fate improved as the team won three of its next four to enter the final weekend with a 4-2 league mark and an outside chance of finishing in a four-way tie for the conference title. To do so, however, would require a win over East and losses by both DeKalb and Larkin.

Beating the high-powered Tomcats, however, was no easy feat for anyone that year. Led by Hicks, future Tomcat head football and basketball coach Wendell Jeffries and all-state defensive back Bill McCue, who also quarterbacked the wishbone offense Wrenn had installed to take full advantage of East's superior quickness, the 7-1 Cats entered Ken Zimmerman Field averaging nearly 32 points per game. West could not keep up, as East ran for over three hundred yards on the ground en route to a 42–6 victory that left the Tomcats in a three-way tie with DeKalb and Larkin for conference honors. Under the expanded playoff format, all three Upstate 8 schools qualified for the playoffs, with East Aurora and Larkin entering Class 6A (largest schools) and DeKalb in 4A.

East hosted Villa Park's Willowbrook High School in a Wednesday afternoon affair that was played in front of five thousand fans packed into Roy E. Davis Field. In a spectacularly entertaining ball game, East held a 22–21 fourth-quarter lead until the Warriors scored a go-ahead touchdown with 1:16 left to play. A failed two-point conversion attempt left the Tomcats down 27–22, with time for one final drive to win the game. Starting at their own twenty-four-yard line, the Tomcats quickly drove to the Willowbrook six-yard line before McCue's fourth-down desperation pass was intercepted in the end zone, ending the Tomcat's hopes and a great season.

Alvin Ross, West Class of 1981. A three-year starter at running back for the Blackhawks, the six-foot-one, 190-pound Ross was widely regarded as the top high school running back in Illinois, and possibly the nation, in 1980. A member of every Illinois all-state team and winner of the 1980 *Champaign News-Gazette* Player of the Year Award, Ross accepted a scholarship to play for coach Barry Switzer at the University of Oklahoma. Unfortunately, after an outstanding freshman year for the Sooners, questions about Ross's involvement with a sports agent brought his college career to an end. He later played briefly for the Philadelphia Eagles and the Arena Football League's Pittsburgh Gladiators before retiring from football.

In 1981, John Wrenn left teaching altogether to pursue a business opportunity, and East hired Pete Ventrelli from West Leyden High School to lead the program. Building on the success of the previous seasons, the Tomcats fielded a competitive team that handed conference champion DeKalb its only Upstate 8 loss, but they ultimately lacked the firepower to contend for the league title and finished fourth. Meanwhile, it took the '81 Blackhawks until the eighth week to score more than one touchdown in a game, and the team finished with a record of 2-7, including a 21–14 upset of East in what turned out to be Jim Czocher's final game as West's head coach. He resigned after the season.

With three consecutive winning seasons fueling football optimism for a successful '82 campaign east of the Fox River, west-siders also got excited after learning that after one year in the business world, the popular John Wrenn would be returning to the sidelines as the Blackhawks' new coach. Others had served both districts as assistants, but Wrenn was the first to be head coach at both East and West.

The year 1982 turned out to be one of rebuilding for the Blackhawks, who lost their first six games but won two of the last three to end the season on the upswing. East's '82 squad was once again loaded with speed, but the offense and quarterback Jim McCue showed some early inconsistency running Ventrelli's option offense, averaging 14 points while splitting the first four games. The Cats began to click at mid-season, however, as scoring increased to 20 points per game, and East won four of its final five regular-season games. The only setback during that span was a 1-point loss to Elgin in mid-October. West entered the season finale with a two-game winning streak and hopes of dashing East's playoff aspirations, but McCue's three touchdowns and 191 rushing yards, together with Kevin Wilson's 140 yards on twenty-five carries, wore the Blackhawks down in the second half. East's 19–7 victory put the Tomcats in a three-way tie with DeKalb and Lake Park for the Upstate 8 championship and earned them a playoff spot.

In the playoff opener at Rock Island High School, the Tomcats got first-half touchdowns from Wilson and McCue but could not find the end zone in the second half and fell to the Rocks, 17–14, to end the season with a 6-4 record.

***

Budget cuts imposed by East Aurora District 131 during the early 1980s resulted in the suspension of the district's junior high football programs and cost Pete Ventrelli his job, as his contract was not renewed despite back-to-back winning seasons. From East, Ventrelli moved on to Berwyn's Morton West High School and, later, to Downers Grove North High School. After sixteen seasons at Downers Grove North, Ventrelli retired after a career that included a total of twelve playoff appearances at four different schools, including East Aurora; one second-place finish; and election to the Illinois Football Coaches Association Hall of Fame.

Action from the 1982 East-West game, which East won 19–7. *Courtesy of East Aurora High School Speculum.*

To replace Ventrelli, East turned to 1966 East alumnus and football letterman Dick Schindel, who had been teaching in the district and coaching football at K.D. Waldo Junior High. While Schindel's '83 Tomcats produced a winning season for the fifth consecutive year, Aurora's football spotlight shifted to the west side, where the Blackhawks were ready to fly.

During the offseason, Coach Wrenn had scrapped the run-oriented wishbone offense he implemented with great success at East in favor of a passing offense that maximized the talents of senior quarterback Jim Bennett and junior wide receiver Kenny Page. Although the new offense sputtered in a season-opening 8–7 loss at Dundee-Crown High School, the Hawks quickly got on track and averaged 28 points while ending the regular season with eight consecutive victories. Against East Aurora, Bennett threw for over 250 yards and four touchdowns in the first half of a 41–6 rout that capped an undefeated Upstate 8 championship and sent the Blackhawks to the playoffs for the second time. Over the course of the season, Bennett would twice be named the *Chicago Tribune*'s Player of the Week and would receive all-state honors at season's end.

Days prior to West's first-round matchup with Addison Trail High School, Wrenn was hospitalized with an illness that prevented him from attending practices and forced him to watch the Blackhawks' playoff game from an ambulance parked next to the field. In a disappointing end to the season, Addison Trail's staunch defense and grinding running game stymied West and carried the Blazers to a 20–7 victory. Addison Trail ultimately advanced

West Aurora coach John Wrenn circles the troops in 1984. *Courtesy of West Aurora High School Eos and the Aurora Historical Society.*

to the state championship game before losing to East St. Louis Senior High School, 13–0.

With Bennett graduated and playing football for the University of Illinois in 1984, Jeff Voris took the reigns of the West offense, and the Blackhawks did not miss a beat as Voris matched Bennett's performance of a year earlier by breaking some of Bennett's school passing records, leading West to a second consecutive playoff appearance and earning all-state honors. Favorite target Kenny Page set several school receiving records and earned all-state honors as well. The Blackhawks won their first

Coach John Wrenn

For eight years beginning in 1977, Aurora served as a springboard for aspiring John Wrenn, an ambitious, bright and charismatic young coach whose journey to the pinnacle of the high school coaching profession included stops on both sides of town.

A 1969 graduate of DeKalb (Illinois) High School, Wrenn played college football at Western Illinois University, where he received honorable mention as a Division II all-American. He began his coaching career as an assistant at Larkin High School in Elgin before joining West Aurora's staff in a similar role under Bob Quinn in 1977. Wrenn's first head coaching opportunity came two years later, when he replaced the iconic Del Dufrain at East Aurora.

After leading the Tomcats to a 5-4 record in his first year, Wrenn's 1980 squad finished the regular season with an 8-1 record and in a three-way tie with Larkin and DeKalb for the Upstate 8 Conference championship, which earned the Cats a playoff berth. After the Tomcats lost a thrilling first-round game to Willowbrook, Wrenn announced he was leaving coaching to pursue a business career.

Being away from the game for a year taught Wrenn that football was his passion, and he returned to coaching in 1982, this time at West Aurora. In what would prove to be the only losing season in his twenty-three years as a head coach, Wrenn's first Blackhawk team posted a 2-7 record. The experience led him to replace the run-oriented option offense he had favored at East Aurora and in his first year at West with a virtual aerial circus that produced back-to-back all-state quarterbacks Jim Bennett and Jeff Voris, as well as consecutive Blackhawk playoff appearances. After three seasons at West, Wrenn left to take an assistant's role under Mike White at the University of Illinois.

Wrenn returned to high school coaching at Homewood-Flossmoor High School in 1986, where his ten-year record of 99-18 included five undefeated regular seasons, nine playoff appearances and one state championship. After the 1995 season, Wrenn moved from the Chicago area to Chandler, Arizona, where he resurfaced three years later as the first head football coach at newly opened Hamilton High

School. Under Wrenn's leadership, Hamilton quickly became one of Arizona's top football programs, compiling a 91-11 record that included two state championships and two second-place finishes in eight years.

In 2006, Coach Wrenn left high school coaching for Arizona State University, where he served as running backs coach and, later, as assistant director of football operations. Despite his departure, the program he established at Hamilton continued to flourish, as the Huskies added five more state championships from 2007 to 2013 and were named Arizona's greatest high school dynasty by MaxPreps.com.

Wrenn retired from Arizona State in the spring of 2014. His twenty-three-year career as a head high school coach produced an overall record of 221-47, nineteen playoff appearances, seven undefeated regular seasons, three state championships and numerous Coach of the Year awards. His five years at East and West produced a combined 31-17 record, two conference championships and three playoff appearances.

seven contests by an average of 25 points and rose to second in the *Chicago Tribune*'s area rankings before suffering a 20–18 loss to Elgin in a battle of conference unbeatens in week eight.

Meanwhile, east-siders were beginning to feel the impact of budget cuts imposed on their athletic programs. The Tomcats only win in '84 was the result of a teachers' strike that caused Hillcrest to forfeit the season opener. Several games were close until the fourth quarter, when a lack of depth caused the Tomcats to wear down. The East-West season finale, however, was not close, as the Blackhawks, frustrated by their loss to Elgin the previous week, gained a small measure of redemption by pounding East 55-7. Kendrick Cross led the way with three touchdown receptions as West set a new series scoring record.

In the playoffs, the Blackhawks had the misfortune of having to travel to East St. Louis for an opening-round match with the defending state champions. The Flyers were in the second year of a historic run in which they won forty-four consecutive games and three straight state titles. In their

Jeff Voris, West Class of 1985. As a senior, Voris set several school passing records and earned all-state honors while leading the Blackhawks to a state playoff appearance in 1984. He accepted a football scholarship to Southwest Missouri State University but transferred to DePauw University in Greencastle, Indiana, after one year. At DePauw, Voris started at quarterback for four years, was named the Tigers' most valuable player three times and served as team captain as a senior. At the time of his graduation, he held numerous DePauw passing records.

When his playing days ended, Voris entered college coaching as a graduate assistant under John Makovic at Illinois and later followed Makovic to the University of Texas. During this time, he earned a graduate degree in athletic administration. In 1994, Voris returned to DePauw, where he worked for six seasons in various coaching capacities, and then served for one season as offensive coordinator under coach Lou Tepper at Edinboro University.

In 2001, Voris became head coach at Carroll University, an NCAA Division III school in Waukesha, Wisconsin. After five years at Carroll, Voris moved up to Division I at Butler University, where he has been head coach for the past eight years. The Bulldogs have won three conference championships during the Voris tenure thus far.

game with West, the Flyers scored on their opening drive and dominated play throughout a 35–13 victory.

West's 1984 playoff loss brought an end to an exciting nine-year period in which both East and West Aurora experienced a football revival that featured five conference championships, six playoff appearances, dynamic and innovative coaches and several highly talented athletes recognized for their outstanding individual performances. At this point in time, East continued to lead the East-West series at 44-36-12.

***

West-siders were disappointed when John Wrenn resigned to take an assistant coaching position under Mike White at the University of Illinois.

Homecoming at West Aurora in 1986. *Courtesy of the Aurora Historical Society.*

He was replaced by twenty-six-year-old Randy Melvin, a 1977 West alumnus who had gone on to play football at Eastern Illinois University and returned to serve as a Blackhawk assistant for the two previous seasons. Melvin's head coaching debut was a rough one. The Blackhawks did not win a game in 1985. Dick Schindel's Tomcats, on the other hand, rebounded a bit from the previous one-win season to finish 3-6, including a 20–13 win over the Blackhawks.

Although neither East nor West were affected, the IHSA doubled the size of the post-season playoffs by expanding the field for each of the six classes from sixteen to thirty-two teams in 1985. The controversial Wednesday–Saturday format used to complete rounds one and two remained unchanged, however.

The Tomcats were 3-6 again in 1986, while West improved to 2-7. In the East-West game, Blackhawk quarterback Bill Pfeiffer and receiver John Laurx combined for four touchdowns and Pfeiffer added two more TD passes in West's 48–14 win, leaving the two schools tied for fifth in the Upstate 8.

While East fell to 1-8 in 1987, Melvin's Blackhawks put together a winning season at 5-4, and their 4-3-league mark was good for fourth place in the Upstate 8. West's 28–6 victory over East in the season finale would be the last

Randy Melvin, West Class of 1977. A three-sport athlete who competed for the Blackhawks in football, wrestling and track and field, Melvin started for three seasons on both the offensive and defensive lines and earned all-state football honors as a senior. The following spring, Melvin also qualified for the Illinois State Track and Field Championships in both shot put and discus, and he placed second in discus. From West, Melvin went to Eastern Illinois University, where he earned Division II all-American honors in 1979 and '80 and helped lead the Panthers to the 1980 Division II Championship Game.

In 1983, Melvin returned to West Aurora as an assistant coach under John Wrenn and assumed the head coaching role when Wrenn resigned two years later. After three seasons at West's helm, Melvin returned to Eastern Illinois to embark on a nomadic thirty-year career as a defensive line coach that has taken him to collegiate jobs at Wyoming, Purdue, Rutgers and Temple, as well as stints with pro football's New England Patriots, Cleveland Browns, British Columbia Lions and Tampa Bay Buccaneers. With New England and British Columbia, Melvin won both a Super Bowl and a Grey Cup. In February 2014, Randy Melvin was named defensive line coach at Florida International University.

games for both Melvin and Schindel, as Melvin moved on to an assistant's job at Eastern Illinois University, while Schindel, feeling the impact of the elimination of junior high football five years earlier, resigned.

West Aurora replaced Melvin with Tim Cedarblad, who had had a successful run at Benet Academy in Lisle, Illinois, where his teams had earned eight playoff appearances in his twelve seasons. East, meanwhile, hired Ed Gavigan, who had spent the previous season at Harlem High School in Machesney Park, Illinois, after fifteen years coaching high school football in Wisconsin.

Gavigan's Tomcats started the season 1-6 before pulling off one of the year's biggest upsets, a shocking 14–7 victory over a playoff-bound St. Charles squad that cost the Saints a share of the Upstate 8 title. West, meanwhile, with a 5-3 record and one of the top defensive teams in

WMRO Radio

Aurora's own WMRO radio first took to the airwaves on December 13, 1938, with a format built around local events, personalities and issues. It included organ recitals from the Paramount Theater; an amateur hour; a popular show called *Aurora Answers*, which featured live interviews with random people in the streets of downtown Aurora; and, of course, plenty of local sports.

The station broadcast its first East-West football game on Thanksgiving Day 1939, with station owner Martin O'Brien, whose initials inspired WMRO's call letters, and Bob Diller calling the game. The Blackhawks won that day, 20–7.

Over the next fifty years, the station's sports coverage became an Aurora institution. On Friday and Saturday nights, Aurorans could tune in to a live broadcast of whichever East or West game was deemed more interesting that evening, followed by a tape-delayed broadcast of the other. Over the years, coverage of the city's other high schools, including Aurora Central Catholic, Marmion Academy and Waubonsie Valley, was added to the mix.

In addition to local high school coverage, WMRO began covering the Illinois State High School Basketball Tournament in 1939, a tradition that continued until the station signed off for good fifty years later. The station broadcast Aurora University football and basketball games and enabled local citizens to follow the Sealmasters and Aurora Home Savings and Loan fast-pitch softball teams as they traveled across the country competing for national titles during the '50s, '60s and '70s. Even local youth league baseball teams had their day, as WMRO broadcast league championship games.

The station gave West Aurora graduate and future Chicago on-air personality John Drury his start, and a young Chick Hearn, who captained East Aurora's basketball team before transferring to Marmion, was on the staff long before he began his Hall of Fame broadcasting career covering the Los Angeles Lakers.

In 1960, Bob Locke joined the station as sports director and spent the next thirty-five years covering the Tomcats and just about everything else. A few years later, Locke encouraged young Neal

Ormond to start covering West's games. Fifty years later, Ormond was still at the mic.

In 1957, failing health forced O'Brien to sell WMRO to Vincent Coffey and Ben Oswalt for a reported $85,000. The station changed hands a couple times after that, with Dale Stevens taking ownership in the late '60s, followed by Beasely Broadcasting Inc. in 1986. Then, suddenly, one Friday in December 1989, Beasley pulled the plug on WMRO, and the station went off the air. Within hours, WKKD sports director Bill Baker arranged for Ormond to broadcast that night's basketball game over his station, and for the next couple years Locke, Ormond and others continued covering the Aurora sports on WKKD and, later, WBIG.

By 2010, East and West Aurora no longer offered the only game in town, and declining interest led WBIG to begin squeezing their games off the airwaves in favor of other area events. In response, West Aurora and Ormond, together with students of the Blackhawk Broadcast Club, began pioneering Internet webcasts, first as audio only and then as video. Over the next three years, a new industry developed, and nearly every area school was streaming video of football games, basketball games and other events via one of several Internet providers that had entered the market.

Chicagoland through eight weeks, needed only to beat the Tomcats to earn a trip to the 1988 playoffs.

In the final game of the regular season, West's James Hale, who rushed for 197 yards and three touchdowns on the night, helped stake the Blackhawks to a 27–14 fourth-quarter lead that had Tomcat fans heading to the exits with seven minutes remaining. At about that time, East caught fire as quarterback Lou Hernandez led the Cats on a 74-yard drive that culminated with Hernandez throwing a touchdown pass to Derrick House. East's attempt at a 2-point conversion failed, and West led by 7 with 2:17 to play. The touchdown made the game a bit more interesting, but it was still seemingly out of the Tomcat's reach. However, when the radio call by Neal Ormond and Dick Schindel reported that East's ensuing onside kick was recovered by Tomcat Tahece Clayton, cars began turning around in the parking lot. A minute later, a Hernandez pass found John Blassingame in the corner of the end zone, and East trailed by just one, 27–26. Rather than play for overtime, Coach Gavigan decided to go for 2 points and the win, and his gamble paid off as Hernandez dove into the end zone to give East a 28–27 lead with just over 1:00 left in regulation time. Desperate for a score that would secure a playoff spot, West's Rich Becker drove the Blackhawks to East's 23-yard line, where West lined up for what appeared to be an attempt at a game-winning, 40-yard field goal. But Coach Cedarblad had called for a fake, and on the game's final play, holder Tim Wagner picked up the snap and took off around end with several Tomcats in pursuit. Wagner made it as far as the 10-yard line before he was pushed out of bounds, bringing a wild end to one of the wildest East-West games ever. The Blackhawks ended the year with a record of 5-4, third in the Upstate 8 but not good enough to make the playoffs.

Ed Gavigan left East after just one year to take the head coaching position at Rock Valley Community College in Winnebago County. Don Williams, who had been an assistant at East for three seasons, replaced him.

East opened the '89 season by defeating Waubonsie Valley 26–13. Although the schools were just four miles apart, it was the first meeting between the Tomcats and Warriors since Waubonsie had opened its doors on Aurora's Far East Side sixteen years earlier. The Cats' only other win that year was a forfeit by Streamwood during a teachers' strike. On the west side, Cedarblad's Blackhawks finished 4-5 overall, including a 44–12 victory over East.

***

As the 1980s turned to the '90s, Aurora football's downward trend continued as both East and West produced identical 2-7 overall records in 1990. The Blackhawks' 28–0 victory over East in the season finale elevated West to a sixth-place tie with DeKalb in conference play, while the Cats finished eighth.

At the start of the 1991–92 school year, Waubonsie Valley, having outgrown the old Little 7 Conference, joined the Upstate 8. The addition of a ninth school complicated scheduling, as each school now played eight league games, with a different conference member playing a non-conference game each week. West defeated East 19–8 to end the season with a 4-5 record, while East won two games by forfeit to finish 2-7 for the third straight year under Don Williams. Neither Tim Cedarblad nor Williams returned the following year.

Wendell Jeffries was promoted to coach the Tomcats prior to the 1992–93 school year. A 1981 East graduate and a member of the Tomcats' 1980 conference championship team, Jeffries provided a link to more successful times. Meanwhile, West Aurora replaced Cedarblad with veteran Bob Williams, brother of East's Don Williams, who came to West after leading nearby Yorkville High School to four consecutive playoff appearances.

The 100th East-West game and the festivities that surrounded it were the highlight of the 1992 season. The game itself took place at Ken Zimmerman Field on October 30, but as had been the custom in bygone days when the games were played on Thanksgiving, the entire week was one big celebration. Former players and coaches from past eras came to town from throughout the country. The *Beacon* offered expanded coverage of the big game all week long, including daily accounts of the various festivities, historical recaps of past games and interviews with past performers and media observers. Players wore commemorative T-shirts to school. As Friday night approached, no one seemed to care that the teams entered the game with identical 1-7 records, as the night was meant to celebrate the past. It was a reunion of sorts, filled with nostalgia, ceremony, community spirit and fireworks. In what was almost an afterthought to everyone but the players and coaches, the Tomcats defeated the Blackhawks 19–8, claiming the newly created Century Trophy and stretching their series lead to 47-41-12.

After just one year at West, Bob Williams opted to return to Yorkville, and Blackhawk assistant Ira Jefferson was promoted to replace him. Jefferson, who had come to West Aurora in 1983, had been a teammate of former Blackhawk coach Randy Melvin at Eastern Illinois University, where he had played linebacker in the NCAA's Division II football championship game as a junior and led the Panthers in tackles while earning honorable mention all-American honors as a senior.

Leagues with an odd number of members face scheduling complications, and with nine schools to consider, the Upstate 8 schedule makers could no longer equitably slot Aurora's rivalry game into the last week of each season. Thus, in 1993, the Blackhawks and Tomcats met in the season's second week. West avenged the previous year's loss with a 29-8 win over East in Jefferson's first East-West game. After starting 4-0, the Blackhawks faded and finished 4-5 on the year. The '93 Tomcats, featuring future Air Force Academy running back Tobin Ruff, finished 3-6 and tied with West for fifth place in the conference.

While the Tomcats were winless in 1994, Jefferson's Blackhawks put together their best season in ten years. Led by all-state linebacker Jeff

Program from the 100th East-West game. *Author's private collection.*

Weisse, who would go on to earn a football scholarship to the University of Illinois, and running backs Joe Howell and Elvis Hernandez, West surprised prognosticators by winning its first six games, including a 35–0 route of East Aurora and a shockingly one-sided upset of previously undefeated Lake Park by the same score. In the East-West game, Howell and quarterback Ted Schroeder paced the Blackhawks with a combined 307 yards rushing and three touchdowns.

The Hawks stumbled a bit in their last three games, losing an 18–12 decision to eventual league champ Waubonsie Valley and suffering a 39–12 loss to St. Charles in the season finale. Nonetheless, they finished in a three-way tie with St. Charles and Lake Park for second place in the Upstate 8 and qualified for the state playoffs for the first time since 1984.

After twenty years of hearing coaches and others complain about the Wednesday–Saturday scheduling format used for rounds one and two of the state playoffs, the IHSA addressed the issue by moving the start of the regular season up one week to provide a full week's rest between the close of the regular season and the first round of playoff games. The Blackhawks drew Chicago's Bogan High School as their first-round opponent.

On October 28, a contingent of west-siders accompanied the Blackhawks to Rockne Stadium in Chicago, where the Blackhawks combined a methodical, ball-control attack with solid defense to earn a 21–8 victory. Schroeder opened the scoring with a twenty-one-yard touchdown run in the first quarter, and Hernandez punched one in from a yard out late in the second quarter to give the Hawks a 14–0 halftime lead. Although Bogan cut the deficit to 14–8 in the third quarter, the Blackhawks were never

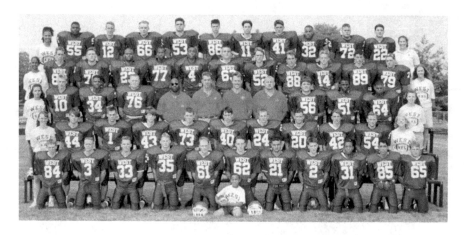

West Aurora's 1994 playoff qualifiers. *Courtesy of Blackhawk Joe Howell.*

seriously threatened, and when Howell answered with the Blackhawks' third touchdown, the win was sealed. For the first time in history, West Aurora advanced to the second round.

On a drizzly Friday night a week later, Naperville Central visited Ken Zimmerman Field, where the 8-2 Blackhawks went toe to toe with the 9-1 Redhawks in an epic battle that wasn't decided until the game's final moments. West led 7–6 after one quarter, but Central scored 18 unanswered points to forge a 24–7 lead midway through the third period. Two Hernandez touchdowns cut Central's lead to 3 points, but the Redhawks extended the lead to 10 before West Aurora mounted a furious fourth-quarter rally. Howell scored a four-yard touchdown to pull West back within 4, and a late fumble recovery gave the Blackhawks one last opportunity. In front of a roaring crowd, Schroeder completed three consecutive passes that moved the ball to the Redhawks' twelve-yard line with less than a minute to play. Unfortunately, that was as close as West would get, as four passes fell incomplete in the end zone, and Naperville Central prevailed. It was a thrilling end to an exciting season, and it left Blackhawk fans optimistic about the future.

In 1995, Joe Howell was joined in the backfield by transfer student Jamal Campbell, a nephew of Ira Jefferson's who had had an outstanding junior year as a running back for the south suburbs' Bradley-Bourbonnais High School. Campbell's presence, together with the success of 1994, gave West high hopes for another playoff run. The Hawks opened the season by pounding conference pre-season favorite Lake Park 26–7. They played well for a few games after that, but by midseason, the Blackhawks had lost their

Tobin Ruff, East Class of 1994. An excellent student who ranked fourth in his graduating class, Ruff was also an outstanding athlete who's size, speed and skill caught the attention of Upstate 8 coaches, who conspired to keep the ball out of his hands, and recruiters from major college football programs. With offers from Northwestern, Wisconsin and others on the table, Ruff chose to enter the Air Force Academy, where he played football for four seasons. As a running back and kick returner, Ruff scored a game-tying touchdown in the Falcons' 1996 upset of Notre Dame, appeared in the Copper Bowl as a freshman and played in the Las Vegas Bowl as a senior. He averaged 6.6 yards per carry over his college career. Upon graduating from the Academy in 1998, Ruff served four years as a U.S. Air Force network officer before returning to civilian life, where, as of 2014, he was reportedly working for the Department of Homeland Security.

rhythm and fallen to 4-5 for the year. East, meanwhile, won just one game all year, a 19–6 victory over Streamwood. The season ended with an exciting East-West game that ended with a flurry of activity. With 1:19 to go in the game, a West touchdown by Howell stretched the Blackhawks' lead to 30–19 and seemingly put the game away, but East's Ken Stone breathed new life into the Tomcats by returning the ensuing kickoff for a touchdown. The Cats got the ball back for one last opportunity with 0:35 remaining, but an interception by West's Russell Harris ended the threat, and the Blackhawks prevailed 30–25.

***

In the fall of 1995, the DuPage Valley Conference began soliciting bids from area schools to replace Glenbard South High School after the Raiders announced they were leaving the DVC to join the Suburban Prairie Conference. In addition to Glenbard South, the DVC consisted of Glenbard East, Glenbard North, Naperville Central, Naperville North, West Chicago, Wheaton North and Wheaton-Warrenville South High Schools. It was a top-notch league of excellent, well-funded, suburban schools with outstanding facilities and highly developed academic and athletic programs. Unlike the Upstate 8 at the time, all DVC schools competed in all sports at all levels. As a football conference, the league was second to none.

Recognizing the unevenness of the Upstate 8 schools, the awkwardness of scheduling a nine-school conference and the opportunity to join a more prestigious league, four Upstate 8 schools—West Aurora, Lake Park, St. Charles and Waubonsie Valley—submitted proposals to join the DVC, with West emerging from the selection process with an invitation to join.

After being notified of their selection, West Aurora officials presented the idea to the community and solicited input over the next several weeks. The community's initial reaction, which centered primarily on whether the move meant an end to the annual East-West football and basketball games, was mostly negative. Others were concerned that West would be unable to succeed in a more competitive environment, and some wondered whether the DVC had selected West to be the league's "doormat."

To address these concerns, West Aurora principal Mark McDonald and athletic director John Bauer began by working with East Aurora to secure the continuation of the annual East-West football game by scheduling it as a non-conference season opener for the foreseeable future. The schools also agreed to schedule one non-conference basketball game each year. Once it was established that the East-West rivalry would live on, the primary advantages of aligning with the DuPage Valley Conference were spelled out: DVC schools represented more stable districts with no foreseeable plans to build additional schools that might disrupt the league's ideal eight-school alignment, and league-wide, DVC schools offered more students more opportunities to participate in more sports than the Upstate 8 schools.

Certainly, West Aurora would have to upgrade some programs by increasing the size of coaching staffs, improving facilities and generally holding some programs to higher standards, but a commitment to self-improvement was presented as a good thing. Besides, across the board, West programs were competitive in nearly all sports. The school had highly successful basketball, wrestling and tennis programs, and over the years, its other programs had produced their fair share of winners. Even the football program, which admittedly had been through a down cycle in recent years, was just one year removed from pushing state semi-finalist Naperville Central to the limit in a playoff game. As the apparent advantages of joining the DVC became clear, the community warmed to the idea, and West Aurora accepted the invitation. The 1996–97 season would be West's last in the Upstate 8.

***

The Blackhawks produced a 4-5 record again in 1996 and finished seventh in their final Upstate 8 season, while East finished 0-9, including a 39–20 loss to West. After winning just one game in three seasons, Wendell Jeffries resigned as East's head coach. He was replaced by thirty-one-year-old Art Panka, who had coached the freshmen and sophomore teams and been a varsity assistant at Amos Alonzo Stagg High School in Palos Hills, Illinois.

West entered the DuPage Valley Conference in 1997, and East-West football began a new tradition with the annual season opener. Intended or not, ideal August weather coupled with the festive atmosphere and pre-season optimism normally associated with the beginning of each school year seemed to reinvigorate East-West games, as interest and attendance remained as high as ever. Coach Panka made an immediate contribution to the East-West mystique when he accused Ira Jefferson of sending spies to watch East practices during the week prior to the game. Whether West spied on the Tomcats' practices or not, it was the speed of the Blackhawks' LesRoy Tittle that made the difference on opening night, as Tittle scored on a forty-three-yard pass and an eighty-yard punt return to help stake West to a 21–0 first-quarter lead. The Red and Blue never looked back in the 36–0 victory.

In their first DVC season, the Blackhawks had little trouble scoring, but the defense gave up thirty-six points per game as West finished 2-5 in the conference and 4-5 overall. East finished 1-8 in Panka's first season.

Prior to the 1998–99 school year, Bartlett and Neuqua Valley High Schools joined the Upstate 8 Conference. With ten teams, it became impossible for every school to play all the other schools each year, which resulted in the introduction of a rotating seven-game schedule. Sadly, after eighty-seven consecutive years, this new scheduling arrangement marked the end of annual East Aurora-Elgin games.

The Blackhawks, having won five straight and eight of the last nine games with East, began the '98 season knowing that a win in the season opener would even the East-West series for the first time since the Red and Black took the lead seventy-one years earlier. The Tomcats took an early 6–0 lead on a forty-two-yard touchdown pass from Brad Brueckner to Jeremy Von Behren, but the Blackhawks combined two interceptions by sophomore linebacker Nate Eimer and two second-half touchdowns to gain a 12–6 victory. The series now stood tied at forty-six wins apiece, with twelve ties.

East showed considerable improvement on both offense and defense throughout the '98 season to finish 3-6 on the season and 3-4 in the Upstate

8. It was the Cats' best conference showing in fifteen years. Meanwhile, with all-state defensive lineman and DVC Defensive Player of the Year Jeff Ruffin, speedster LesRoy Tittle and quarterback Kevin Presbrey leading the way, West finished with an overall record of 5-4 and tied for fourth in the conference with a record of 3-4.

The 1999 season opened with West beating East 23–0 to take the lead in the series. It was the Blackhawks' seventh consecutive win over the east-siders. The rebuilding Blackhawks added a non-conference win over Elgin the following week but went winless in league play to finish the year at 2-7 and last in the DVC. The Tomcats, with victories over Streamwood and DeKalb, also finished the '99 season with a 2-7 mark. It was East's sixteenth consecutive losing season. During that same span, West had had eleven losing seasons. How had things gotten so bad?

***

By the year 2000, Aurora's population had reached 143,000. Over the previous thirty years, the city's Far East Side in DuPage County had become a fully established suburban entity, very different from traditional Aurora. Only a few of the area's old-line manufacturers—Caterpillar, Aurora Pump, Henry Pratt Company and Lyon Metal—remained. After Caterpillar, the town's largest employers in 2000 were the three local school districts, the two hospitals, the park district and Hollywood Casino. The downtown area had not recovered from the exodus of the 1970s. Were it not for the continued presence of Aurora National, Old Second and Merchants banks; the restored Paramount Theatre; the casino; city hall; the library; and a handful of small businesses, the once-bustling downtown would have been virtually abandoned.

The population growth that occurred since 1970 was not distributed evenly. While the new Far East Side and Indian Prairie School District 204 grew exponentially, landlocked East Aurora School District 131 grew more modestly. West Aurora School District 129, which included developing areas on the city's western edges as well as in the adjacent towns of North Aurora and Montgomery, grew at a more controlled, albeit steady, pace.

In 2000, Aurora's Hispanic population, which represented 7 percent of the total population in 1970, had grown to represent one-third of the city's residents by 2000. And although recent Hispanic immigrants were settling in all three local school districts, the concentration was highest in District 131 and lowest in District 204, with District 129 falling in the middle.

The preponderance of new arrivals in the city's older sections had turned many of Aurora's traditionally multigenerational middle-class neighborhoods into low-income, transient communities. Crime throughout the city was on the rise. Infrastructure in the older sections of town was decaying. Aurora had become a unique blend of post-industrial rust belt and modern suburbia located in the midst of some of Chicagoland's trendiest and fastest-growing suburbs.

As all this was going on in the city of Aurora, nearby communities were taking the concept of competitive high school football to a higher level than ever before. While many Upstate 8 and DuPage Valley Conference communities offered competitive park district football programs to grade school–age boys (and girls) of the 1980s and '90s, similar programs were not introduced in Aurora until the late 1990s. In some neighboring communities, private citizens and businesses organized and sponsored traveling football clubs for more serious youth players, but no one in Aurora stepped up to do the same. While other school districts offered well-developed middle school programs that were often coordinated with the local high school program, East and West Aurora's middle school football programs were often curtailed or suspended by budget cuts. When middle school programs were available, they were generally too inconsistent to effectively prepare players for the rigors of competing in high school. During the 1990s, Aurora's Catholic schools offered the best grade school football programs in town, and although it was available to seventh and eighth graders only, that early training helped propel Aurora Central Catholic High School and Marmion Academy to eleven playoff appearances during the decade.

The absence of effective youth football feeder programs, demographic challenges presented by increasingly larger portions of student populations from homes that did not immerse their children in the culture of football and a lack of success at the high school level combined to discourage students from even trying out for the high school team. The result was that throughout the '90s, both East and West often entered games with half the number of players as their opponents and were challenging other schools' well-trained players with students who were learning the most basic fundamentals of the game at the high school level. Given these circumstances, it is not hard to see why West Aurora was having a difficult time competing with the DuPage Valley Conference's power programs or why East was having trouble competing with anyone at all.

***

Both East and West entered the new millennium with new coaches—thirty-year-old assistant coach Mike Runge replaced Ira Jefferson at West, while the east-siders tabbed Al Tamberelli to replace Art Panka. Runge had played high school football at Waubonsie Valley and college football at Illinois Wesleyan University before starting his teaching career at West. Tamberelli had most recently been an assistant coach at North Central College in Naperville, and prior to that he had been head coach at tiny Culver-Stockton College in Canton, Missouri.

In the season opener at Ken Zimmerman Field, the Tomcats' Ajarus Jones ran for 171 yards and four touchdowns to lead East to an exciting 26–23 victory over the Blackhawks. East built a 20–7 lead after three quarters, but West rallied to go ahead on a 20-yard touchdown scamper by quarterback John Slocum before Jones's fourth touchdown of the night put East up for good. The victory ended the Blackhawks' seven-game series winning streak and served as a springboard for East's first winning season since 1983, as the Cats finished 5-4 overall and 4-3 in the conference. The Blackhawks, meanwhile, finished 2-7 and in sixth place in the DVC.

In 2001, the IHSA expanded the playoff format to eight thirty-two-team classes, meaning that 256 schools would qualify for the post-season each year. Under this new format, most teams with at least five wins would qualify for the playoffs. That same year, St. Charles North High School entered the Upstate 8 Conference, bringing the league to eleven members. Moving forward, some teams would play seven league games, while others played six.

Both East and West came into 2001 with a host of new starters, and it showed in the first half of the ragged season opener. The Blackhawks opened the scoring in the second quarter when quarterback Adam Solarz connected with Brandon Foster on a nineteen-yard touchdown pass. West added second-half touchdown runs by Solarz and Marquis Hubbard and a fifty-nine-yard fumble return by Ben Knight to cap a 29–0 victory. Unfortunately, neither school won a game for the remainder of the season, and East seemingly fell to an all-time low as the Tomcats scored just 14 points over the entire year.

In 2002, West reported that more students were playing football at the district's middle schools than ever before. Furthermore, in an effort to become more competitive, the high school introduced a year-round weight training program, something other DVC schools had had in place for years. It was also around this time that students who had played in the Aurora

Superstars Youth Football League, a league launched in the late 1990s to provide recreational football opportunities to grade school children from both sides of town, were beginning to enter high school.

The '02 season opened with West routing the Tomcats 41–6 and winning the next two as well, but the Blackhawks dropped their last six to finish 3-6 and last in the DVC, while East Aurora was 0-9 for the second straight season.

East began the 2003 season with ten sophomores on its roster, and the results were predictable. In the season opener, West rolled up over four hundred yards of total offense in a second consecutive 41–6 victory. The Cats' losing would continue until October, when a 32–7 win over Rockford Jefferson ended the losing streak at twenty-four games. The Blackhawks, meanwhile, did not fare any better as they, too, finished 1-8 and last in the DVC for the third consecutive season.

Despite the poor showings of the previous three years, the Blackhawks entered 2004 with high hopes, as twelve returning starters were joined by an outstanding junior class who had posted winning seasons as both freshman and sophomores. West was quarterbacked by six-foot-four Matt McGary, son of John McGary, a teacher in East District 131 who had played for the Blackhawks in the 1970s and spent several years coaching various levels of football at West.

The Tomcats were also cautiously optimistic that things were heading in the right direction, as last year's sophomores were now battle-tested juniors. East's optimism proved to be unfounded, however, as in the season opener, the Blackhawks opened the scoring with a twenty-six-yard pass from McGary to Ben Petry and were not seriously challenged on their way to a 30–6 victory. The following week, West beat Elgin and later added conference victories over Glenbard East, West Chicago and Wheaton North to finish the season with a record of 5-4 and hopes of qualifying for the post-season. Unfortunately, the Blackhawks' five victories came against teams that combined to win just seven games between them, which, in the IHSA's final calculation, was not enough to earn that elusive playoff invitation. The Tomcats posted a 1-8 record for the year, beating Streamwood 19–18 in the third game of the season.

With twenty seniors—including three-year starters Julius Tucker; six-foot-four, 290-pound tackle John Berrios; and seven others who had played on the varsity as sophomores—the 2005 Tomcats were East's most experienced team in years. West, meanwhile, returned nine offensive and four defensive starters from the previous year's 5-4 team.

The 2005 season opened with the Blackhawks earning the school's 500th all-time victory in a 33–0 shutout of East. Unfortunately, after following that up with a 21–14 victory over Elgin, the Blackhawks' season disintegrated, and they were winless in league play. On the east side, Tucker and Berrios would earn all-conference honors, but it was another long year, nonetheless, as the Tomcats' lone victory came in a 41–6 rout of Streamwood in the season finale. It was the Cats' third consecutive one-win season under Coach Tamberelli.

Coaches Tamberelli and Runge had assumed their head coaching responsibilities together in 2000, and as it turned out, they would step down together following the 2005 season. In Runge's six seasons, the Blackhawks were 8-4 against their traditional non-conference foes East Aurora and Elgin but just 6-36 against DVC competition. West-siders were finding out that while the Blackhawks could compete in other sports, competing in the state's strongest football conference was a tough proposition—and while the competition in the Upstate 8 was not as uniformly high as in the DuPage Valley Conference, East faced similar challenges. After compiling an 8-46 mark over six years, Tamberelli, too, had had enough.

West went outside the district to hire Roger "Buck" Drach to lead the Blackhawks beginning in 2006. In twenty-three years at Bartonville-Limestone and St. Charles High Schools, Drach's teams had compiled a record of 158-75, with thirteen playoff appearances. He had retired from coaching to spend more time with his family following the death of his wife, Rose, in 1999 but eased back in to coaching as an assistant at Batavia High School before coming to West Aurora. East, meanwhile, hired forty-eight-year-old Bill Bryant, an assistant at Plainfield Central. The bulk of Bryant's teaching and coaching career had been spent in Texas, where he had spent several years as an assistant football coach and head baseball, softball and basketball coach. He came to East intending to work on building successful middle school programs to feed the high school, a common model used by high schools in Texas.

With two new coaches roaming the sidelines, the 2006 season opened with West Aurora defeating East 33–0. The Blackhawks gained 378 yards on the evening compared to just 60 for the east-siders. Neither coaching change would have an immediate impact on results, as the Blackhawks again won their non-conference games with East and Elgin but were winless in the DVC, while East beat South Elgin High School, which had recently replaced DeKalb as the Upstate 8's eleventh member, and was competing in its first year of varsity football.

Ongoing efforts to "change the culture" on both sides of town resulted in small improvements at both schools in 2007. At East, Coach Bryant preached self-discipline while initiating a weight program and improved summer camps. For the first time in years, the Tomcat roster reached forty players. Unfortunately, the inroads Bryant made did not produce on-field results, as the Cats went 0-9 on the year, including a 38–6 loss to West Aurora. Meanwhile, through the season's first eight weeks, the '07 Blackhawks were 4-4 and would qualify for the playoffs for the first time in thirteen years with a win over Glenbard North. The Panthers entered the game in an identical situation: 4-4 and needing to beat the Blackhawks to earn a playoff spot. To the dismay of Blackhawk fans, the Panthers emerged with a 14–7 victory and went on to demonstrate the top-to-bottom strength of the DuPage Valley Conference by advancing to the Class 8A championship game before losing to conference rival Naperville North.

From 2008 to 2010, Drach's Blackhawks fell into what had become a familiar pattern: able to win non-conference games with East Aurora and Elgin and to compete with conference foes Glenbard East and West Chicago but unable to crack the DVC's five upper-echelon programs. As Drach retired after the 2010 season, west-siders were wondering whether West would ever compete in the DuPage Valley Conference.

On the east side, the '08 Tomcats beat South Elgin and Thornwood to post their first two-win season in seven years but went 0-27 from 2009 to 2011.

***

Ken Zimmerman's tenure as West Aurora's head football coach had lasted twenty-six years; the eleven coaches who followed averaged three and a half. Zim's teams won 54 percent of the games he coached. The eleven coaches who followed won 30 percent. In past coaching searches, West Aurora had seemingly tried everything from seasoned veterans who had had success at other schools (Dick Munn, Tim Cedarblad, Bob Williams, Buck Drach) to young but inexperienced assistants who had demonstrated they could connect with kids and were up for a challenge (Randy Melvin, Ira Jefferson, Mike Runge). All came in with good intentions. Several went on to achieve great success at other schools. But in the forty years since Zimmerman retired from coaching, not a one had built sustainable success at West Aurora.

In 2011, West Aurora turned to twenty-eight-year-old Nate Eimer to lead the program. A 2001 West graduate, Eimer had been a three-year starter at tight end and linebacker for the Blackhawks. With an eye on the long term, Eimer came into the role focused on building a foundation by working

Nate Eimer, West Class of 2001. A product of Aurora's west side, Eimer graduated from Holy Angels Grade School before entering West Aurora as a freshman in 1997. The six-two, 230-pound Eimer was a three-year starter at tight end and linebacker who earned DVC all-conference, *Beacon* all-area and academic all-state honors as a junior and senior. He was also a three-year varsity basketball player and key member of West Aurora's 2000 Class AA state basketball champions.

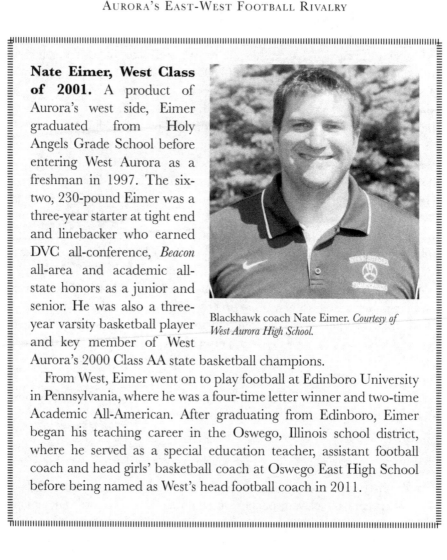

Blackhawk coach Nate Eimer. *Courtesy of West Aurora High School.*

From West, Eimer went on to play football at Edinboro University in Pennsylvania, where he was a four-time letter winner and two-time Academic All-American. After graduating from Edinboro, Eimer began his teaching career in the Oswego, Illinois school district, where he served as a special education teacher, assistant football coach and head girls' basketball coach at Oswego East High School before being named as West's head football coach in 2011.

to get kids who were serious about football involved in youth programs, on upgrading the middle school programs and on taking the high school's weight program to the next level. None of these initiatives were new. The question was: would he be the one to deliver?

The 2011 season brought an end to the Blackhawks' long-running series with Elgin High School, which had appeared on West's schedule every year since 1914. After beating East Aurora and St. Charles East in the non-conference portion of the schedule, the Blackhawks finished 2-5 in conference play, with wins over West Chicago and Glenbard East. East Aurora was 0-9 in Bill Bryant's last season.

Kurt Becker, East Class of 1977. Born in Aurora in 1958, Becker grew up on the city's east side, where he attended Simmons Junior High School (now Simmons Middle School) and East Aurora High School. As a senior, he was captain of East's 1976 conference championship football team and a track and field athlete.

Recruited by legendary University of Michigan coach Bo Schembechler, Becker played for the Wolverines for four seasons while earning his degree in business administration. As an offensive guard, Becker was twice named All Big Ten and, as a senior, was a consensus all-American and finalist for the Lombardi Award, given each year to college football's top lineman. Drafted by the Chicago Bears in 1982, the versatile Becker played every offensive line position except center during his nine-year NFL career and was part of the Bears' 1985 Super Bowl championship team.

Tomcat coach Kurt Becker. Courtesy of East Aurora High School.

When his playing days ended, Becker returned to the Aurora area to pursue business interests. He also served as a volunteer assistant at Marmion Academy for four years before responding to a call to return "home" to the Tomcats in 2012. In addition to his business and coaching responsibilities, Becker has been an officer and fundraiser for the East Aurora Football Old-Timers Association and chairman of the East Aurora Youth Tackle Football organization, which was admitted into the Chicagoland Youth Football League in 2013.

At the time Bryant left, the Tomcat program was at an all-time low. East had lost thirty straight games. Generational ties to the Tomcat legacy, which had been so strong for so long, barely existed. The existing feeder program continued to be ineffective in turning out players. Sure, the program always turned out a handful of dedicated, football-minded kids, but there was simply never enough talent, and each new school year began with a challenge to round up enough players to field a team. What aspiring coach would want such a job? Enter East Aurora's most accomplished alumnus, Kurt Becker.

With his east-side roots, collegiate and professional success and connections to people throughout the game, the physically imposing Becker offered the name recognition and credibility needed to lead a comprehensive effort to rebuild the Tomcat program. With an emphasis on history and tradition, self-discipline, grades and commitment to team as an extension of family, Becker's rebuilding process began in 2012.

Prior to the 2012–13 school year, West Chicago and Lake Park High Schools traded places, as West Chicago moved to the Upstate 8 Conference while Lake Park took West Chicago's place in the DVC. On the gridiron, the 2012 season began like most other recent years, as West Aurora routed East 59–19 on opening night. Despite the presence of three exciting offensive players in quarterback Quintez Jones, wide receiver Cole Childs and back Booker Ross, the Blackhawks did not have enough firepower to break into the DVC's upper echelon and finished the season 3-6 overall and 2-5 in the conference. The Tomcats endured their fourth straight winless season.

***

By 2013, Aurora's population had reached 200,000 people, and although it was now Illinois' second-largest municipality, its economic base was fully intertwined with the rest of the Chicago metropolitan area. Positive signs of progress could be seen around the city. Crime, which had risen to untenable levels in the mid-1990s, had fallen to the point of making national news, as the city experienced not a single murder in 2012. Old neighborhoods were starting to come back as the Hispanic immigrants of twenty and thirty years earlier became fully assimilated second- and third-generation residents. Aurora was receiving accolades as a good place to live. The Paramount Theater had become the jewel of the western suburbs' arts and entertainment scene. Abandoned industrial wastelands along the banks of the Fox River had been cleared to make way for RiverEdge Park, an open-air concert venue. Downtown was now home to Waubonsee Community College's gleaming new campus, and a new library was under construction. And although the city center continued to struggle to find its identity, at least many of the old abandoned buildings had been cleared away.

East and West took steps toward brighter football futures as well. West Chicago's decision to leave the DuPage Valley Conference for the Upstate 8 started a chain reaction of moves involving schools from both conferences that resulted in West Aurora's decision to return to the Upstate 8 Conference beginning with the 2014–15 school year. The competition won't be easy for West, but nothing could be as difficult as the DVC. Later in 2013, east-siders took the long-discussed step of establishing an advanced youth football program that began competing on three levels in the Chicagoland Youth Football League.

***

In August 2013, Neal Ormond's call of his fiftieth East-West football game was delayed by one day as area storms postponed Friday night's game until Saturday. But when the whistle finally blew, the 121st game of the series that began in 1893 started with a bang as East's Desmond Gant returned the opening kickoff for a touchdown. No one could remember if the Tomcats had led the Blackhawks at any time since their last series victory thirteen years earlier. The lead didn't last long, however, as the Blackhawks went on to hand East its fortieth consecutive loss by a score of 46–18. Unfortunately for the Blackhawks, that would be the high point of the season, as they finished the year 1-8 and last in the DuPage Valley Conference.

On October 4, 2013, East Aurora's losing streak stood at forty-four games as the Tomcats prepared to meet Elgin High School for the 112th time since 1893. The Maroons slowly built a 22-8 second-half lead and controlled the game until Gant shifted the momentum with a 98-yard kickoff return that brought the Tomcats back to within striking distance. From there, running back Jamaria Littleton took over, running for 134 yards in the second half and scoring a fourth-quarter touchdown that knotted the score at 22. A few minutes later, an Elgin fumble gave the ball back to East, and after several nice runs by Littleton, East had the ball in position for a last-minute field goal attempt. A nervous Richard Barajas, who had not kicked all game, then booted the ball through the uprights to propel the Tomcats to their first victory in five years! It was a glorious evening.

Although both East and West ended 2013 with identical 1-8 records, both were excited for the future. East was honored with an IHSA "Sport a Winning Attitude" award during the season, and Desmond Gant was named honorable mention all-state by the Illinois High School Football Coaches' Association. Six of nine graduating Tomcat seniors were either going on

Neal Ormond III, West Class of 1958. Born in New York, Neal Ormond moved to Aurora's west side as a child in the 1940s, attended West Aurora schools and, after spending six years away at college, returned to become a local institution as the "Voice of the Blackhawks," a school board member and volunteer coach.

In addition to participating on West's varsity tennis team, Ormond played on the 1957–58 Blackhawk basketball team that finished fourth in the state tournament. After graduating from West, he studied engineering at Yale University and covered Bulldog sports for the school radio station. From Yale, Ormond headed west to Stanford University, where he continued his broadcasting career while earning a master's in business administration.

After Stanford, Ormond accepted a position with Standard Oil in downtown Chicago and returned to the Aurora area, where, at the urging of WMRO's Bob Locke, he began moonlighting as a high school sports broadcaster. He called his first game, an 18–7 Blackhawk victory over St. Charles, on September 18, 1964, and over the next fifty years was at the mic for more than 450 football games, at least 1,500 basketball games and numerous other events, including fast-pitch softball and local youth baseball and softball games. He has been heard on three radio stations, cable television and, most recently, the Internet.

When he wasn't announcing local sporting events, Ormond built a thirty-year career as an executive with Standard Oil, Quaker Oats and W.W. Grainger. He and his wife, Mary Clark Ormond, raised a family of three West Aurora graduates before he "retired" to a career of community service that as of 2014 included seventeen years as a three-sport volunteer Blackhawk coach and nineteen years on the West Aurora School Board, including five as president. Ormond has also served on the Blackhawk Sports Booster Board and as chairman of the Community Foundation of the Fox River Valley.

On January 25, 2014, the night of the 217th East-West basketball game, Aurorans from both sides of the Fox River gathered to honor Ormond for his fifty years of broadcasting. When the ceremonies ended, Ormond sat at the mic and delivered his 108th East-West basketball broadcast.

The 2013 Blackhawks. *Courtesy of West Aurora High School.*

The 2013 Tomcats. *Courtesy of East Aurora High School.*

to play football in college or were entering the military. West of the river, fans cheered 2013 West graduate Booker Ross as he played for the NCAA Division III University of Wisconsin-Whitewater national champions and congratulated Quintez Jones, Alex Shire and Matt Williams on receiving scholarships to play college football.

A lot has happened in the 120 years since Aurora's first East-West game. Over those years, both schools have reached the highest of highs and endured the lowest of lows. But through it all, they have been together. May the rivalry live on!

EAST AURORA

WEST AURORA

1974

	W	L	Coach			W	L	Coach
Overall Record:	5	4	Del Dufrain	Overall Record:		2	7	Dick Munn
Conference Record:	4	3		Conference Record:		1	6	

Date	Opponent		EA	Opp	Date	Opponent		WA	Opp
09.06	Joliet East	W	6	0	09.07	Hinsdale Central	L	0	60
09.13	LaSalle-Peru	L	6	30	09.13	Joliet West	W	33	12
09.20	**Naperville**	L	13	34	09.20	**Wheaton Central**	L	14	20
09.27	**St. Charles**	W	37	7	09.27	**DeKalb**	L	15	18
10.05	**Elgin Central**	W	15	8	10.04	**Larkin**	L	22	38
10.11	**Wheaton Central**	L	6	20	10.11	**Naperville**	L	0	28
10.18	**DeKalb**	L	13	27	10.18	**St. Charles**	L	8	16
10.25	**Larkin**	W	14	8	10.25	**Elgin Central**	W	20	6
11.01	**West Aurora**	W	15	14	11.01	**East Aurora**	L	14	15

1975

	W	L	Coach			W	L	Coach
Overall Record:	3	6	Del Dufrain	Overall Record:		1	8	Dick Munn
Conference Record:	2	3		Conference Record:		1	4	

Date	Opponent		EA	Opp	Date	Opponent		WA	Opp
09.05	Freeport	L	16	19	09.05	Wheaton Central	L	0	33
09.12	LaSalle-Peru	L	6	24	09.12	Naperville Central	L	16	42
09.19	**DeKalb**	W	14	10	09.19	**St. Charles**	L	6	14
09.26	**Larkin**	L	6	20	09.26	**Elgin Central**	L	12	26
10.03	Boylan	L	0	3	10.03	Horlick (Racine, WI)	L	6	14
10.10	**St. Charles**	L	13	14	10.10	**DeKalb**	L	6	40
10.17	**Elgin**	W	14	0	10.17	**Larkin**	L	8	28
10.24	St. Patrick	W	6	2	10.24	Joliet Catholic	L	0	20
10.31	**West Aurora**	L	3	8	10.31	**East Aurora**	W	8	3

Key: W = Win, L = Loss, T = Tie, WF = Win by forfeit, LF = Loss by forfeit, **Bold** = Conference game, *Italics* = state playoff game

EAST AURORA

WEST AURORA

1976

	W	L	Coach			W	L	Coach
Overall Record:	8	3	Del Dufrain		Overall Record:	3	6	Dick Munn
Conference Record:	4	1			Conference Record:	1	4	

Date	Opponent		EA	Opp	Date	Opponent		WA	Opp
09.10	Freeport	W	21	7	09.10	Wheaton Central	L	6	27
09.17	LaSalle-Peru	W	22	20	09.17	Naperville Central	W	40	12
09.24	**DeKalb**	W	14	7	09.24	**St. Charles**	W	20	13
10.01	**Larkin**	W	25	23	10.01	**Elgin Central**	L	13	21
10.08	Boylan	L	14	43	10.09	Bollingbrook	W	27	14
10.15	**St. Charles**	W	48	20	10.15	**DeKalb**	L	0	25
10.22	**Elgin**	L	16	28	10.22	**Larkin**	L	0	25
10.29	St. Viator	W	22	21	10.29	Joliet Catholic	L	8	26
11.05	**West Aurora**	W	34	0	11.05	**East Aurora**	L	0	34
11.10	*Eisenhower*	W	41	13					
11.13	*Glenbard East*	L	7	20					

Conference Co-champions

State Playoff Qualifier

1977

	W	L	Coach			W	L	Coach
Overall Record:	3	6	Del Dufrain		Overall Record:	5	4	Bob Quinn
Conference Record:	1	4			Conference Record:	2	3	

Date	Opponent		EA	Opp	Date	Opponent		WA	Opp
09.09	Freeport	L	19	22	09.09	Joliet West	W	27	0
09.16	LaSalle-Peru	L	6	14	09.16	Naperville Central	W	29	0
09.23	**Larkin**	L	14	15	09.23	**Elgin Central**	L	6	26
09.30	**DeKalb**	W	33	13	09.30	**St. Charles**	W	9	6
10.07	**St. Charles**	L	0	16	10.07	**DeKalb**	L	3	12
10.14	Boylan	W	26	0	10.14	Glenbrook North	L	10	12
10.21	Westview	W	12	10	10.21	Freeport	W	14	0
10.28	**Elgin**	L	6	12	10.28	**Larkin**	L	7	12
11.04	**West Aurora**	L	14	20	11.04	**East Aurora**	W	20	14

EAST AURORA   WEST AURORA

1978

	W	L	Coach			W	L	Coach
Overall Record:	3	6	Del Dufrain		Overall Record:	7	3	Bob Quinn
Conference Record:	2	3			Conference Record:	4	1	

Date	Opponent		EA	Opp	Date	Opponent		WA	Opp
09.08	Freeport	L	12	16	09.08	Joliet West	W	24	0
09.15	LaSalle-Peru	W	13	8	09.15	Naperville Central	W	10	0
09.22	**Larkin**	L	20	28	09.22	**Elgin Central**	W	31	0
09.29	**DeKalb**	W	9	0	09.29	**St. Charles**	W	17	6
10.06	**St. Charles**	L	7	20	10.06	**DeKalb**	W	17	6
10.13	Boylan	L	6	7	10.13	Glenbrook North	W	9	0
10.20	Ridgewood	L	9	13	10.20	Freeport	L	10	13
10.27	**Elgin**	W	27	0	10.27	**Larkin**	L	0	22
11.03	**West Aurora**	L	0	3	11.03	**East Aurora**	W	3	0
					11.08	*Forest View*	L	9	15

Conference Champions

State Playoff Qualifier

1979

	W	L	Coach			W	L	Coach
Overall Record:	5	4	John Wrenn		Overall Record:	6	3	Bob Quinn
Conference Record:	4	3			Conference Record:	4	3	

Date	Opponent		EA	Opp	Date	Opponent		WA	Opp
09.08	Downers Grove South	W	31	0	09.07	Naperville Central	W	28	0
09.14	LaSalle-Peru	L	16	30	09.14	Joliet West	W	28	8
09.21	**Streamwood**	L	7	13	09.22	**Lake Park**	W	29	7
09.28	**Elgin**	W	28	0	09.28	**Larkin**	L	13	14
10.06	**Larkin**	L	0	28	10.05	**Elgin**	W	35	7
10.12	**DeKalb**	W	14	6	10.12	**St. Charles**	L	12	21
10.19	**St. Charles**	L	20	34	10.19	**DeKalb**	W	25	14
10.26	**Lake Park**	W	52	20	10.26	**Streamwood**	W	21	6
11.02	**West Aurora**	W	13	7	11.02	**East Aurora**	L	7	13

Key: W = Win, L = Loss, T = Tie, WF = Win by forfeit, LF = Loss by forfeit, **Bold** = Conference game, *Italics* = state playoff game

EAST AURORA

WEST AURORA

1980

	W	L	Coach			W	L	Coach
Overall Record:	8	2	John Wrenn	Overall Record:		4	5	Jim Czocher
Conference Record:	6	1		Conference Record:		4	3	

Date	Opponent		EA	Opp	Date	Opponent		WA	Opp
09.05	Morgan Park	W	38	0	09.05	Naperville Central	L	20	21
09.12	LaSalle-Peru	W	36	22	09.12	Wheaton North	L	14	15
09.20	**Streamwood**	W	28	0	09.20	**Lake Park**	W	26	8
09.26	**Elgin**	W	40	6	09.26	**Larkin**	L	13	14
10.03	**Larkin**	W	49	7	10.03	**Elgin**	W	37	19
10.10	**DeKalb**	L	0	14	10.10	**St. Charles**	W	35	33
10.17	**St. Charles**	W	35	16	10.17	**DeKalb**	L	7	12
10.25	**Lake Park**	W	27	8	10.24	**Streamwood**	W	22	14
10.31	**West Aurora**	W	42	6	10.31	**East Aurora**	L	6	42
11.05	*Willowbrook*	L	22	27					

Conference Champions

State Playoff Qualifier

1981

	W	L	Coach			W	L	Coach
Overall Record:	6	3	Pete Ventrelli	Overall Record:		2	7	Jim Czocher
Conference Record:	4	3		Conference Record:		2	5	

Date	Opponent		EA	Opp	Date	Opponent		WA	Opp
09.11	Niles West	W	29	21	09.12	Benet Academy	L	0	7
09.18	LaSalle-Peru	W	19	12	09.18	Wheaton North	L	0	25
09.25	**St. Charles**	W	17	14	09.25	**DeKalb**	L	8	12
10.02	**Lake Park**	W	28	6	10.02	**Streamwood**	W	7	0
10.09	**Streamwood**	L	7	12	10.10	**Lake Park**	L	7	20
10.16	**Elgin**	W	24	22	10.16	**Larkin**	L	6	39
10.23	**Larkin**	L	0	14	10.23	**Elgin**	L	6	10
10.30	**DeKalb**	W	15	8	10.30	**St. Charles**	L	14	21
11.06	**West Aurora**	L	14	21	11.06	**East Aurora**	W	21	14

EAST AURORA

WEST AURORA

1982

	W	L	Coach			W	L	Coach
Overall Record:	6	4	Pete Ventrelli	Overall Record:		2	7	John Wrenn
Conference Record:	5	2		Conference Record:		2	5	

Date	Opponent		EA	Opp	Date	Opponent		WA	Opp
09.10	Niles West	L	14	18	09.10	Benet Academy	L	14	20
09.17	LaSalle-Peru	W	20	0	09.17	Downers Grove North	L	0	6
09.24	**St. Charles**	W	11	8	09.24	**DeKalb**	L	7	24
10.01	**Lake Park**	L	12	14	10.01	**Streamwood**	L	0	12
10.08	**Streamwood**	W	28	12	10.08	**Lake Park**	L	13	21
10.15	**Elgin**	L	20	21	10.15	**Larkin**	L	7	13
10.22	**Larkin**	W	14	13	10.22	**Elgin**	W	27	20
10.29	**DeKalb**	W	27	6	10.29	**St. Charles**	W	26	0
11.05	**West Aurora**	W	19	7	11.05	**East Aurora**	L	7	19
11.10	*Rock Island*	L	14	17					

Conference Tri-champions

State Playoff Qualifier

1983

	W	L	Coach			W	L	Coach
Overall Record:	5	4	Dick Schindel	Overall Record:		8	2	John Wrenn
Conference Record:	4	3		Conference Record:		7	0	

Date	Opponent		EA	Opp	Date	Opponent		WA	Opp
09.09	Hillcrest	W	20	13	09.10	Dundee-Crown	L	7	8
09.16	LaSalle-Peru	L	19	24	09.16	Ottawa	W	34	6
09.24	**Lake Park**	L	13	21	09.24	**Streamwood**	W	21	6
09.30	**St. Charles**	W	7	6	09.30	**DeKalb**	W	21	20
10.08	**Elgin**	W	13	7	10.07	**Larkin**	W	35	14
10.14	**Streamwood**	L	2	6	10.15	**Lake Park**	W	29	15
10.21	**DeKalb**	W	13	3	10.21	**St. Charles**	W	13	0
10.28	**Larkin**	W	23	10	10.28	**Elgin**	W	32	0
11.04	**West Aurora**	L	6	41	11.04	**East Aurora**	W	41	6
					11.09	*Addison Trail*	L	7	20

Conference Champions

State Playoff Qualifier

East Aurora

West Aurora

1984

	W	L	Coach			W	L	Coach
Overall Record:	1	8	Dick Schindel	Overall Record:		8	2	John Wrenn
Conference Record:	0	7		Conference Record:		6	1	

Date	Opponent		EA	Opp	Date	Opponent		WA	Opp
09.08	Freeport	NA	6	13	09.07	Harlem	NA	34	0
09.08	Hillcrest	WF	1	0	09.07	Oak Forest	WF	1	0
09.14	LaSalle-Peru	L	6	34	09.14	Ottawa	W	42	7
09.22	**Lake Park**	L	12	21	09.21	**Streamwood**	W	26	12
09.28	**St. Charles**	L	12	14	09.28	**DeKalb**	W	21	12
10.05	**Elgin**	L	7	13	10.05	**Larkin**	W	34	0
10.13	**Streamwood**	L	14	19	10.12	**Lake Park**	W	35	12
10.19	**DeKalb**	L	16	20	10.19	**St. Charles**	W	32	6
10.26	**Larkin**	L	13	24	10.26	**Elgin**	L	18	20
11.02	**West Aurora**	L	7	55	11.02	**East Aurora**	W	55	7
					11.07	*East St. Louis*	L	13	35

State Playoff Qualifier

1985

	W	L	Coach			W	L	Coach
Overall Record:	3	6	Dick Schindel	Overall Record:		0	9	Randy Melvin
Conference Record:	2	5		Conference Record:		0	7	

Date	Opponent		EA	Opp	Date	Opponent		WA	Opp
08.30	Rock Island	NA	8	14					
08.30	Wheaton North	WF	1	0	08.30	Oak Forest	L	14	20
09.06	LaSalle-Peru	L	8	24	09.06	Proviso East	L	0	36
09.13	**DeKalb**	L	6	26	09.13	**St. Charles**	L	7	36
09.20	**Larkin**	L	6	28	09.20	**Elgin**	L	0	26
09.28	**Lake Park**	L	6	40	09.28	**Streamwood**	L	10	32
10.04	**St. Charles**	L	16	47	10.04	**DeKalb**	L	19	20
10.11	**Elgin**	L	6	36	10.11	**Larkin**	L	0	35
10.19	**Streamwood**	W	14	7	10.19	**Lake Park**	L	7	20
10.25	**West Aurora**	W	20	13	10.25	**East Aurora**	L	13	20

Key: W = Win, L = Loss, T = Tie, WF = Win by forfeit, LF = Loss by forfeit, **Bold** = Conference game, *Italics* = state playoff game

EAST AURORA

WEST AURORA

1986

	W	L	Coach				W	L	Coach
Overall Record:	3	6	Dick Schindel		Overall Record:		2	7	Randy Melvin
Conference Record:	2	5			Conference Record:		2	5	

Date	Opponent		EA	Opp	Date	Opponent		WA	Opp
09.05	Wheaton North	L	6	29	09.05	Wheaton Central	L	7	13
09.12	LaSalle-Peru	W	12	0	09.12	Naperville Central	L	3	14
09.19	**DeKalb**	L	14	21	09.19	**St. Charles**	L	0	19
09.27	**Larkin**	L	6	28	09.27	**Elgin**	L	35	36
10.04	**Lake Park**	L	14	38	10.04	**Streamwood**	L	7	24
10.10	**St. Charles**	L	16	26	10.10	**DeKalb**	W	20	14
10.17	**Elgin**	W	35	21	10.17	**Larkin**	L	24	42
10.25	**Streamwood**	W	42	20	10.25	**Lake Park**	L	11	28
10.31	**West Aurora**	L	14	48	10.31	**East Aurora**	W	48	14

1987

	W	L	Coach				W	L	Coach
Overall Record:	1	8	Dick Schindel		Overall Record:		5	4	Randy Melvin
Conference Record:	0	7			Conference Record:		4	3	

Date	Opponent		EA	Opp	Date	Opponent		WA	Opp
09.04	Wheaton North	L	0	15	09.04	Wheaton Central	W	19	7
09.11	LaSalle-Peru	W	13	8	09.11	Naperville Central	L	7	27
09.18	**Elgin**	L	0	20	09.18	**Larkin**	W	14	6
09.26	**Streamwood**	L	0	25	09.25	**Lake Park**	L	15	49
10.02	**DeKalb**	L	7	20	10.02	**St. Charles**	W	20	14
10.09	**Larkin**	L	7	20	10.09	**Elgin**	L	7	33
10.16	**Lake Park**	L	7	34	10.16	**Streamwood**	L	0	34
10.23	**St. Charles**	L	3	14	10.23	**DeKalb**	W	12	7
10.30	**West Aurora**	L	6	27	10.30	**East Aurora**	W	27	6

Key: W = Win, L = Loss, T = Tie, WF = Win by forfeit, LF = Loss by forfeit, **Bold** = Conference game, *Italics* = state playoff game

EAST AURORA

WEST AURORA

1988

	W	L	Coach			W	L	Coach
Overall Record:	3	6	Ed Gavigan	Overall Record:		5	4	Tim Cedarblad
Conference Record:	2	5		Conference Record:		4	3	

Date	Opponent		EA	Opp	Date	Opponent		WA	Opp
09.03	Wheaton North	L	0	35	09.03	Bremen	W	21	8
09.09	LaSalle-Peru	W	16	13	09.09	Naperville Central	L	6	7
09.16	Elgin	L	6	22	09.16	Larkin	L	6	19
09.24	Streamwood	L	13	54	09.24	Lake Park	W	26	0
09.30	DeKalb	L	6	20	09.30	St. Charles	L	2	14
10.07	Larkin	L	14	38	10.07	Elgin	W	13	3
10.15	Lake Park	L	6	26	10.15	Streamwood	W	13	6
10.21	St. Charles	W	14	7	10.21	DeKalb	W	8	3
10.28	West Aurora	W	28	27	10.28	East Aurora	L	27	28

1989

	W	L	Coach			W	L	Coach
Overall Record:	2	7	Don Williams	Overall Record:		4	5	Tim Cedarblad
Conference Record:	1	6		Conference Record:		3	4	

Date	Opponent		EA	Opp	Date	Opponent		WA	Opp
09.01	Waubonsie Valley	W	26	13	09.01	Bremen	W	33	12
09.08	LaSalle-Peru	L	6	36	09.08	Naperville Central	L	16	20
09.16	Streamwood	WF	1	0	09.15	Lake Park	WF	1	0
09.22	Elgin	L	8	24	09.22	Larkin	W	32	8
09.29	Larkin	L	0	44	09.29	Elgin	L	14	19
10.06	DeKalb	L	6	42	10.06	St. Charles	L	9	10
10.13	St. Charles	L	0	27	10.13	DeKalb	L	22	28
10.20	Lake Park	L	6	41	10.20	Streamwood	L	9	24
10.27	West Aurora	L	12	44	10.27	East Aurora	W	44	12

EAST AURORA   WEST AURORA

1990

	W	L	Coach			W	L	Coach
Overall Record:	2	7	Don Williams	Overall Record:		2	7	Tim Cedarblad
Conference Record:	1	6		Conference Record:		2	5	

Date	Opponent		EA	Opp	Date	Opponent		WA	Opp
08.31	Waubonsie Valley	L	8	30	08.31	Bollingbrook	L	0	20
09.07	LaSalle-Peru	W	9	0	09.07	Naperville Central	L	0	21
09.14	**Streamwood**	L	19	42	09.14	**Lake Park**	L	14	21
09.21	**Elgin**	L	0	42	09.21	**Larkin**	L	7	12
09.28	**Larkin**	L	6	34	09.28	**Elgin**	L	13	41
10.05	**DeKalb**	W	19	16	10.05	**St. Charles**	W	19	13
10.12	**St. Charles**	L	22	35	10.12	**DeKalb**	L	19	34
10.19	**Lake Park**	L	14	24	10.19	**Streamwood**	L	19	25
10.26	**West Aurora**	L	0	28	10.26	**East Aurora**	W	28	0

1991

	W	L	Coach			W	L	Coach
Overall Record:	2	7	Don Williams	Overall Record:		4	5	Tim Cedarblad
Conference Record:	2	6		Conference Record:		4	4	

Date	Opponent		EA	Opp	Date	Opponent		WA	Opp
09.06	**St. Charles**	L	7	48	09.06	**Larkin**	L	20	24
09.13	**Waubonsie Valley**	L	20	33	09.13	**Lake Park**	W	10	3
09.21	**Streamwood**	WF	1	0	09.20	**DeKalb**	W	12	10
09.27	Stagg	L	0	47	09.28	**Elgin**	WF	1	0
10.04	**Larkin**	WF	1	0	10.05	Joliet West	L	7	25
10.11	**Lake Park**	L	8	32	10.12	**St. Charles**	L	7	13
10.18	**DeKalb**	L	21	25	10.19	**Waubonsie Valley**	L	0	39
10.25	**Elgin**	L	0	15	10.25	**Streamwood**	L	14	26
11.01	**West Aurora**	L	8	19	11.01	**East Aurora**	W	19	14

Key: W = Win, L = Loss, T = Tie, WF = Win by forfeit, LF = Loss by forfeit, **Bold** = Conference game, *Italics* = state playoff game

174

EAST AURORA

WEST AURORA

1992

	W	L	Coach		W	L	Coach
Overall Record:	2	7	Wendell Jeffries	Overall Record:	1	8	Bob Williams
Conference Record:	1	7		Conference Record:	1	7	

Date	Opponent		EA	Opp	Date	Opponent		WA	Opp
09.04	St. Charles	L	3	28	09.05	Larkin	W	21	20
09.11	Waubonsie Valley	L	8	38	09.11	Lake Park	L	6	25
09.18	Streamwood	L	8	30	09.18	DeKalb	L	7	28
09.25	Stagg	W	19	12	09.25	Elgin	L	3	14
10.02	Larkin	L	7	14	10.02	Joliet West	L	0	21
10.09	Lake Park	L	13	36	10.09	St. Charles	L	3	24
10.16	DeKalb	L	19	31	10.16	Waubonsie Valley	L	20	58
10.23	Elgin	L	26	32	10.23	Streamwood	L	19	21
10.30	West Aurora	W	20	6	10.30	East Aurora	L	6	20

1993

	W	L	Coach		W	L	Coach
Overall Record:	3	6	Wendell Jeffries	Overall Record:	4	5	Ira Jefferson
Conference Record:	3	5		Conference Record:	3	5	

Date	Opponent		EA	Opp	Date	Opponent		WA	Opp
					09.03	Joliet	NA	8	14
09.03	Elgin	W	21	14	09.03	DeKalb	WF	1	0
09.10	West Aurora	L	8	29	09.10	East Aurora	W	29	8
09.17	Streamwood	W	7	6	09.17	Elgin	W	19	13
09.24	Lake Park	L	6	21	09.24	Lockport	W	12	7
10.01	Waubonsie Valley	L	22	34	10.01	Streamwood	L	2	6
10.08	Larkin	L	0	19	10.08	Lake Park	L	0	35
10.15	St. Charles	L	6	54	10.15	Waubonsie Valley	L	7	14
10.22	DeKalb	W	40	7	10.22	Larkin	L	7	35
10.29	Homewood-Flossmoor	L	6	38	10.29	St. Charles	L	13	32

EAST AURORA   WEST AURORA

1994

	W	L	Coach		W	L	Coach
Overall Record:	0	9	Wendell Jeffries	Overall Record:	8	3	Ira Jefferson
Conference Record:	0	8		Conference Record:	6	2	

Date	Opponent		EA	Opp	Date	Opponent		WA	Opp
08.26	**Elgin**	L	7	38	08.26	**DeKalb**	W	27	14
09.02	**West Aurora**	L	0	35	09.02	**East Aurora**	W	35	0
09.10	**Streamwood**	L	0	6	09.09	**Elgin**	W	30	29
09.16	**Lake Park**	L	0	21	09.16	Lockport	W	36	24
09.23	**Waubonsie Valley**	L	6	48	09.24	**Streamwood**	W	20	7
09.30	**Larkin**	L	18	20	09.30	**Lake Park**	W	35	0
10.07	**St. Charles**	L	16	48	10.07	**Waubonsie Valley**	L	12	18
10.14	**DeKalb**	L	6	35	10.14	**Larkin**	W	24	12
10.21	Homewood-Flossmoor	L	10	48	10.21	**St. Charles**	L	12	39
					10.28	*Bogan*	W	21	8
					11.04	*Naperville Central*	L	27	31

State Playoff Qualifier

1995

	W	L	Coach		W	L	Coach
Overall Record:	2	7	Wendell Jeffries	Overall Record:	4	5	Ira Jefferson
Conference Record:	1	7		Conference Record:	4	4	

Date	Opponent		EA	Opp	Date	Opponent		WA	Opp
08.25	**Larkin**	L	0	56	08.25	**Lake Park**	W	26	7
09.01	**St. Charles**	L	0	47	09.01	**DeKalb**	W	14	6
09.09	**Streamwood**	W	19	6	09.09	Libertyville	L	19	39
09.15	**Waubonsie Valley**	L	0	12	09.15	**Larkin**	L	26	34
09.22	**Elgin**	L	0	13	09.22	**St. Charles**	L	6	34
09.29	Antioch	L	19	20	09.29	**Streamwood**	W	18	9
10.06	**Lake Park**	L	14	34	10.06	**Waubonsie Valley**	L	15	24
10.13	**DeKalb**	L	12	20	10.13	**Elgin**	L	37	38
10.20	**West Aurora**	L	25	30	10.20	**East Aurora**	W	30	25

Key: W = Win, L = Loss, T = Tie, WF = Win by forfeit, LF = Loss by forfeit, **Bold** = Conference game, *Italics* = state playoff game

EAST AURORA

WEST AURORA

1996

	W	L	Coach				W	L	Coach
Overall Record:	0	9	Wendell Jeffries		Overall Record:		4	5	Ira Jefferson
Conference Record:	0	8			Conference Record:		3	5	

Date	Opponent		EA	Opp	Date	Opponent		WA	Opp
08.30	**Larkin**	L	6	48	08.30	**Lake Park**	L	10	20
09.06	**St. Charles**	L	0	41	09.06	**DeKalb**	W	14	8
09.13	**Streamwood**	L	0	35	09.13	Libertyville	W	21	7
09.20	**Waubonsie Valley**	L	14	40	09.20	**Larkin**	L	19	46
09.27	**Elgin**	L	0	40	09.27	**St Charles**	L	14	35
10.05	Antioch	L	7	27	10.05	**Streamwood**	L	9	17
10.11	**Lake Park**	L	7	42	10.11	**Waubonsie Valley**	W	19	13
10.18	**DeKalb**	L	14	28	10.18	**Elgin**	L	14	28
10.25	**West Aurora**	L	20	39	10.25	**East Aurora**	W	39	20

1997

	W	L	Coach				W	L	Coach
Overall Record:	1	8	Art Panka		Overall Record:		4	5	Ira Jefferson
Conference Record:	1	6			Conference Record:		2	5	

Date	Opponent		EA	Opp	Date	Opponent		WA	Opp
08.29	West Aurora	L	0	36	08.29	East Aurora	W	36	0
09.05	Zion-Benton	L	0	41	09.05	Elgin	W	13	3
09.12	**Streamwood**	L	14	34	09.12	**Naperville North**	L	28	43
09.19	**Elgin**	L	6	14	09.19	**Wheaton North**	W	35	20
09.26	**Waubonsie Valley**	L	0	48	09.26	**Glenbard North**	L	21	42
10.03	**Lake Park**	L	7	34	10.03	**Naperville Central**	L	23	49
10.10	**Larkin**	L	7	43	10.10	**Glenbard East**	L	10	37
10.17	**DeKalb**	W	26	7	10.17	**West Chicago**	W	35	32
10.24	**St. Charles**	L	12	48	10.24	**Wheaton-Warrenville S.**	L	2	35

EAST AURORA   WEST AURORA

1998

	W	L	Coach			W	L	Coach
Overall Record:	3	6	Art Panka		Overall Record:	5	4	Ira Jefferson
Conference Record:	3	4			Conference Record:	3	4	

Date	Opponent		EA	Opp	Date	Opponent		WA	Opp
08.28	West Aurora	L	6	12	08.28	East Aurora	W	12	6
09.04	Zion-Benton	L	6	27	09.04	Elgin	W	12	3
09.11	**DeKalb**	W	21	0	09.11	**Naperville North**	L	19	45
09.18	**St. Charles**	L	0	42	09.18	**Wheaton North**	L	14	27
09.25	**Waubonsie Valley**	L	6	41	09.25	**Glenbard North**	W	26	21
10.02	**Bartlett**	W	21	6	10.02	**Naperville Central**	L	6	12
10.09	**Streamwood**	L	19	40	10.09	**Glenbard East**	W	21	17
10.16	**Larkin**	L	14	35	10.16	**West Chicago**	W	26	7
10.23	**Neuqua Valley**	W	20	15	10.23	**Wheaton-Warrenville S.**	L	6	49

1999

	W	L	Coach			W	L	Coach
Overall Record:	2	7	Art Panka		Overall Record:	2	7	Ira Jefferson
Conference Record:	2	5			Conference Record:	0	7	

Date	Opponent		EA	Opp	Date	Opponent		WA	Opp
08.27	West Aurora	L	0	23	08.27	East Aurora	W	23	0
09.03	Minooka	L	0	41	09.03	Elgin	W	39	9
09.10	**Waubonsie Valley**	L	0	44	09.10	**Wheaton North**	L	0	42
09.17	**Streamwood**	W	36	30	09.17	**Glenbard North**	L	12	26
09.24	**Bartlett**	L	14	34	09.24	**Naperville Central**	L	16	49
10.01	**Larkin**	L	13	51	10.01	**Glenbard East**	L	20	40
10.08	**Elgin**	L	21	28	10.08	**West Chicago**	L	9	31
10.15	**DeKalb**	W	39	6	10.15	**Wheaton-Warrenville S.**	L	14	62
10.22	**Lake Park**	L	6	40	10.22	**Naperville North**	L	6	34

Key: W = Win, L = Loss, T = Tie, WF = Win by forfeit, LF = Loss by forfeit, **Bold** = Conference game, *Italics* = state playoff game

EAST AURORA

WEST AURORA

2000

	W	L	Coach		W	L	Coach
Overall Record:	5	4	Al Tamberelli	Overall Record:	2	7	Mike Runge
Conference Record:	4	3		Conference Record:	2	5	

Date	Opponent		EA	Opp	Date	Opponent		WA	Opp
08.25	West Aurora	W	26	23	08.25	East Aurora	L	23	26
09.01	Minooka	L	0	25	09.01	Elgin	L	7	35
09.08	**Waubonsie Valley**	L	6	45	09.08	**Wheaton North**	W	13	7
09.15	**Streamwood**	W	34	30	09.15	**Glenbard North**	L	0	40
09.22	**Bartlett**	L	0	24	09.22	**Naperville Central**	L	0	42
09.29	**Larkin**	W	35	26	09.29	**Glenbard East**	L	7	34
10.06	**Elgin**	L	7	24	10.06	**West Chicago**	W	28	22
10.13	**DeKalb**	W	38	14	10.13	**Wheaton-Warrenville S.**	L	16	21
10.20	**Lake Park**	W	34	28	10.20	**Naperville North**	L	19	22

2001

	W	L	Coach		W	L	Coach
Overall Record:	0	9	Al Tamberelli	Overall Record:	1	8	Mike Runge
Conference Record:	0	6		Conference Record:	0	7	

Date	Opponent		EA	Opp	Date	Opponent		WA	Opp
08.24	West Aurora	L	0	29	08.24	East Aurora	W	29	0
08.31	Minooka	L	6	28	08.31	Elgin	L	6	20
09.07	**Neuqua Valley**	L	0	46	09.07	**Glenbard North**	L	13	34
09.14	Belvidere	L	0	42	09.14	**Naperville Central**	L	0	41
09.21	**Lake Park**	L	0	45	09.21	**Glenbard East**	L	28	34
09.28	**Elgin**	L	8	44	09.28	**West Chicago**	L	9	28
10.05	**St. Charles East**	L	0	40	10.05	**Wheaton-Warrenville S.**	L	0	21
10.12	**Streamwood**	L	0	8	10.12	**Naperville North**	L	20	44
10.19	**St. Charles North**	L	0	12	10.19	**Wheaton North**	L	0	44

EAST AURORA | WEST AURORA

2002

	W	L	Coach		W	L	Coach
Overall Record:	0	9	Al Tamberelli	Overall Record:	3	6	Mike Runge
Conference Record:	0	6		Conference Record:	1	6	

Date	Opponent		EA	Opp	Date	Opponent		WA	Opp
08.30	West Aurora	L	6	41	08.30	East Aurora	W	41	6
09.06	Minooka	L	0	20	09.06	Elgin	W	27	25
09.13	**Neuqua Valley**	L	18	46	09.13	**Glenbard North**	W	34	27
09.20	Belvidere	L	14	27	09.20	**Naperville Central**	L	7	20
09.27	**Lake Park**	L	6	41	09.27	**Glenbard East**	L	28	42
10.04	**Elgin**	L	13	34	10.04	**West Chicago**	L	19	40
10.11	**St. Charles East**	L	19	34	10.11	**Wheaton-Warrenville S.**	L	6	35
10.18	**Streamwood**	L	17	34	10.18	**Naperville North**	L	0	55
10.25	**St. Charles North**	L	7	27	10.25	**Wheaton North**	L	8	48

2003

	W	L	Coach		W	L	Coach
Overall Record:	1	8	Al Tamberelli	Overall Record:	1	8	Mike Runge
Conference Record:	0	6		Conference Record:	0	7	

Date	Opponent		EA	Opp	Date	Opponent		WA	Opp
08.29	West Aurora	L	6	41	08.29	East Aurora	W	41	6
09.05	Oak Lawn Community	L	6	18	09.05	Elgin	L	9	21
09.12	**Streamwood**	L	14	35	09.12	**Naperville Central**	L	0	40
09.19	**St. Charles East**	L	20	31	09.19	**Glenbard East**	L	12	20
09.26	**Elgin**	L	12	20	09.26	**West Chicago**	L	14	38
10.03	**Lake Park**	L	6	42	10.03	**Wheaton-Warrenville S.**	L	14	49
10.10	Jefferson	W	32	7	10.10	**Naperville North**	L	6	34
10.17	**Waubonsie Valley**	L	14	50	10.17	**Wheaton North**	L	8	42
10.24	**St. Charles North**	L	6	7	10.24	**Glenbard North**	L	0	28

Key: W = Win, L = Loss, T = Tie, WF = Win by forfeit, LF = Loss by forfeit, **Bold** = Conference game, *Italics* = state playoff game

EAST AURORA

WEST AURORA

2004

	W	L	Coach		W	L	Coach
Overall Record:	1	8	Al Tamberelli	Overall Record:	5	4	Mike Runge
Conference Record:	1	5		Conference Record:	3	4	

Date	Opponent		EA	Opp	Date	Opponent		WA	Opp
08.27	West Aurora	L	6	30	08.27	East Aurora	W	30	6
09.03	Oak Lawn Community	L	21	31	09.03	Elgin	W	40	7
09.10	**Streamwood**	W	19	18	09.10	**Naperville Central**	L	7	47
09.17	**St. Charles East**	L	19	33	09.17	**Glenbard East**	W	14	0
09.24	**Elgin**	L	18	28	09.24	**West Chicago**	W	40	19
10.01	**Lake Park**	L	14	34	10.01	**Wheaton-Warrenville S.**	L	0	34
10.08	Jefferson	L	7	28	10.08	**Naperville North**	L	28	41
10.15	**Waubonsie Valley**	L	14	48	10.15	**Wheaton North**	W	18	14
10.22	**St. Charles North**	L	0	43	10.22	**Glenbard North**	L	0	34

2005

	W	L	Coach		W	L	Coach
Overall Record:	1	8	Al Tamberelli	Overall Record:	2	7	Mike Runge
Conference Record:	1	5		Conference Record:	0	7	

Date	Opponent		EA	Opp	Date	Opponent		WA	Opp
08.26	West Aurora	L	0	33	08.26	East Aurora	W	33	0
09.02	Oak Lawn Community	L	0	14	09.02	Elgin	W	21	14
09.09	Hononegah	L	6	24	09.09	**West Chicago**	L	18	21
09.16	**DeKalb**	L	19	24	09.16	**Naperville Central**	L	13	41
09.23	**Bartlett**	L	7	25	09.23	**Wheaton North**	L	6	41
09.30	**Lake Park**	L	13	31	09.30	**Glenbard East**	L	19	20
10.07	**St. Charles North**	L	14	42	10.07	**Wheaton-Warrenville S.**	L	0	52
10.14	**Waubonsie Valley**	L	0	13	10.14	**Naperville North**	L	40	42
10.21	**Streamwood**	W	41	6	10.21	**Glenbard North**	L	26	46

EAST AURORA

WEST AURORA

2006

	W	L	Coach			W	L	Coach
Overall Record:	1	8	Bill Bryant	Overall Record:		2	7	Buck Drach
Conference Record:	1	5		Conference Record:		0	7	

Date	Opponent		EA	Opp	Date	Opponent		WA	Opp
08.25	West Aurora	L	0	33	08.25	East Aurora	W	33	0
09.01	Oak Lawn Community	L	0	37	09.01	Elgin	W	27	12
09.08	Hononegah	L	0	28	09.08	**West Chicago**	L	17	19
09.15	**South Elgin**	W	30	20	09.15	**Naperville Central**	L	3	12
09.23	**Bartlett**	L	0	51	09.23	**Wheaton North**	L	7	12
09.29	**Lake Park**	L	13	44	09.29	**Glenbard East**	L	8	34
10.06	**St. Charles North**	L	7	54	10.06	**Wheaton-Warrenville S.**	L	13	69
10.13	**Waubonsie Valley**	L	6	49	10.13	**Naperville North**	L	12	47
10.20	**Streamwood**	L	6	57	10.20	**Glenbard North**	L	7	41

2007

	W	L	Coach			W	L	Coach
Overall Record:	0	9	Bill Bryant	Overall Record:		4	5	Buck Drach
Conference Record:	0	7		Conference Record:		2	5	

Date	Opponent		EA	Opp	Date	Opponent		WA	Opp
08.25	West Aurora	L	6	38	08.25	East Aurora	W	38	6
08.31	Lake Zurich	L	0	65	08.31	Elgin	W	21	13
09.07	**South Elgin**	L	2	42	09.07	**Naperville Central**	L	13	27
09.14	**Larkin**	L	14	46	09.14	**Glenbard East**	W	9	6
09.21	**Streamwood**	L	14	19	09.21	**Wheaton North**	L	15	28
09.28	Thornwood	L	12	41	09.28	**Wheaton-Warrenville S.**	L	6	35
10.05	**Elgin**	L	6	40	10.05	**Naperville North**	L	0	37
10.12	**Lake Park**	L	3	36	10.12	**West Chicago**	W	48	27
10.19	**Bartlett**	L	6	55	10.19	**Glenbard North**	L	7	14

Key: W = Win, L = Loss, T = Tie, WF = Win by forfeit, LF = Loss by forfeit, **Bold** = Conference game, *Italics* = state playoff game

EAST AURORA

WEST AURORA

2008

	W	L	Coach
Overall Record:	2	7	Bill Bryant
Conference Record:	1	5	

	W	L	Coach
Overall Record:	3	6	Buck Drach
Conference Record:	1	6	

Date	Opponent		EA	Opp
08.29	West Aurora	L	0	46
09.05	Yorkville	L	8	21
09.12	**South Elgin**	W	6	3
09.19	**Larkin**	L	20	38
09.26	**Streamwood**	L	21	40
10.03	Thornwood	W	14	0
10.10	**Elgin**	L	13	47
10.17	**Lake Park**	L	12	49
10.24	**Bartlett**	L	6	51

Date	Opponent		WA	Opp
08.29	East Aurora	W	46	0
09.05	Elgin	W	41	26
09.12	**Naperville Central**	L	2	41
09.19	**Glenbard East**	W	33	27
09.26	**Wheaton North**	L	27	38
10.03	**Wheaton-Warrenville S.**	L	7	41
10.10	**Naperville North**	L	12	48
10.17	**West Chicago**	L	28	42
10.24	**Glenbard North**	L	0	26

2009

	W	L	Coach
Overall Record:	0	9	Bill Bryant
Conference Record:	0	6	

	W	L	Coach
Overall Record:	3	6	Buck Drach
Conference Record:	1	6	

Date	Opponent		EA	Opp
08.28	West Aurora	L	13	46
09.04	Yorkville	L	22	50
09.11	**St. Charles North**	L	6	55
09.18	**Elgin**	L	19	20
09.25	**St. Charles East**	L	0	41
10.02	**Lake Park**	L	0	28
10.09	St. Ignatius	L	5	46
10.16	**Larkin**	L	14	58
10.23	**Waubonsie Valley**	L	6	42

Date	Opponent		WA	Opp
08.28	East Aurora	W	46	13
09.04	Elgin	W	28	6
09.11	**Naperville Central**	L	19	41
09.18	**Naperville North**	L	25	55
09.25	**Wheaton North**	L	13	24
10.02	**West Chicago**	W	20	7
10.09	**Glenbard North**	L	6	42
10.16	**Glenbard East**	L	33	35
10.23	**Wheaton-Warrenville S.**	L	0	61

EAST AURORA

WEST AURORA

2010

	W	L	Coach			W	L	Coach
Overall Record:	0	9	Bill Bryant		Overall Record:	4	5	Buck Drach
Conference Record:	0	7			Conference Record:	2	5	

Date	Opponent		EA	Opp	Date	Opponent		WA	Opp
08.27	West Aurora	L	12	52	08.27	East Aurora	W	52	12
09.03	Yorkville	L	0	23	09.03	Elgin	W	23	7
09.10	**Metea Valley**	L	6	39	09.10	**Naperville Central**	L	6	45
09.17	**Neuqua Valley**	L	0	43	09.17	**Naperville North**	L	7	21
09.24	**Streamwood**	L	8	34	09.24	**Wheaton North**	L	13	21
10.01	**Lake Park**	L	0	42	10.01	**West Chicago**	W	29	28
10.08	**South Elgin**	L	8	52	10.08	**Glenbard North**	L	21	34
10.15	**Waubonsie Valley**	L	0	51	10.15	**Glenbard East**	W	55	32
10.22	**Bartlett**	L	13	62	10.22	**Wheaton-Warrenville S.**	L	6	42

2011

	W	L	Coach			W	L	Coach
Overall Record:	0	9	Bill Bryant		Overall Record:	4	5	Nate Eimer
Conference Record:	0	7			Conference Record:	2	5	

Date	Opponent		EA	Opp	Date	Opponent		WA	Opp
08.26	West Aurora	L	6	48	08.26	East Aurora	W	48	6
09.02	Yorkville	L	6	42	09.02	St. Charles East	W	20	7
09.09	**Metea Valley**	L	0	47	09.09	**Wheaton-Warrenville S.**	L	6	20
09.16	**Neuqua Valley**	L	7	56	09.16	**Naperville Central**	L	14	35
09.23	**Streamwood**	L	0	49	09.23	**Glenbard North**	L	21	31
09.30	**Lake Park**	L	0	49	09.30	**Wheaton North**	L	7	38
10.08	**South Elgin**	L	6	52	10.07	**Naperville North**	L	21	45
10.14	**Waubonsie Valley**	L	0	68	10.14	**West Chicago**	W	41	0
10.21	**Bartlett**	L	0	59	10.21	**Glenbard East**	W	17	14

Key: W = Win, L = Loss, T = Tie, WF = Win by forfeit, LF = Loss by forfeit, **Bold** = Conference game, *Italics* = state playoff game

EAST AURORA   WEST AURORA

2012

	W	L	Coach			W	L	Coach
Overall Record:	0	9	Kurt Becker		Overall Record:	3	6	Nate Eimer
Conference Record:	0	6			Conference Record:	2	5	

Date	Opponent		EA	Opp	Date	Opponent		WA	Opp
08.25	West Aurora	L	6	38	08.24	East Aurora	W	59	19
08.31	Lake Zurich	L	0	65	08.31	St. Charles East	L	21	26
09.07	**South Elgin**	L	2	42	09.07	**Wheaton-Warrenville S.**	L	7	14
09.14	**Larkin**	L	14	46	09.14	**Naperville Central**	L	7	42
09.21	**Streamwood**	L	14	19	09.21	**Glenbard North**	L	14	28
09.28	Thornwood	L	12	41	09.28	**Wheaton North**	L	28	41
10.05	**Elgin**	L	6	40	10.05	**Naperville North**	L	2	38
10.12	**Lake Park**	L	3	36	10.12	**West Chicago**	W	35	9
10.19	**Bartlett**	L	6	55	10.19	**Glenbard East**	W	52	18

2013

	W	L	Coach			W	L	Coach
Overall Record:	1	8	Kurt Becker		Overall Record:	1	8	Nate Eimer
Conference Record:	0	6			Conference Record:	0	7	

Date	Opponent		EA	Opp	Date	Opponent		WA	Opp
08.31	West Aurora	L	18	46	08.31	East Aurora	W	46	18
09.06	Yorkville	L	14	38	09.06	Plainfield East	L	12	35
09.13	**Bartlett**	L	6	40	09.13	**Glenbard East**	L	0	21
09.20	**South Elgin**	L	20	48	09.20	**Wheaton-Warrenville S.**	L	7	42
09.27	**Neuqua Valley**	L	6	52	09.27	**Naperville Central**	L	0	56
10.04	Elgin	W	25	22	10.04	**Glenbard North**	L	13	34
10.11	**Metea Valley**	L	28	52	10.11	**Wheaton North**	L	7	48
10.18	**Waubonsie Valley**	L	0	49	10.18	**Naperville North**	L	30	52
10.25	**West Chicago**	L	24	29	10.25	**Lake Park**	L	0	35

THE ELGIN HIGH SCHOOL MAROONS

No history of Aurora high school football would be complete without special mention of Elgin High School. For while the East-West rivalry is the longest-running football rivalry in Illinois, the rivalries between both Aurora schools and Elgin are not far behind.

The cities of Aurora and Elgin share a rich history as rival towns. Located just twenty-two miles apart, the communities were founded on the banks of the Fox River within one year of one another in the mid-1830s. Both were incorporated as cities twenty years later and, for much of the first half of the twentieth century, were joined together by the Chicago, Aurora and Elgin Interurban Railroad. These facts, coupled with the cities' similar developmental and economic histories, served to create a long-lasting community rivalry that intensified the natural athletic rivalries of their high schools.

On November 11, 1893, one week before the inaugural East-West game, East Aurora's players traveled to the "Watch City" for a match with the local high school team and returned with a hard-fought 20–12 victory. In what was its first significant coverage of high school football, the front page of the *Beacon*'s November 13, 1893 edition hailed the east-siders as conquering heroes. A scheduled rematch was postponed twice and eventually abandoned. East Aurora and Elgin met twice in 1894 and then were on-again, off-again until 1902, when the schools began a string of 102 games in 103 years from that year to 2004, missing in 1910 and 1998 but playing twice in 1908. Through 2013, the schools had met 108 times, with the Maroons leading the series 52-49-7.

West Aurora and Elgin first met in 1896, and until the series was suspended following the 2010 season, the teams played in every year except 1902 and 1914. The series includes Illinois' first night game, played in Elgin under temporary lights on October 27, 1898. The Maroons won that one 12–5 (sometimes reported 15–5). Through 2013, West Aurora and Elgin met on the gridiron 116 times, with West leading the series 56-50-10.

Together, East Aurora, West Aurora and Elgin were charter members of the Northern Illinois High School Conference (informally known as the Big 8, Big 7 or Big 6, depending on the year) and competed as conference foes for forty-six years before leaving in 1963 to help form the Upstate 8 Conference. The three schools combined to win twenty-six of forty-six conference championships from 1916 to 1962. In the Upstate 8, the schools combined to win ten of thirty-four conference championships before West left to join the DuPage Valley Conference after the 1996–97 school year.

This three-cornered rivalry is truly one of Illinois' finest.

East Aurora vs. Elgin
Game Log

Year	Home	Score	Away	Score
1893	*EAST AURORA*	20	Elgin	12
1894 A	*EAST AURORA*	18	Elgin	0
1894 B	*EAST AURORA*	14	Elgin	0
1895		*No game*		
1896	East Aurora	0	*ELGIN*	10
1897	*EAST AURORA*	10	Elgin	0
1898		*No game*		
1899		*No game*		
1900		*No game*		
1901		*No game*		
1902	*EAST AURORA*	12	Elgin	6
1903	East Aurora	0	*ELGIN*	12
1904	*EAST AURORA*	17	Elgin	5
1905	East Aurora	0	*ELGIN*	5
1906	*EAST AURORA*	18	Elgin	4
1907	East Aurora	0	*ELGIN*	7
1908 A	East Aurora	0	*ELGIN*	9
1908 B	East Aurora	0	*ELGIN*	5
1909	East Aurora	0	Elgin	0
1910		*No game*		
1911	*EAST AURORA*	21	Elgin	0
1912	East Aurora	0	*ELGIN*	16
1913	East Aurora	0	*ELGIN*	16
1914	*EAST AURORA*	6	Elgin	0
1915	*EAST AURORA*	40	Elgin	3
1916	*EAST AURORA*	3	Elgin	0
1917	*EAST AURORA*	13	Elgin	0
1918	East Aurora	0	*ELGIN*	26
1919	*EAST AURORA*	13	Elgin	6
1920	East Aurora	7	*ELGIN*	34
1921	East Aurora	0	*ELGIN*	7
1922	*EAST AURORA*	6	Elgin	0
1923	East Aurora	0	*ELGIN*	9
1924	East Aurora	14	*ELGIN*	16
1925	East Aurora	0	*ELGIN*	7

1926	East Aurora	0	ELGIN	6
1927	East Aurora	6	Elgin	6
1928	East Aurora	7	ELGIN	38
1929	East Aurora	6	ELGIN	7
1930	EAST AURORA	14	Elgin	7
1931	EAST AURORA	19	Elgin	0
1932	East Aurora	0	ELGIN	6
1933	EAST AURORA	7	Elgin	6
1934	EAST AURORA	19	Elgin	7
1935	EAST AURORA	25	Elgin	0
1936	East Aurora	0	Elgin	0
1937	EAST AURORA	19	Elgin	0
1938	EAST AURORA	14	Elgin	0
1939	East Aurora	6	Elgin	6
1940	EAST AURORA	12	Elgin	6
1941	East Aurora	6	ELGIN	19
1942	East Aurora	12	Elgin	12
1943	EAST AURORA	19	Elgin	0
1944	East Aurora	19	Elgin	19
1945	East Aurora	0	ELGIN	19
1946	EAST AURORA	6	Elgin	0
1947	EAST AURORA	12	Elgin	6
1948	East Aurora	7	Elgin	7
1949	East Aurora	6	ELGIN	14
1950	East Aurora	7	ELGIN	17
1951	EAST AURORA	21	Elgin	13
1952	East Aurora	13	ELGIN	20
1953	East Aurora	6	ELGIN	32
1954	EAST AURORA	20	Elgin	12
1955	East Aurora	7	ELGIN	20
1956	EAST AURORA	23	Elgin	13
1957	EAST AURORA	25	Elgin	6
1958	East Aurora	13	ELGIN	27
1959	East Aurora	0	ELGIN	20
1960	EAST AURORA	14	Elgin	7
1961	East Aurora	0	ELGIN	14
1962	EAST AURORA	22	Elgin	7
1963	EAST AURORA	19	Elgin	7
1964	EAST AURORA	18	Elgin Cen	0

1965	*EAST AURORA*	27	Elgin Cen	6
1966	*EAST AURORA*	16	Elgin Cen	12
1967	East Aurora	13	*ELGIN CEN*	24
1968	*EAST AURORA*	26	Elgin Cen	7
1969	*EAST AURORA*	14	Elgin Cen	8
1970 (1)	East Aurora	27	*ELGIN CEN*	8
1971	East Aurora	20	*ELGIN CEN*	28
1972	*EAST AURORA*	21	Elgin Cen	20
1973	*EAST AURORA*	16	Elgin Cen	8
1974	*EAST AURORA*	15	Elgin Cen	8
1975	*EAST AURORA*	14	Elgin	0
1976	East Aurora	16	*ELGIN*	28
1977	East Aurora	6	*ELGIN*	12
1978	*EAST AURORA*	27	Elgin	0
1979	*EAST AURORA*	28	Elgin	0
1980	*EAST AURORA*	40	Elgin	6
1981	*EAST AURORA*	24	Elgin	22
1982	East Aurora	20	*ELGIN*	21
1983	*EAST AURORA*	13	Elgin	7
1984	East Aurora	7	*ELGIN*	13
1985	East Aurora	6	*ELGIN*	36
1986	*EAST AURORA*	35	Elgin	21
1987	East Aurora	0	*ELGIN*	20
1988	East Aurora	6	*ELGIN*	22
1989	East Aurora	8	*ELGIN*	24
1990	East Aurora	0	*ELGIN*	42
1991	East Aurora	0	*ELGIN*	15
1992	East Aurora	26	*ELGIN*	32
1993	*EAST AURORA*	21	Elgin	14
1994	East Aurora	7	*ELGIN*	38
1995	East Aurora	0	*ELGIN*	13
1996	East Aurora	0	*ELGIN*	40
1997	East Aurora	6	*ELGIN*	14
1998		*No game*		

1999	East Aurora	21	***ELGIN***	28
2000	East Aurora	7	***ELGIN***	24
2001	East Aurora	8	***ELGIN***	44
2002	East Aurora	13	***ELGIN***	34
2003	East Aurora	12	***ELGIN***	20
2004	East Aurora	18	***ELGIN***	28
2005		*No game*		
2006		*No game*		
2007	East Aurora	6	***ELGIN***	40
2008	East Aurora	13	***ELGIN***	47
2009	East Aurora	19	***ELGIN***	20
2010		*No game*		
2011		*No game*		
2012	East Aurora	0	***ELGIN***	35
2013	***EAST AURORA***	25	Elgin	22

1. East Aurora won on game day but later forfeited.

2. Elgin leads the series 53-49-7.

West Aurora vs. Elgin
Game Log

1896	***WEST AURORA***	6	Elgin	0
1897	***WEST AURORA***	24	Elgin	6
1898 A	West Aurora	0	***ELGIN***	2
1898 B (1)	West Aurora	5	***ELGIN***	12
1899 A	West Aurora	6	***ELGIN***	17
1899 B	West Aurora	0	***ELGIN***	16
1900	West Aurora	0	Elgin	0
1901	West Aurora	5	***ELGIN***	18
1902		*No game*		
1903	West Aurora	5	Elgin	5
1904	West Aurora	0	***ELGIN***	10
1905	***WEST AURORA***	45	Elgin	0
1906	***WEST AURORA***	15	Elgin	5
1907	***WEST AURORA***	12	Elgin	0
1908	West Aurora	0	Elgin	0
1909	***WEST AURORA***	2	Elgin	0

1910	*WEST AURORA*	6	Elgin	0
1911	West Aurora	0	Elgin	0
1912	*WEST AURORA*	10	Elgin	9
1913	*WEST AURORA*	19	Elgin	3
1914			*No game*	
1915	*WEST AURORA*	12	Elgin	6
1916	*WEST AURORA*	6	Elgin	0
1917	West Aurora	6	*ELGIN*	13
1918	West Aurora	7	Elgin	7
1919	*WEST AURORA*	13	Elgin	6
1920	West Aurora	6	*ELGIN*	13
1921	West Aurora	7	*ELGIN*	10
1922	*WEST AURORA*	13	Elgin	0
1923	*WEST AURORA*	7	Elgin	3
1924	West Aurora	0	*ELGIN*	16
1925	West Aurora	0	*ELGIN*	7
1926	West Aurora	0	*ELGIN*	6
1927	West Aurora	0	Elgin	0
1928	West Aurora	0	Elgin	0
1929 A	West Aurora	6	*ELGIN*	18
1929 B	West Aurora	0	*ELGIN*	21
1930	West Aurora	12	*ELGIN*	20
1931	West Aurora	14	Elgin	14
1932	West Aurora	0	Elgin	0
1933	West Aurora	7	*ELGIN*	10
1934	*WEST AURORA*	6	Elgin	0
1935	*WEST AURORA*	14	Elgin	13
1936	*WEST AURORA*	34	Elgin	7
1937	*WEST AURORA*	14	Elgin	0
1938	West Aurora	7	*ELGIN*	19
1939	West Aurora	0	Elgin	0
1940	*WEST AURORA*	13	Elgin	6
1941	*WEST AURORA*	6	Elgin	0
1942	*WEST AURORA*	13	Elgin	6
1943	West Aurora	7	*ELGIN*	27
1944	West Aurora	13	*ELGIN*	37
1945	*WEST AURORA*	19	Elgin	13
1946	*WEST AURORA*	34	Elgin	0
1947	*WEST AURORA*	7	Elgin	6

1948	*WEST AURORA*	14	Elgin	12
1949	West Aurora	31	*ELGIN*	39
1950	West Aurora	13	*ELGIN*	31
1951	*WEST AURORA*	7	Elgin	6
1952	West Aurora	13	*ELGIN*	49
1953	West Aurora	7	*ELGIN*	13
1954	West Aurora	6	*ELGIN*	20
1955	West Aurora	7	*ELGIN*	33
1956	West Aurora	14	*ELGIN*	26
1957	West Aurora	0	*ELGIN*	25
1958	West Aurora	12	*ELGIN*	13
1959	*WEST AURORA*	24	Elgin	20
1960	*WEST AURORA*	6	Elgin	0
1961	*WEST AURORA*	7	Elgin	0
1962	West Aurora	7	*ELGIN*	21
1963	West Aurora	6	*ELGIN*	19
1964	*WEST AURORA*	51	Elgin	0
1965	*WEST AURORA*	26	Elgin	12
1966	*WEST AURORA*	27	Elgin	7
1967	*WEST AURORA*	8	Elgin	0
1968	*WEST AURORA*	14	Elgin	12
1969	West Aurora	6	*ELGIN*	36
1970	*WEST AURORA*	12	Elgin	8
1971	West Aurora	28	*ELGIN*	30
1972	West Aurora	6	*ELGIN*	38
1973	West Aurora	6	*ELGIN*	30
1974	*WEST AURORA*	20	Elgin	6
1975	West Aurora	12	*ELGIN*	26
1976	West Aurora	13	*ELGIN*	21
1977	West Aurora	6	*ELGIN*	26
1978	*WEST AURORA*	31	Elgin	0
1979	*WEST AURORA*	35	Elgin	7
1980	*WEST AURORA*	37	Elgin	19
1981	West Aurora	6	*ELGIN*	10
1982	*WEST AURORA*	27	Elgin	20
1983	*WEST AURORA*	32	Elgin	0
1984	West Aurora	18	*ELGIN*	20
1985	West Aurora	0	*ELGIN*	26
1986	West Aurora	35	*ELGIN*	36

1987	West Aurora	7	***ELGIN***	33
1988	***WEST AURORA***	13	Elgin	3
1989	West Aurora	14	***ELGIN***	19
1990	West Aurora	13	***ELGIN***	41
1991	***WEST AURORA***	2	Elgin	0
1992	West Aurora	3	***ELGIN***	14
1993	***WEST AURORA***	19	Elgin	13
1994	***WEST AURORA***	30	Elgin	29
1995	West Aurora	37	***ELGIN***	38
1996	West Aurora	14	***ELGIN***	28
1997	***WEST AURORA***	13	Elgin	3
1998	***WEST AURORA***	12	Elgin	3
1999	***WEST AURORA***	39	Elgin	9
2000	West Aurora	7	***ELGIN***	35
2001	West Aurora	6	***ELGIN***	20
2002	***WEST AURORA***	27	Elgin	25
2003	West Aurora	9	***ELGIN***	21
2004	***WEST AURORA***	40	Elgin	7
2005	***WEST AURORA***	21	Elgin	14
2006	***WEST AURORA***	27	Elgin	12
2007	***WEST AURORA***	21	Elgin	13
2008	***WEST AURORA***	41	Elgin	26
2009	***WEST AURORA***	28	Elgin	6
2010	***WEST AURORA***	23	Elgin	7

1. On October 27, 1898, Elgin hosted West in the state's first night football game.

2. West Aurora leads the series 56-50-10.

EAST AURORA VS. WEST AURORA, 1893–2013

Game Log

1893	*EAST AURORA*	28	West Aurora	0
1894			*No Game*		
1895	*EAST AURORA*	12	West Aurora	6
1896 A (1)	East Aurora	0	West Aurora	0
1896 B	East Aurora	10	West Aurora	10
1897			*No Game*		
1898 A	East Aurora	6	West Aurora	6
1898 B	*EAST AURORA*	34	West Aurora	0
1899	*EAST AURORA*	33	West Aurora	0
1900	*EAST AURORA*	17	West Aurora	0
1901	*EAST AURORA*	6	West Aurora	0
1902	East Aurora	0	*WEST AURORA*	22
1903	East Aurora	0	*WEST AURORA*	6
1904	*EAST AURORA*	5	West Aurora	0
1905	East Aurora	5	*WEST AURORA*	6
1906	East Aurora	10	*WEST AURORA*	12
1907	*EAST AURORA*	13	West Aurora	4
1908	East Aurora	6	West Aurora	6
1909	East Aurora	5	West Aurora	5

1910	East Aurora	0	West Aurora	0
1911	East Aurora	0	West Aurora	0
1912	East Aurora	0	*WEST AURORA*	37
1913	East Aurora	3	*WEST AURORA*	13
1914	*EAST AURORA*	14	West Aurora	7
1915	*EAST AURORA*	25	West Aurora	0
1916	East Aurora	7	*WEST AURORA*	20
1917	East Aurora	0	West Aurora	0
1918	East Aurora	0	*WEST AURORA*	6
1919	East Aurora	0	*WEST AURORA*	13
1920	*EAST AURORA*	14	West Aurora	6
1921	East Aurora	0	*WEST AURORA*	7
1922	East Aurora	0	*WEST AURORA*	6
1923	East Aurora	3	West Aurora	3
1924	East Aurora	0	*WEST AURORA*	28
1925	*EAST AURORA*	3	West Aurora	0
1926	East Aurora	0	*WEST AURORA*	6
1927	*EAST AURORA*	30	West Aurora	0
1928	*EAST AURORA*	12	West Aurora	6
1929	*EAST AURORA*	28	West Aurora	0
1930	*EAST AURORA*	13	West Aurora	0
1931	East Aurora	0	*WEST AURORA*	13
1932	*EAST AURORA*	31	West Aurora	0
1933	*EAST AURORA*	13	West Aurora	0
1934	*EAST AURORA*	7	West Aurora	0
1935	*EAST AURORA*	20	West Aurora	0
1936	East Aurora	12	*WEST AURORA*	18
1937	East Aurora	7	*WEST AURORA*	9
1938	*EAST AURORA*	19	West Aurora	6
1939	East Aurora	7	*WEST AURORA*	20
1940	*EAST AURORA*	25	West Aurora	6
1941	East Aurora	6	*WEST AURORA*	34
1942	East Aurora	8	*WEST AURORA*	13
1943	*EAST AURORA*	12	West Aurora	0
1944	*EAST AURORA*	14	West Aurora	13
1945	*EAST AURORA*	6	West Aurora	0
1946	East Aurora	0	*WEST AURORA*	41
1947	East Aurora	0	West Aurora	0
1948	East Aurora	0	West Aurora	0

1949	East Aurora	13	WEST AURORA	20
1950	East Aurora	13	WEST AURORA	19
1951	East Aurora	18	WEST AURORA	32
1952	EAST AURORA	29	West Aurora	7
1953	EAST AURORA	19	West Aurora	7
1954	East Aurora	13	WEST AURORA	19
1955	EAST AURORA	26	West Aurora	0
1956	EAST AURORA	25	West Aurora	6
1957	East Aurora	19	West Aurora	19
1958	East Aurora	0	WEST AURORA	34
1959	East Aurora	0	WEST AURORA	19
1960	East Aurora	6	WEST AURORA	12
1961	EAST AURORA	14	West Aurora	6
1962	EAST AURORA	21	West Aurora	7
1963	EAST AURORA	27	West Aurora	0
1964	EAST AURORA	21	West Aurora	6
1965	East Aurora	13	WEST AURORA	26
1966	East Aurora	7	WEST AURORA	34
1967	EAST AURORA	14	West Aurora	13
1968	EAST AURORA	27	West Aurora	6
1969	EAST AURORA	25	West Aurora	14
1970 (2)	East Aurora	19	WEST AURORA	8
1971	EAST AURORA	21	West Aurora	18
1972	EAST AURORA	47	West Aurora	6
1973	EAST AURORA	31	West Aurora	16
1974	EAST AURORA	15	West Aurora	14
1975	East Aurora	3	WEST AURORA	8
1976	EAST AURORA	34	West Aurora	0
1977	East Aurora	14	WEST AURORA	20
1978	East Aurora	0	WEST AURORA	3
1979	EAST AURORA	13	West Aurora	7
1980	EAST AURORA	42	West Aurora	6
1981	East Aurora	14	WEST AURORA	21
1982	EAST AURORA	19	West Aurora	7
1983	East Aurora	6	WEST AURORA	41
1984	East Aurora	7	WEST AURORA	55
1985	EAST AURORA	20	West Aurora	13
1986	East Aurora	14	WEST AURORA	48
1987	East Aurora	6	WEST AURORA	27

1988	**EAST AURORA**	28	West Aurora	27
1989	East Aurora	12	**WEST AURORA**	44
1990	East Aurora	0	**WEST AURORA**	28
1991	East Aurora	14	**WEST AURORA**	19
1992	**EAST AURORA**	20	West Aurora	6
1993	East Aurora	8	**WEST AURORA**	29
1994	East Aurora	0	**WEST AURORA**	35
1995	East Aurora	25	**WEST AURORA**	30
1996	East Aurora	20	**WEST AURORA**	39
1997	East Aurora	0	**WEST AURORA**	36
1998	East Aurora	6	**WEST AURORA**	12
1999	East Aurora	0	**WEST AURORA**	23
2000	**EAST AURORA**	26	West Aurora	23
2001	East Aurora	0	**WEST AURORA**	29
2002	East Aurora	6	**WEST AURORA**	41
2003	East Aurora	6	**WEST AURORA**	41
2004	East Aurora	6	**WEST AURORA**	30
2005	East Aurora	0	**WEST AURORA**	33
2006	East Aurora	0	**WEST AURORA**	33
2007	East Aurora	6	**WEST AURORA**	38
2008	East Aurora	0	**WEST AURORA**	46
2009	East Aurora	13	**WEST AURORA**	46
2010	East Aurora	12	**WEST AURORA**	52
2011	East Aurora	6	**WEST AURORA**	48
2012	East Aurora	19	**WEST AURORA**	59
2013	East Aurora	18	**WEST AURORA**	46

Notes:

1. Details of game are unknown.

2. East Aurora won on game day but later forfeited.

3. West Aurora leads the series at 61-48-12.

EAST AURORA
SEASON RECORDS

Season	Coach	W	L	T	Pct.	PF	PA	Conf.	W	L	T	Pct.	Place
1893	Frank Darby	2	0	0	1.000	48	12						
1894	Frank Darby	3	0	1	0.875	50	10						
1895	Tom Reid	3	2	4	0.556	40	26						
1896	T. Darby / H. Willard	5	2	2	0.667	120	36						
1897	Unknown	7	1	1	0.833	178	16						
1898	Bill Hazard	4	3	1	0.625	138	59						
1899	Coach Harris	8	1	0	0.889	132	37						
1900	Coach Stewart	9	0	2	0.909	122	16						
1901	Billy Lindsey	10	2	1	0.808	206	48						
1902	Billy Lindsey	7	4	0	0.636	190	104						
1903	Coach Johnson	3	5	0	0.375	77	101						
1904	O.A. Rawlings	6	3	0	0.667	87	61						
1905	O.A. Rawlings	4	4	1	0.500	93	69						
1906	O.A. Rawlings	6	1	0	0.857	63	16						
1907	W.F. Shirley	5	3	1	0.611	97	44						

Season	Coach	W	L	T	Pct.	PF	PA	Conf.	W	L	T	Pct.	Place
1908	W.F. Shirley	3	4	2	0.444	47	74						
1909	W.F. Shirley	3	2	3	0.563	56	38						
1910	Boyd Lehman	3	2	1	0.583	35	61						
1911	Boyd Lehman	5	2	1	0.688	83	23						
1912	Boyd Lehman	2	7	0	0.222	31	199						
1913	Walter Dyer	4	6	0	0.400	261	33						
1914	George Stuart	8	0	0	1.000	262	17						
1915	Martin Shale	9	1	0	0.900	418	29						
1916	Telford Mead	5	2	0	0.714	122	43	NIHSC	4	2	0	0.667	4th
1917	Telford Mead	5	1	2	0.750	105	14	NIHSC	2	1	2	0.600	2nd
1918	Tracey Cone	2	5	0	0.286	50	119	NIHSC	Season cancelled				
1919	David Glascock	5	4	0	0.556	106	101	NIHSC	5	1	0	0.833	1st (tie
1920	Billy Robinson	2	6	1	0.278	81	159	Big 7	2	4	0	0.333	5th
1921	Billy Robinson	6	4	0	0.556	108	63	Big 7	3	3	0	0.500	4th
1922	Billy Robinson	4	4	0	0.500	45	43	Big 7	3	3	0	0.500	3rd
1923	Johnny Sabo	2	3	3	0.438	54	43	Big 7	1	2	3	0.417	5th
1924	Johnny Sabo	3	7	0	0.300	108	170	Big 7	0	6	0	0.000	7th
1925	Glen Thompson	6	4	0	0.600	52	88	Big 7	3	3	0	0.500	3rd
1926	Glen Thompson	5	4	1	0.550	179	35	Big 7	1	4	1	0.250	6th
1927	Glen Thompson	8	0	1	0.944	238	15	Big 7	5	0	1	0.917	1st
1928	Glen Thompson	4	4	2	0.500	101	82	Big 7	2	3	1	0.417	5th
1929	Glen Thompson	8	1	0	0.889	227	19	Big 6	4	1	0	0.800	2nd
1930	Glen Thompson	8	1	0	0.889	307	50	Big 6	4	1	0	0.800	2nd
1931	Glen Thompson	5	4	0	0.556	91	67	Big 6	3	2	0	0.600	3rd
1932	Glen Thompson	5	3	1	0.611	56	32	Big 6	2	2	1	0.500	4th
1933	Glen Thompson	7	1	1	0.833	135	15	Big 6	3	1	1	0.700	3rd
1934	Glen Thompson	5	5	0	0.500	71	80	Big 6	2	3	0	0.400	4th
1935	Glen Thompson	6	3	0	0.667	132	63	Big 7	4	2	0	0.667	2nd

Season	Coach	W	L	T	Pct.	PF	PA	Conf.	W	L	T	Pct.	Place
1936	Glen Thompson	5	2	2	0.667	136	52	Big 7	3	2	1	0.583	3rd
1937	Glen Thompson	7	3	0	0.700	174	71	Big 7	4	2	0	0.667	2nd
1938	Glen Thompson	9	0	0	1.000	188	6	Big 7	6	0	0	1.000	1st
1939	Glen Thompson	3	5	1	0.389	84	87	Big 7	2	3	1	0.417	4th
1940	Glen Thompson	8	2	0	0.800	127	81	Big 8	5	2	0	0.714	2nd
1941	Glen Thompson	4	5	0	0.444	72	106	Big 8	1	4	0	0.200	5th
1942	G. Thompson / J. Maze	2	5	2	0.333	60	120	Big 8	2	4	1	0.357	6th
1943	Joe Maze	5	4	0	0.556	107	66	Big 8	4	3	0	0.571	3rd
1944	Joe Maze	7	1	1	0.833	184	78	Big 8	5	1	1	0.786	1st
1945	Joe Maze	3	6	0	0.333	49	113	Big 8	1	3	0	0.250	4th
1946	Joe Maze	1	7	2	0.200	37	176	Big 8	1	5	1	0.214	8th
1947	Joe Maze	3	6	1	0.350	50	109	Big 8	2	4	1	0.357	5th
1948	Joe Maze	7	1	2	0.800	174	79	Big 8	5	0	2	0.857	2nd
1949	Joe Maze	6	3	1	0.650	192	109	Big 8	3	3	1	0.500	5th
1950	Don Griffin	5	5	0	0.500	162	113	Big 8	4	3	0	0.571	3rd
1951	Don Griffin	7	3	0	0.700	165	115	Big 8	5	2	0	0.714	2nd
1952	Don Griffin	5	3	1	0.611	151	99	Big 8	5	1	1	0.786	3rd
1953	Don Griffin	4	4	1	0.500	83	92	Big 8	3	3	0	0.500	5th
1954	Don Griffin	8	1	0	0.889	185	71	Big 8	6	1	0	0.857	1st
1955	Art Court	7	1	1	0.833	168	49	Big 8	5	1	1	0.786	2nd
1956	Art Court	7	1	1	0.833	210	64	Big 8	7	0	0	1.000	1st
1957	Art Court	5	3	1	0.611	155	97	Big 8	5	1	1	0.786	1st
1958	Art Court	3	5	1	0.389	158	169	Big 8	2	4	1	0.357	5th
1959	Art Court	1	7	1	0.167	28	170	Big 8	1	6	0	0.143	8th
1960	Art Court	6	2	1	0.722	139	84	Big 8	4	2	1	0.643	4th
1961	Del Dufrain	2	6	1	0.278	46	175	Big 8	2	4	1	0.357	6th
1962	Del Dufrain	6	3	0	0.667	149	86	Big 8	5	2	0	0.714	1st (tie)
1963	Del Dufrain	9	0	0	1.000	209	41	UEC	7	0	0	1.000	1st

Season	Coach	W	L	T	Pct.	PF	PA	Conf.	W	L	T	Pct.	Place
1964	Del Dufrain	7	1	1	0.833	132	45	UEC	6	0	1	0.929	**1st**
1965	Del Dufrain	5	2	2	0.667	121	117	UEC	3	2	2	0.571	4th
1966	Del Dufrain	6	3	0	0.667	156	125	UEC	5	2	0	0.714	**1st (tie)**
1967	Del Dufrain	2	7	0	0.222	74	218	UEC	2	5	0	0.286	5th
1968	Del Dufrain	6	3	0	0.667	173	81	UEC	4	3	0	0.571	3rd
1969	Del Dufrain	5	4	0	0.556	173	110	UEC	4	3	0	0.571	3rd
1970	Del Dufrain	0	9	0	0.000	229	99	UEC	0	7	0	0.000	8th*
1971	Del Dufrain	3	6	0	0.333	166	193	UEC	1	6	0	0.143	8th
1972	Del Dufrain	5	4	0	0.556	154	115	UEC	4	3	0	0.571	4th
1973	Del Dufrain	6	4	0	0.600	192	114	UEC	4	3	0	0.571	4th
1974	Del Dufrain	5	4		0.556	125	148	UEC	4	3	0	0.571	3rd
1975	Del Dufrain	3	6		0.333	78	100	UEC	2	3	0	0.400	3rd
1976	Del Dufrain	8	3		0.727	264	202	UEC	4	1	0	0.800	**1st (tie)**
1977	Del Dufrain	3	6		0.333	130	122	UEC	1	4	0	0.200	6th
1978	Del Dufrain	3	6		0.333	103	95	UEC	2	3	0	0.400	5th
1979	John Wrenn	5	4		0.556	181	138	UEC	4	3		0.571	3rd
1980	John Wrenn	8	2		0.800	317	106	UEC	6	1		0.857	**1st (tie)**
1981	Pete Ventrelli	6	3		0.667	153	130	UEC	4	3		0.571	4th
1982	Pete Ventrelli	6	4		0.600	165	99	UEC	5	2		0.714	**1st (tie)**
1983	Dick Schindel	5	4		0.556	116	131	UEC	4	3		0.571	4th
1984	Dick Schindel	1	8		0.111	93	213	UEC	0	7		0.000	8th
1985	Dick Schindel	3	6		0.333	90	235	UEC	2	5		0.286	6th
1986	Dick Schindel	3	6		0.333	159	231	UEC	2	5		0.286	5th
1987	Dick Schindel	1	8		0.111	43	183	UEC	0	7		0.000	8th
1988	Ed Gavigan	3	6		0.333	203	242	UEC	2	5		0.286	6th
1989	Don Williams	2	7		0.222	64	271	UEC	1	6		0.143	8th
1990	Don Williams	2	7		0.222	97	251	UEC	1	6		0.143	8th
1991	Don Williams	2	7		0.222	64	219	UEC	2	6		0.250	9th

Season	Coach	W	L	T	Pct.	PF	PA	Conf.	W	L	T	Pct.	Place
1992	Wendell Jeffries	2	7		0.222	123	227	UEC	1	7		0.125	8th
1993	Wendell Jeffries	3	6		0.333	97	164	UEC	3	5		0.375	5th
1994	Wendell Jeffries	0	9		0.000	63	299	UEC	0	8		0.000	9th
1995	Wendell Jeffries	1	8		0.111	89	238	UEC	1	7		0.125	8th
1996	Wendell Jeffries	0	9		0.000	68	340	UEC	0	8		0.000	9th
1997	Art Panka	1	8		0.111	72	305	UEC	1	6		0.143	7th
1998	Art Panka	3	6		0.333	113	218	UEC	3	4		0.429	6th
1999	Art Panka	2	7		0.222	129	297	UEC	2	5		0.286	8th
2000	Al Tamberelli	5	4		0.556	180	239	UEC	4	3		0.571	4th
2001	Al Tamberelli	0	9		0.000	14	294	UEC	0	6		0.000	11th
2002	Al Tamberelli	0	9		0.000	100	304	UEC	0	6		0.000	11th
2003	Al Tamberelli	1	8		0.111	116	251	UEC	0	6		0.000	11th
2004	Al Tamberelli	1	8		0.111	118	293	UEC	1	5		0.167	8th
2005	Al Tamberelli	1	8		0.111	100	212	UEC	1	5		0.167	9th
2006	Bill Bryant	1	8		0.111	62	373	UEC	1	5		0.167	9th
2007	Bill Bryant	0	9		0.000	63	382	UEC	0	6		0.000	11th
2008	Bill Bryant	2	7		0.222	100	295	UEC	1	5		0.167	9th
2009	Bill Bryant	0	9		0.000	85	386	UEC	0	6		0.000	10th
2010	Bill Bryant	0	9		0.000	47	398	UEC	0	6		0.000	7th
2011	Bill Bryant	0	9		0.000	25	470	UEC	0	6		0.000	7th
2012	Kurt Becker	0	9		0.000	51	437	UEC	0	6		0.000	7th
2013	Kurt Becker	1	8		0.111	141	376	UEC	0	6		0.000	7th
		503	528	57	0.489	14,779	16233		257	343	28	0.432	

EAST AURORA COACHES' RECORDS

Coach	Seasons	Years	Games	W	L	T	Pct.
Glen Thompson	17+	1925–42	167	105	51	11	0.662
Del Dufrain	18	1961–78	165	84	77	4	0.521
Joe Maze	7+	1942–49	68	32	29	7	0.522
Bill Bryant	6	2006–11	54	3	51		0.056
Al Tamberelli	6	2000–05	54	8	46		0.148
Art Court	6	1955–60	54	29	19	6	0.593
Don Griffin	5	1950–54	47	29	16	2	0.638
Wendell Jeffries	5	1992–96	45	6	39	0	0.133
Dick Schindel	5	1983–87	45	13	32	0	0.289
Art Panka	3	1997–99	27	6	21	0	0.222
Don Williams	3	1989–91	27	6	21		0.222
Billy Robinson	3	1920–22	26	11	14	1	0.442
W.F. Shirley	3	1907–09	26	11	9	6	0.538
Coach Rawlings	3	1904–06	25	16	8	1	0.660
Coach Lehman	3	1910–12	23	10	11	2	0.478
Billy Lindsey	2	1901–02	24	17	6	1	0.729
Pete Ventrelli	2	1981–82	19	12	7	0	0.632
John Wrenn	2	1979–80	19	13	6	0	0.684
Johnny Sabo	2	1923–24	18	5	10	3	0.361
Telford Mead	2	1916–17	15	10	3	2	0.733
Kurt Becker	2	2012–13	18	1	17	0	0.056
Coach Stewart	1	1900	11	9	0	2	0.909

Coach	Seasons	Years	Games	W	L	T	Pct.
Martin Shale	1	1915	10	9	1	0	0.900
Coach Dyer	1	1913	10	4	6	0	0.400
Ed Gavigan	1	1988	9	3	6		0.333
David Glascock	1	1919	9	5	4	0	0.556
Coach Harris	1	1899	9	8	1	0	0.889
Tom Reid	1	1895	9	3	2	4	0.556
George Stuart	1	1914	8	8	0	0	1.000
Coach Johnson	1	1903	8	3	5	0	0.375
Bill Hazard	1	1898	8	4	2	2	0.625
Tracey Cone	1	1918	7	2	5	0	0.286
Frank Darby	2	1893–94	6	5	0	1	0.917
T. Darby.H. Willard	1	1896	9	5	2	2	0.667
Unknown	1	1897	9	7	1	1	0.833

WEST AURORA SEASON RECORDS

Season	Coach	W	L	T	Pct.	PF	PA	Conf.	W	L	T	Pct.	Place
1893		0	1	0	0.000	0	28						
1894		5	0	0	1.000	110	14						
1895	George Nichols	2	3	0	0.400	34	36						
1896	Walter Garrey	6	1	2	0.778	88	36						
1897		4	0	1	0.900	102	12						
1898		0	3	2	0.200	11	54						
1899		4	3	0	0.571	29	71						
1900	George Wilbert	7	1	1	0.833	99	17						
1901	Claude Briggs	7	2	0	0.778	82	35						
1902	Claude Briggs	4	5	0	0.444	57	72						
1903	Claude Briggs	5	3	1	0.611	39	84						
1904	Claude Briggs	7	3	1	0.682	86	35						
1905	Claude Briggs	8	1	1	0.850	164	17						
1906	Claude Briggs	6	1	2	0.778	84	27						
1907	Claude Briggs	4	4	1	0.500	115	84						
1908	J.L. Stevenson	4	2	4	0.600	90	37						
1909	J.L. Stevenson	2	3	2	0.429	13	137						

Season	Coach	W	L	T	Pct.	PF	PA	Conf.	W	L	T	Pct.	Place
1910	Harry Smith	6	2	1	0.722	126	72						
1911	Elven Berkheiser	5	2	3	0.650	133	55						
1912	Elven Berkheiser	10	0	0	1.000	317	40						
1913	Byron Chappel	9	0	0	1.000	261	33						
1914	Byron Chappel	6	2	0	0.750	352	34						
1916	Carl Breneman	7	2	0	0.778	195	24	NIHSC	3	1	0	0.750	*
1917	George Bogard	3	4	1	0.438	56	92	NIHSC	1	3	1	0.300	5th
1918	J. McGough / R. Valentine	4	2	2	0.625	114	81	NIHSC	Season cancelled				
1919	George Bogard	7	2	0	0.778	161	39	NIHSC	5	1	0	0.833	1st (tie)
1920	Russell Courtwright	3	5	1	0.389	86	135	Big 7	3	3	0	0.500	3rd
1921	Ralph Fletcher	4	4	0	0.500	80	86	Big 7	4	2	0	0.667	3rd
1922	Ralph Fletcher	10	0	1	0.955	250	38	Big 7	6	0	0	1.000	1st
1923	Ralph Fletcher	5	1	1	0.786	47	31	Big 7	5	0	1	0.917	1st
1924	Ralph Fletcher	5	3	0	0.625	109	56	Big 7	3	3	0	0.500	4th
1925	Ralph Fletcher	2	5	1	0.313	40	105	Big 7	2	3	1	0.417	4th
1926	Ralph Fletcher	5	3	0	0.625	69	34	Big 7	4	2	0	0.667	3rd
1927	Ralph Fletcher	1	2	5	0.438	33	57	Big 7	0	2	4	0.333	5th
1928	Emil Schultz	5	3	0	0.625	83	72	Big 7	3	3	0	0.500	4th
1929	Emil Schultz	2	5	2	0.333	99	145	Big 6	0	3	2	0.200	5th
1930	Ralph Fletcher	3	6	0	0.333	64	124	Big 6	1	4	0	0.200	5th
1931	Ralph Fletcher	6	0	3	0.833	130	65	Big 6	2	0	3	0.700	1st
1932	Ralph Fletcher	2	4	3	0.389	60	81	Big 6	0	3	2	0.200	6th
1933	Ralph Fletcher	3	6	0	0.333	86	69	Big 6	0	5	0	0.000	6th
1934	Ralph Fletcher	3	4	2	0.444	78	83	Big 6	1	3	1	0.300	5th
1935	Marger Apsit	4	6	0	0.400	69	98	Big 7	2	4	0	0.333	5th
1936	Marger Apsit	9	0	0	1.000	144	38	Big 7	6	0	0	1.000	1st
1937	Marger Apsit	7	2	0	0.778	136	39	Big 7	4	2	0	0.667	2nd
1938	Marger Apsit	5	4	0	0.556	85	106	Big 7	3	3	0	0.500	4th

Season	Coach	W	L	T	Pct.	PF	PA	Conf.	W	L	T	Pct.	Place
1939	Marger Apsit	5	2	3	0.650	117	89	Big 7	3	2	1	0.583	3rd
1940	Marger Apsit	5	5	0	0.500	90	77	Big 8	4	3	0	0.571	3rd
1941	Marger Apsit	6	2	1	0.722	169	56	Big 8	3	1	1	0.700	2nd
1942	Marger Apsit	6	3	0	0.667	109	86	Big 8	5	2	0	0.714	3rd
1943	Leo Tilly	3	5	1	0.389	113	150	Big 8	1	5	1	0.214	8th
1944	Ken Zimmerman	3	6	0	0.333	129	139	Big 8	1	6	0	0.143	8th
1945	Ken Zimmerman	6	3	0	0.667	117	70	Big 8	2	2	0	0.500	3rd
1946	Ken Zimmerman	10	0	0	1.000	244	64	Big 8	7	0	0	1.000	**1st**
1947	Ken Zimmerman	4	4	2	0.500	59	92	Big 8	2	3	2	0.429	4th
1948	Ken Zimmerman	9	0	1	0.950	128	56	Big 8	6	0	1	0.929	**1st**
1949	Ken Zimmerman	9	1	0	0.900	283	153	Big 8	6	1	0	0.857	**1st**
1950	Ken Zimmerman	6	2	1	0.722	205	124	Big 8	5	2	0	0.714	3rd
1951	Ken Zimmerman	5	4	0	0.556	156	111	Big 8	5	2	0	0.714	2nd
1952	Ken Zimmerman	1	8	0	0.111	79	226	Big 8	1	6	0	0.143	7th
1953	Ken Zimmerman	3	6	0	0.333	81	158	Big 8	1	6	0	0.143	7th
1954	Ken Zimmerman	3	5	1	0.389	109	144	Big 8	3	4	0	0.429	4th
1955	Ken Zimmerman	4	5	0	0.444	104	140	Big 8	3	4	0	0.429	4th
1956	Ken Zimmerman	6	3	0	0.667	145	109	Big 8	4	3	0	0.571	4th
1957	Ken Zimmerman	4	4	1	0.500	152	148	Big 8	4	2	1	0.643	4th
1958	Ken Zimmerman	7	2	0	0.778	241	116	Big 8	5	2	0	0.714	3rd
1959	Ken Zimmerman	6	2	1	0.722	173	142	Big 8	5	2	0	0.714	2nd
1960	Ken Zimmerman	7	1	1	0.833	139	70	Big 8	7	0	0	1.000	**1st**
1961	Ken Zimmerman	3	6	0	0.333	45	118	Big 8	3	4	0	0.429	4th
1962	Ken Zimmerman	2	6	1	0.278	65	159	Big 8	1	5	1	0.214	8th
1963	Ken Zimmerman	1	8	0	0.111	79	191	UEC	0	7	0	0.000	8th
1964	Ken Zimmerman	4	4	1	0.500	132	119	UEC	3	4	0	0.429	5th
1965	Ken Zimmerman	6	3	0	0.667	119	107	UEC	5	2	0	0.714	3rd
1966	Ken Zimmerman	7	2	0	0.778	250	119	UEC	5	2	0	0.714	**1st (tie)**

Season	Coach	W	L	T	Pct.	PF	PA	Conf.	W	L	T	Pct.	Place
1967	Ken Zimmerman	3	6	0	0.333	84	145	UEC	2	5	0	0.286	5th
1968	Ken Zimmerman	3	6	0	0.333	131	208	UEC	3	4	0	0.429	6th
1969	Ken Zimmerman	3	6	0	0.333	114	177	UEC	2	5	0	0.286	6th
1970	Zimmerman / Zuege	7	2	0	0.778	156	135	UEC	5	2	0	0.714	2nd
1971	Dick Zuege	4	5	0	0.444	154	162	UEC	2	5	0	0.286	7th
1972	Dick Zuege	1	8	0	0.111	95	256	UEC	0	7	0	0.000	8th
1973	Dick Zuege	2	7	1	0.250	101	197	UEC	1	6	0	0.143	6th
1974	Dick Munn	2	7		0.222	126	213	UEC	1	6	0	0.143	7th
1975	Dick Munn	1	8		0.111	62	220	UEC	1	4	0	0.200	6th
1976	Dick Munn	3	6		0.333	114	197	UEC	1	4	0	0.200	5th
1977	Bob Quinn	5	4		0.556	125	82	UEC	2	3	0	0.400	3rd
1978	Bob Quinn	7	3		0.700	130	62	UEC	4	1	0	0.800	**1st**
1979	Bob Quinn	6	3		0.667	198	90	UEC	4	3		0.571	3rd
1980	Jim Czocher	4	5		0.444	180	178	UEC	4	3		0.571	4th
1981	Jim Czocher	2	7		0.222	69	148	UEC	2	5		0.286	6th
1982	John Wrenn	2	7		0.222	101	135	UEC	2	5		0.286	6th
1983	John Wrenn	8	2		0.800	240	95	UEC	7	0		1.000	**1st**
1984	John Wrenn	8	2		0.800	310	111	UEC	6	1		0.857	2nd
1985	Randy Melvin	0	9		0.000	70	245	UEC	0	7		0.000	8th
1986	Randy Melvin	2	7		0.222	155	204	UEC	2	5		0.286	5th
1987	Randy Melvin	5	4		0.556	121	183	UEC	4	3		0.571	4th
1988	Tim Cedarblad	5	4		0.556	122	88	UEC	4	3		0.571	3rd
1989	Tim Cedarblad	4	5		0.444	179	133	UEC	3	4		0.429	5th
1990	Tim Cedarblad	2	7		0.222	119	187	UEC	2	5		0.286	6th
1991	Tim Cedarblad	4	5		0.444	89	154	UEC	4	4		0.500	4th
1992	Bob Williams	1	8		0.111	85	231	UEC	1	7		0.125	8th
1993	Ira Jefferson	4	5		0.444	97	164	UEC	3	5		0.375	5th
1994	Ira Jefferson	8	3		0.727	279	182	UEC	6	2		0.750	2nd

Season	Coach	W	L	T	Pct.	PF	PA	Conf.	W	L	T	Pct.	Place
1995	Ira Jefferson	4	5		0.444	191	216	UEC	4	4		0.500	5th
1996	Ira Jefferson	4	5		0.444	159	194	UEC	3	5		0.375	7th
1997	Ira Jefferson	4	5		0.444	203	261	DVC	2	5		0.286	6th
1998	Ira Jefferson	5	4		0.556	142	187	DVC	3	4		0.429	4th
1999	Ira Jefferson	2	7		0.222	139	293	DVC	0	7		0.000	8th
2000	Mike Runge	2	7		0.222	113	249	DVC	2	5		0.286	6th
2001	Mike Runge	1	8		0.111	105	266	DVC	0	7		0.000	8th
2002	Mike Runge	3	6		0.333	170	298	DVC	1	6		0.143	8th
2003	Mike Runge	1	8		0.111	104	278	DVC	0	7		0.000	8th
2004	Mike Runge	5	4		0.556	177	202	DVC	3	4		0.429	5th
2005	Mike Runge	2	7		0.222	176	277	DVC	0	7		0.000	8th
2006	Buck Drach	2	7		0.222	127	246	DVC	0	7		0.000	8th
2007	Buck Drach	4	5		0.444	157	193	DVC	2	5		0.286	6th
2008	Buck Drach	3	6		0.333	196	289	DVC	1	6		0.143	6th
2009	Buck Drach	3	6		0.333	190	284	DVC	1	6		0.143	7th
2010	Buck Drach	4	5		0.444	212	242	DVC	2	5		0.286	6th
2011	Nate Eimer	4	5		0.444	195	196	DVC	2	5		0.286	6th
2012	Nate Eimer	3	6		0.333	225	235	DVC	2	5		0.286	6th
2013	Nate Eimer	1	8		0.111	115	341	DVC	0	7		0.000	8th
		525	485	61	.519	15,502	15,459		260	352	20	.427	

WEST AURORA COACHES' RECORDS

Coach	Seasons	Years	Games	W	L	T	Pct.
Ken Zimmerman	26+	1944–70*	239	125	104	10	0.544
Ralph Fletcher	12	1921–27, 1930–34	103	49	38	16	0.553
Marger Apsit	8	1935–42	75	47	24	4	0.653
Claude Briggs	7	1901–07	66	41	19	6	0.667
Ira Jefferson	7	1993–99	65	31	34	0	0.477
Mike Runge	6	2000–05	54	14	40	0	0.259
Buck Drach	5	2006–10	45	16	29	0	0.356
Tim Cedarblad	4	1988–91	36	15	21	0	0.417
Dick Zuege	3+	1970–73	36	14	21	1	0.403
Randy Melvin	3	1985–87	27	7	20	0	0.259
John Wrenn	3	1982–84	29	18	11	0	0.621
Bob Quinn	3	1977–79	28	18	10	0	0.643
Dick Munn	3	1974–76	27	6	21	0	0.222
Nate Eimer	3	2011–13	27	8	19	0	0.296
Elven Berkheiser	2	1911–12	20	15	2	3	0.825
Jim Czocher	2	1980–81	18	6	12	0	0.333
Byron Chappel	2	1913–14	17	15	2	0	0.882
George Bogard	2	1917, 1919	17	10	6	1	0.618
J.L. Stevenson	2	1908–09	17	6	5	6	0.529
Emil Schultz	2	1928–29	17	7	8	2	0.471
George Wilbert	1	1900	9	7	1	1	0.833
Carl Brenneman	1	1916	9	7	2	0	0.778

Coach	Seasons	Years	Games	W	L	T	Pct.
Harry Smith	1	1910	9	6	2	1	0.722
J.D. Fletcher	1	1915	9	5	3	1	0.611
Russell Courtwright	1	1920	9	3	5	1	0.389
Leo Tilly	1	1943	9	3	5	1	0.389
Bob Williams	1	1992	9	1	8	0	0.111
Walter Garrey	1	1896	9	6	1	2	0.813
George Nichols	1	1895	5	2	3	0	0.400
R.E. Valentine	partial	1918	5	3	1	1	0.700
John McGough	partial	1918	3	1	1	1	0.500
Unknown	5	1893–94, 1897–99	23	13	7	3	0.630

NORTHERN ILLINOIS HIGH SCHOOL CONFERENCE (BIG 6, BIG 7, BIG 8)

League Standings 1916 to 1962

1916	W	L
Freeport	4	1
West Aurora	3	1
Elgin	3	1
East Aurora	4	2
Rockford	2	3
Joliet	2	4
DeKalb	0	6

1917	W	L	T
Rockford	4	1	0
East Aurora	2	1	2
Elgin	3	2	0
Freeport	3	2	0
West Aurora	1	3	1
Joliet	0	4	1

*DeKalb withdrew from the conference.

1918
Season cancelled due to the Spanish flu pandemic of 1918

1919	W	L	T
West Aurora	5	1	0
East Aurora	5	1	0
Elgin	4	2	0
Rockford	4	2	0
DeKalb*	2	4	0
Freeport	1	5	0
Joliet	0	6	0

1920	W	L	T
Rockford	5	0	1
Elgin	5	0	1
West Aurora	3	3	0
DeKalb	3	3	0
East Aurora	2	4	0
Freeport	1	4	1
Joliet	0	5	1

1921	W	L	T
Elgin	6	0	0
Rockford	5	1	0
West Aurora	4	2	0
East Aurora	3	3	0
Joliet	1	4	1
DeKalb	0	4	2
Freeport	0	5	1

*DeKalb rejoined the conference.

1922	W	L	T
West Aurora	6	0	0
Rockford	5	1	0
East Aurora	3	3	0
DeKalb	3	3	0
Freeport	2	4	0
Joliet	1	5	0
Elgin	1	5	0

1923	W	L	T
West Aurora	5	0	1
Rockford	3	2	1
Elgin	3	2	1
Freeport	3	3	0
DeKalb	2	3	1
East Aurora	1	2	3
Joliet	0	5	1

1924	W	L	T
Freeport	6	0	0
Rockford	5	1	0
Elgin	4	2	0
West Aurora	3	3	0
Joliet	1	4	1
DeKalb	1	4	1
East Aurora	0	6	0

1925	W	L	T
Freeport	6	0	0
Elgin	5	1	0
East Aurora	3	3	0
West Aurora	2	3	1
Rockford	2	4	0
Joliet	1	4	1
DeKalb	0	4	2

1926	W	L	T
Elgin	5	1	0
Rockford	5	1	0
West Aurora	4	2	0
DeKalb	3	3	0
Freeport	1	3	2
East Aurora	1	4	1
Joliet	0	5	1

1927	W	L	T
East Aurora	5	0	1
Joliet	4	1	1
Elgin	2	1	3
Rockford	2	2	2
West Aurora	0	2	4
Freeport	1	3	2
DeKalb	0	5	1

1928	W	L	T
Elgin	6	0	0
Rockford	4	2	0
Joliet	4	2	0
West Aurora	3	3	0
East Aurora	2	3	1
DeKalb	0	4	2

1929	W	L	T
Elgin	5	0	0
East Aurora	4	1	0
Joliet	3	2	0
Rockford	1	3	1
West Aurora	0	3	2
Freeport	0	4	1

DeKalb withdrew from the conference again.

1930	W	L	T
Rockford	5	0	0
East Aurora	4	1	0
Joliet	2	2	1
Elgin	2	2	1
West Aurora	1	4	0
Freeport	0	5	0

1931	W	L	T
West Aurora	2	0	3
Elgin	3	1	1
East Aurora	3	2	0
Joliet	2	2	1
Freeport	1	3	1
Rockford	1	4	0

1932	W	L	T
Joliet	3	0	2
Rockford	2	0	3
Elgin	2	0	3
East Aurora	2	2	1
West Aurora	0	3	2
Freeport	0	4	1

1933	W	L	T
Joliet	3	0	2
Rockford	3	0	2
East Aurora	3	1	1
Freeport	2	3	0
Elgin	1	3	1
West Aurora	0	5	0

1934	W	L	T
Joliet	4	0	1
Rockford	4	0	1
Freeport	2	2	1
East Aurora	2	3	0
West Aurora	1	3	1
Elgin	0	5	0

1935	W	L	T
Joliet	5	1	0
Rockford	4	2	0
LaSalle-Peru*	4	2	0
East Aurora	4	2	0
West Aurora	2	4	0
Freeport	2	4	0
Elgin	0	6	0

LaSalle-Peru joined the conference.

1936	W	L	T
West Aurora	6	0	0
Freeport	4	2	0
East Aurora	3	2	1
Joliet	3	2	1
Elgin	2	3	1
Rockford	1	4	1
LaSalle-Peru	0	6	0

1937	W	L	T
Rockford	4	1	1
West Aurora	4	2	0
East Aurora	4	2	0
Freeport	3	2	1
Elgin	3	3	0
LaSalle-Peru	2	4	0
Joliet	0	6	0

1938	W	L	T
East Aurora	6	0	0
LaSalle-Peru	4	2	0
Rockford	4	2	0
West Aurora	3	3	0
Elgin	3	3	0
Freeport	1	5	0
Joliet	0	6	0

1939	W	L	T
LaSalle-Peru	6	0	0
Joliet	4	2	0
West Aurora	3	2	1
East Aurora	2	3	1
Elgin	1	2	3
Rockford	1	4	1
Freeport	1	5	0

1940	W	L	T
LaSalle-Peru	5	1	1
East Aurora	5	2	0
West Aurora	4	3	0
Joliet	4	3	0
Rockford West*	3	4	0
Elgin	2	3	2
Rockford East*	2	3	2
Freeport	0	6	1

Rockford split into Rockford East and Rockford West.

1941	W	L	T
Joliet	4	0	1
West Aurora	3	1	1
Elgin	3	2	0
LaSalle-Peru	2	2	0
East Aurora	1	4	0
Freeport	0	4	0

The Rockford schools disbanded at midseason due to a budget crisis that closed the schools.

1942	W	L	T
Rockford West	6	0	1
LaSalle-Peru	6	0	1
West Aurora	5	2	0
Rockford East	4	3	0
Freeport	2	5	0
East Aurora	2	4	1
Elgin	1	5	1
Joliet	1	6	0

1943	W	L	T
Rockford West	6	0	1
Freeport	4	2	1
Elgin	3	2	2
East Aurora	4	3	0
Joliet	3	4	0
Rockford East	2	4	1
LaSalle-Peru	1	4	2
West Aurora	1	5	1

1944	W	L	T
East Aurora	5	1	1
Joliet	4	2	1
Rockford East	4	3	0
Rockford West	4	3	0
LaSalle-Peru	3	4	0
Freeport	3	4	0
Elgin	2	3	2
West Aurora	1	6	0

1945	W	L	T
LaSalle-Peru	3	0	1
Elgin	2	1	1
West Aurora	2	2	0
East Aurora	1	3	0
Joliet	1	3	0

Freeport, Rockford East and Rockford West disbanded due to a polio outbreak.

1946	W	L	T
West Aurora	7	0	0
Rockford West	5	2	0
Rockford East	4	3	0
Joliet	3	4	0
LaSalle-Peru	3	4	0
Freeport	2	4	1
Elgin	2	5	0
East Aurora	1	5	1

1947	W	L	T
LaSalle-Peru	6	1	0
Joliet	5	1	1
Rockford East	5	1	1
West Aurora	2	3	2
Rockford West	2	4	1
East Aurora	2	4	1
Freeport	2	5	0
Elgin	1	6	0

1948	W	L	T
West Aurora	6	0	1
East Aurora	5	0	2
Joliet	5	2	0
Elgin	4	2	1
Freeport	2	4	1
Rockford East	2	5	0
LaSalle-Peru	1	5	1
Rockford West	0	7	0

1949	W	L	T
West Aurora	6	1	0
LaSalle-Peru	5	2	0
Elgin	5	2	0
Rockford West	4	2	1
East Aurora	3	3	1
Joliet	2	4	1
Freeport	1	5	1
Rockford East	0	7	0

1950	W	L	T
Elgin	7	0	0
Joliet	6	1	0
West Aurora	5	2	0
East Aurora	4	3	0
Rockford East	2	5	0
Rockford West	2	5	0
Freeport	2	5	0
LaSalle-Peru	0	7	0

1951	W	L	T
Joliet	6	0	1
West Aurora	5	2	0
East Aurora	5	2	0
Elgin	4	3	0
Rockford West	2	4	1
Freeport	2	5	0
LaSalle-Peru	2	5	0
Rockford East	1	6	0

1952	W	L	T
Joliet	6	0	1
Elgin	6	1	0
East Aurora	5	1	1
Rockford West	3	3	1
Rockford East	3	4	0
LaSalle-Peru	2	4	1
West Aurora	1	6	0
Freeport	0	7	0

1953	W	L	T
Rockford East	5	1	1
Elgin	5	1	1
LaSalle-Peru	4	2	1
Joliet	4	2	1
East Aurora	3	3	1
Rockford West	3	3	1
West Aurora	1	6	0
Freeport	0	7	0

1954	W	L	T
East Aurora	6	1	0
Elgin	5	1	1
LaSalle-Peru	5	1	1
West Aurora	3	4	0
Joliet	3	4	0
Rockford East	2	4	1
Rockford West	2	5	0
Freeport	0	6	1

1955	W	L	T
Elgin	7	0	0
East Aurora	5	1	1
Rockford East	5	2	0
West Aurora	3	4	0
Rockford West	2	4	1
LaSalle-Peru	2	5	0
Freeport	1	4	2
Joliet	1	6	0

1956	W	L	T
East Aurora	7	0	0
Elgin	6	1	0
Rockford East	5	2	0
West Aurora	4	3	0
Freeport	3	4	0
Rockford West	2	5	0
LaSalle-Peru	0	6	1
Joliet	0	6	1

1957	W	L	T
East Aurora	5	1	1
Elgin	5	2	0
LaSalle-Peru	5	2	0
West Aurora	4	2	1
Rockford East	3	3	1
Freeport	2	4	1
Joliet	2	5	0
Rockford West	0	7	0

1958	W	L	T
Elgin	7	0	0
LaSalle-Peru	6	1	0
West Aurora	5	2	0
Rockford East	3	4	0
East Aurora	2	4	1
Rockford West	2	4	1
Freeport	2	5	0
Joliet	0	7	0

1959	W	L	T
Freeport	6	0	1
West Aurora	5	2	0
Rockford East	3	3	1
LaSalle-Peru	3	3	1
Elgin	3	3	1
Rockford West	3	4	0
Joliet	2	5	0
East Aurora	1	6	0

1960	W	L	T
West Aurora	7	0	0
Freeport	5	1	1
LaSalle-Peru	5	2	0
East Aurora	4	2	1
Rockford East	3	4	0
Elgin	2	5	0
Rockford West	1	6	0
Auburn*	0	7	0

Rockford's Auburn replaced Joliet.

1961	W	L	T
Rockford East	7	0	0
Freeport	6	1	0
LaSalle-Peru	5	2	0
Elgin	3	4	0
West Aurora	3	4	0
East Aurora	2	4	1
Rockford West	1	5	1
Auburn*	0	7	0

Auburn went undefeated, but forfeited all games for using an ineligible player

1962	W	L	T
East Aurora	5	2	0
Auburn	5	2	0
Elgin	4	2	1
Rockford West	3	3	1
Rockford East	3	3	1
Freeport	2	3	2
LaSalle-Peru	2	5	0
West Aurora	1	5	1

UPSTATE 8 CONFERENCE

League Standings 1963 to 2013

1963	W	L	T
East Aurora	7	0	0
Naperville	6	1	0
Wheaton	5	2	0
DeKalb	4	3	0
Glenbard East	3	4	0
Elgin	2	5	0
Larkin	1	6	0
West Aurora	0	7	0

1964	W	L	T
East Aurora	6	0	1
Naperville	6	1	0
Wheaton C.*	5	2	0
Glenbard East	3	3	1
Larkin	3	4	0
West Aurora	3	4	0
Elgin	1	6	0
DeKalb	0	7	0

Wheaton became Wheaton Central.

1965	W	L	T
Wheaton C.	6	1	0
DeKalb	5	1	1
West Aurora	5	2	0
East Aurora	3	2	2
Larkin	3	3	1
Naperville	2	5	0
St. Charles*	1	6	0
Elgin	1	6	0

St. Charles replaced Glenbard East

1966	W	L	T
West Aurora	5	2	0
East Aurora	5	2	0
DeKalb	5	2	0
Larkin	4	2	1
Wheaton C.	3	3	1
Naperville	3	4	0
St. Charles	1	6	0
Elgin	1	6	0

1967	W	L	T
Larkin	7	0	0
Wheaton C.	6	1	0
Naperville	5	2	0
Elgin	3	4	0
West Aurora	2	5	0
East Aurora	2	5	0
DeKalb	2	5	0
St. Charles	1	6	0

1968	W	L	T
Wheaton C.	7	0	0
Naperville	5	2	0
Larkin	4	3	0
East Aurora	4	3	0
DeKalb	4	3	0
West Aurora	3	4	0
Elgin	1	6	0
St. Charles	0	7	0

1969	W	L	T
Larkin	7	0	0
Naperville	6	1	0
East Aurora	4	3	0
Elgin Central	3	3	1
DeKalb	3	4	0
Wheaton C.	2	5	0
West Aurora	2	5	0
St. Charles	0	6	1

1970	W	L	T
DeKalb	7	0	0
West Aurora	6	1	0
Wheaton C.	5	2	0
St. Charles	4	3	0
Naperville	3	4	0
Elgin Central	2	5	0
Larkin	1	6	0
East Aurora*	0	7	0

East Aurora went undefeated but forfeited all games for using an ineligible player.

1971	W	L	T
St. Charles	5	1	1
DeKalb	5	2	0
Wheaton C.	5	2	0
Larkin	4	3	0
Naperville	3	4	0
Elgin	2	4	1
West Aurora	2	5	0
East Aurora	1	6	0

1972	W	L	T
Elgin	6	1	0
Larkin	5	2	0
Naperville	5	2	0
St. Charles	4	3	0
East Aurora	4	3	0
Wheaton C.	3	4	0
DeKalb	1	6	0
West Aurora	0	7	0

1973	W	L	T
Naperville	6	1	0
Larkin	6	1	0
Wheaton C.	5	2	0
East Aurora	4	3	0
Elgin	4	3	0
DeKalb	1	6	0
West Aurora	1	6	0
St. Charles	1	6	0

1974	W	L
Naperville C.*	7	0
Larkin	5	2
East Aurora	4	3
DeKalb	4	3
Wheaton C.	4	3
Elgin Central	2	5
West Aurora	1	6
St. Charles	1	6

Naperville became Naperville Central.

1975	W	L
St. Charles	5	0
DeKalb	3	2
Larkin	2	3
Elgin	2	3
East Aurora	2	3
West Aurora	1	4

Wheaton Central and Naperville Central withdrew from the conference.

1976	W	L
Elgin	4	1
East Aurora	4	1
Larkin	3	2
DeKalb	2	3
West Aurora	1	4
St. Charles	1	4

1977	W	L
Elgin	5	0
Larkin	3	2
West Aurora	2	3
St. Charles	2	3
DeKalb	2	3
East Aurora	1	4

1978	W	L
West Aurora	4	1
St. Charles	3	2
Larkin	3	2
Elgin	3	2
East Aurora	2	3
DeKalb	0	5

1979	W	L
Larkin	7	0
St. Charles	6	1
West Aurora	4	3
East Aurora	4	3
DeKalb	3	4
Streamwood*	2	5
Lake Park*	2	5
Elgin	0	7

Streamwood and Lake Park joined the conference.

1980	W	L
DeKalb	6	1
East Aurora	6	1
Larkin	6	1
West Aurora	4	3
St. Charles	3	4
Streamwood	2	5
Lake Park	1	6
Elgin	0	7

1981	W	L
DeKalb	6	1
Larkin	5	2
Streamwood	5	2
East Aurora	4	3
Lake Park	3	4
West Aurora	2	5
St. Charles	2	5
Elgin	1	6

1982	W	L
DeKalb	5	2
East Aurora	5	2
Lake Park	5	2
Larkin	4	3
Elgin	3	4
West Aurora	2	5
Streamwood	2	5
St. Charles	2	5

1983	W	L
West Aurora	7	0
Lake Park	5	2
DeKalb	5	2
East Aurora	4	3
Streamwood	3	4
Larkin	2	5
Elgin	2	5
St. Charles	0	7

1984	W	L
Elgin	7	0
West Aurora	6	1
Larkin	5	2
DeKalb	4	3
Lake Park	3	4
St. Charles	2	5
Streamwood	1	6
East Aurora	0	7

1985	W	L
St. Charles	7	0
Larkin	6	1
Elgin	5	2
Streamwood	3	4
Lake Park	3	4
East Aurora	2	5
DeKalb	2	5
West Aurora	0	7

1986	W	L
Lake Park	7	0
St. Charles	6	1
Larkin	4	3
Elgin	4	3
West Aurora	2	5
East Aurora	2	5
DeKalb	2	5
Streamwood	1	6

1987	W	L
Streamwood	7	0
Lake Park	5	2
Elgin	5	2
West Aurora	4	3
DeKalb	4	3
Larkin	2	5
St. Charles	1	6
East Aurora	0	7

1988	W	L
Streamwood	6	1
St. Charles	5	2
West Aurora	4	3
Lake Park	4	3
Larkin	3	4
East Aurora	2	5
DeKalb	2	5
Elgin	2	5

1989	W	L
DeKalb	6	1
Streamwood	4	3
Larkin	4	3
Lake Park	4	3
West Aurora	3	4
St. Charles	3	4
Elgin	3	4
East Aurora	1	6

1990	W	L
Larkin	6	1
Streamwood	5	2
Elgin	5	2
Lake Park	4	3
St. Charles	3	4
West Aurora	2	5
DeKalb	2	5
East Aurora	1	6

1991	W	L
St. Charles	7	1
Waubonsie Valley*	6	2
Elgin	5	3
West Aurora	4	4
Larkin**	3	4
Lake Park	3	5
DeKalb	3	5
Streamwood**	2	5
East Aurora	2	6

*Waubonsie Valley joined the conference.

**Larkin-Streamwood cancelled by teachers' strike.

1992	W	L
Waubonsie Valley	8	0
St. Charles	7	1
Elgin	6	2
Streamwood	4	4
Larkin	4	4
Lake Park	3	5
DeKalb	2	6
West Aurora	1	7
East Aurora	1	7

1993	W	L
St. Charles	8	0
Lake Park	7	1
Waubonsie Valley	6	2
Larkin	5	3
West Aurora	3	5
East Aurora	3	5
Streamwood	2	6
Elgin	2	6
DeKalb	0	8

1994	W	L
Waubonsie Valley	7	1
West Aurora	6	2
St. Charles	6	2
Lake Park	6	2
Larkin	4	4
Elgin	4	4
DeKalb	2	6
Streamwood	1	7
East Aurora	0	8

1995	W	L
St. Charles	7	1
Lake Park	7	1
Larkin	6	2
Waubonsie Valley	5	3
West Aurora	4	4
Elgin	3	5
DeKalb	2	6
Streamwood	1	7
East Aurora	1	7

1996	W	L
St. Charles	8	0
Larkin	6	2
Lake Park	5	3
Elgin	5	3
Waubonsie Valley	4	4
Streamwood	4	4
West Aurora	3	5
DeKalb	1	7
East Aurora	0	8

1997	W	L
Waubonsie Valley	7	0
St. Charles	6	1
Streamwood	4	3
Larkin	4	3
Lake Park	4	3
Elgin	2	5
East Aurora	1	6
DeKalb	0	7

*West Aurora withdrew from the conference.

1998	W	L
St. Charles	7	0
Streamwood	6	1
Lake Park	5	2
Larkin	5	2
Waubonsie Valley	4	3
East Aurora	3	4
Bartlett*	2	5
Elgin	2	5
DeKalb	1	6

*Bartlett joined the conference.

1999	W	L
Lake Park	7	0
St. Charles	6	1
Larkin	5	2
Bartlett	4	3
Neuqua Valley*	4	3
Elgin	3	4
Waubonsie Valley	3	4
East Aurora	2	5
DeKalb	1	6
Streamwood	0	7

*Neuqua Valley joined the conference.

2000	W	L
Elgin	6	1
Bartlett	5	2
St. Charles East	5	2
East Aurora	4	3
Waubonsie Valley	4	3
Lake Park	3	4
Neuqua Valley	3	4
Streamwood	3	4
Larkin	2	5
DeKalb	0	7

2001	W	L
Bartlett	6	1
Lake Park	6	1
St. Charles East*	5	1
Elgin	5	2
Waubonsie Valley	4	2
Streamwood	3	4
DeKalb	2	4
St. Charles North*	2	4
Larkin	1	5
Neuqua Valley	1	5
East Aurora	0	6

*St. Charles became St. Charles East, and St. Charles North joined the conference.

2002	W	L
Bartlett	6	1
Lake Park	6	1
Neuqua Valley	5	1
St. Charles North	5	1
St. Charles East	4	2
Larkin	3	3
Streamwood	3	4
Elgin	2	5
Waubonsie Valley	1	5
DeKalb	0	6
East Aurora	0	6

2003	W	L
Bartlett	6	0
Neuqua Valley	6	1
Lake Park	5	1
Larkin	5	1
St. Charles North	5	2
Streamwood	3	4
Waubonsie Valley	2	4
DeKalb	1	5
Elgin	1	5
St. Charles East	1	6
East Aurora	0	6

2004	W	L
Neuqua Valley	7	0
St. Charles North	7	0
Bartlett	5	1
Waubonsie Valley	4	2
Lake Park	3	3
Larkin	3	3
St. Charles East	3	4
East Aurora	1	5
Elgin	1	5
Streamwood	1	6
DeKalb	0	6

2005	W	L
Neuqua Valley	6	0
Bartlett	5	1
St. Charles East	5	1
St. Charles North	5	2
Waubonsie Valley	4	2
Lake Park	3	3
Elgin	3	4
Larkin	2	5
East Aurora	1	5
DeKalb	1	6
Streamwood	0	6

2006	W	L
Neuqua Valley	6	0
St. Charles East	5	1
Larkin	5	2
St. Charles North	5	2
Bartlett	4	2
Lake Park	3	3
Waubonsie Valley	3	3
Elgin	2	5
East Aurora	1	5
Streamwood	1	5
South Elgin*	0	7

2007	W	L
St. Charles East	5	1
Waubonsie Valley	5	1
Neuqua Valley	5	2
Bartlett	4	2
St. Charles North	4	2
Larkin	4	3
South Elgin	3	3
Lake Park	3	4
Elgin	1	5
Streamwood	1	6
East Aurora	0	6

*South Elgin replaced DeKalb.

2008	W	L
Bartlett	6	0
St. Charles East	5	1
Waubonsie Valley	5	1
St. Charles North	4	2
Lake Park	4	3
Larkin	3	4
Neuqua Valley	3	4
South Elgin	2	4
East Aurora	1	5
Elgin	1	5
Streamwood	1	6

2009	W	L
St. Charles East	7	0
Lake Park	6	1
Waubonsie Valley	5	2
South Elgin	4	2
St. Charles North	4	3
Neuqua Valley	3	3
Elgin	3	3
Larkin	2	4
Bartlett	1	5
East Aurora	0	6
Streamwood	0	6

2010	W	L
Valley Division		
Bartlett	5	1
Waubonsie Valley	5	1
Neuqua Valley	4	2
South Elgin	4	2
Lake Park	2	4
Metea Valley*	1	5
East Aurora	0	6
River Division		
Geneva*	6	0
Batavia*	4	2
Elgin	4	2
St. Charles North	3	3
St. Charles East	2	4
Larkin	2	4
Streamwood	0	6

Metea Valley, Geneva and Batavia joined the conference, which split into two divisions.

2011	W	L
Valley Division		
Bartlett	6	0
Waubonsie Valley	5	1
Lake Park	3	3
Neuqua Valley	3	3
South Elgin	3	3
Metea Valley	1	5
East Aurora	0	6
River Division		
Batavia	6	0
Geneva	5	1
St. Charles East	3	3
Streamwood	3	3
St. Charles North	2	4
Larkin	2	4
Elgin	0	6

2012	W	L
Valley Division		
Neuqua Valley	6	0
Waubonsie Valley	5	1
Bartlett	4	2
Lake Park	3	3
South Elgin	2	4
Metea Valley	1	5
East Aurora	0	6
River Division		
Batavia	6	0
St. Charles East	5	1
St. Charles North	4	2
Geneva	3	3
Streamwood	2	4
Larkin	1	5
Elgin	0	6

2013	W	L
Valley Division		
Neuqua Valley	6	0
Waubonsie Valley	5	1
Metea Valley	4	2
South Elgin	3	3
Bartlett	2	4
West Chicago*	1	5
East Aurora	0	6
River Division		
Batavia	6	0
Geneva	5	1
St. Charles East	4	2
St. Charles North	3	3
Larkin	2	4
Streamwood	1	5
Elgin	0	6

West Chicago replaced Lake Park.

APPENDIX I

DUPAGE VALLEY CONFERENCE

League Standings 1997 to 2013

1997	W	L	1998	W	L	1999	W	L
Naperville Central	6	1	Wheaton-W. South	7	0	Naperville Central	7	0
Naperville North	6	1	Naperville North	6	1	Wheaton-W. South	5	2
Wheaton-W. South	6	1	Naperville Central	5	2	Naperville North	5	2
Glenbard North	4	3	Wheaton North	3	4	Glenbard East	4	3
Glenbard East	3	4	West Aurora	3	4	Wheaton North	4	3
West Aurora*	2	5	Glenbard East	3	4	Glenbard North	2	5
Wheaton North	1	6	Glenbard North	1	6	West Chicago	1	6
West Chicago	0	7	West Chicago	0	7	West Aurora	0	7

West Aurora replaced Glenbard South.

2000	W	L	2001	W	L	2002	W	L
Naperville Central	7	0	Naperville Central	7	0	Wheaton North	7	0
Naperville North	6	1	Wheaton-W. South	6	1	Naperville North	6	1
Glenbard North	4	3	Wheaton North	4	3	Naperville Central	4	3
Wheaton-W. South	4	3	Glenbard North	4	3	West Chicago	3	4
Glenbard East	3	4	Naperville North	3	4	Wheaton-W. South	3	4
West Aurora	2	5	Glenbard East	3	4	Glenbard North	2	5
Wheaton North	1	6	West Chicago	1	6	Glenbard East	2	5
West Chicago	1	6	West Aurora	0	7	West Aurora	1	6

2003	W	L
Naperville North	7	0
Glenbard North	6	1
Wheaton-W. South	5	2
Naperville Central	3	4
Wheaton North	3	4
Glenbard East	3	4
West Chicago	1	6
West Aurora	0	7

2004	W	L
Naperville North	7	0
Naperville Central	6	1
Wheaton-W. South	5	2
Glenbard North	4	3
West Aurora	3	4
Wheaton North	2	5
West Chicago	1	6
Glenbard East	0	7

2005	W	L
Wheaton-W. South	7	0
Naperville North	6	1
Naperville Central	5	2
Glenbard North	4	3
West Chicago	3	4
Wheaton North	2	5
Glenbard East	1	6
West Aurora	0	7

2006	W	L
Wheaton-W. South	7	0
Naperville Central	6	1
Naperville North	5	2
Glenbard North	4	3
Wheaton North	3	4
Glenbard East	2	5
West Chicago	1	6
West Aurora	0	7

2007	W	L
Wheaton-W. South	7	0
Naperville North	6	1
Naperville Central	5	2
Glenbard North	4	3
Wheaton North	3	4
West Aurora	2	5
West Chicago	1	6
Glenbard East	0	7

2008	W	L
Naperville North	7	0
Wheaton-W. South	6	1
Glenbard North	5	2
Naperville Central	4	3
Wheaton North	3	4
West Aurora	1	6
West Chicago	1	6
Glenbard East	1	6

2009	W	L
Wheaton-W. South	7	0
Glenbard North	6	1
Naperville Central	5	2
Wheaton North	4	3
Naperville North	3	4
Glenbard East	2	5
West Aurora	1	6
West Chicago	0	7

2010	W	L
Wheaton-W. South	7	0
Glenbard North	6	1
Wheaton North	5	2
Naperville North	4	3
Naperville Central	3	4
West Aurora	2	5
Glenbard East	1	6
West Chicago	0	7

2011	W	L
Wheaton-W. South	6	1
Wheaton North	6	1
Naperville Central	5	2
Glenbard North	4	3
Naperville North	4	3
West Aurora	2	5
West Chicago	1	6
Glenbard East	0	7

2012	W	L	2013	W	L
Glenbard North	7	0	Glenbard North	7	0
Wheaton North	6	1	Wheaton North	5	2
Naperville Central	4	3	Wheaton-W. South	5	2
Naperville North	4	3	Naperville Central	4	3
Wheaton-W. South	4	3	Naperville North	4	3
West Aurora	2	5	Lake Park*	2	5
Glenbard East	1	6	Glenbard East	1	6
West Chicago	0	7	West Aurora	0	7

Lake Park replaced West Chicago.

BIBLIOGRAPHY

Newspapers

Aurora Beacon-News
Aurora Daily Beacon
Chicago Tribune
The Daily Herald
Freeport Journal-Standard
The News-Gazette

Books and Articles

Camp, Walter, ed., *Spalding's Official Football Guide.* New York: American Sports Publishing Company, 1893–1921.

East Aurora High School. *Speculum Yearbook.* Aurora, IL. Multiple years, 1914–2013.

Edwards, Jim and Wynette Edwards. *Aurora: A Diverse People Build Their City.* Charleston, SC: Arcadia Publishing, 1998.

Ghrist, John Russell. *Valley Voices: A Radio History.* Carpentersville, IL: Crossroads Communications, 1996.

Higgins, Jo Fredell. *Postcard History Series: Aurora.* Charleston, SC: Arcadia Publishing, 2006.

Pruter, Robert. *The Birth of High School Football in Illinois.* Self published.

———. *A Century of Intersectional and Interstate Football Contests.* Self published.

———. *The Greatest High School Football Rivalry in Illinois: Englewood vs. Hyde Park.* Self published.

West Aurora High School. *Eos Yearbook.* Aurora, IL. Multiple years, 1911–2013.

Websites

www.ancestry.com
www.e-yearbooks.com
www.ihsa.org
www.newspapers.com

Interviews

Kurt Becker, East Aurora Class of 1977, Head Football Coach, 2012–
Ed Colton, East Aurora Class of 1945
Del Dufrain, Head Football Coach, East Aurora, 1961–78
Nate Eimer, West Aurora Class of 2001, Head Football Coach, 2011–
John Jaros, Aurora Historical Society
Steve "Benny" Kenyon, East Aurora, Class of 1968
Neal Ormond, West Aurora Class of 1958
Mike Runge, Head Football Coach, West Aurora, 2000–05
Bob Schindel, East Aurora Class of 1957
Dick Schindel, East Aurora Class of 1966, Head Football Coach 1983–87
Jim Stone, West Aurora Class of 1980
Gary Stutzman, East Aurora Class of 1961
John Wrenn, Head Football Coach, East Aurora 1979-80, West Aurora 1982–84

INDEX

H

I

J

ABOUT THE AUTHOR

S teve Solarz holds undergraduate and graduate degrees from Northern Illinois University and has lived in the city of Aurora, Illinois, for his entire adult life. During that time, he has been a human resources executive, a local high school football fan, a youth baseball and basketball coach, an unsuccessful candidate for school board and a history buff. This is his first book.

CPSIA information can be obtained
at www.ICGtesting.com
Printed in the USA
LVHW080151251119
637818LV00018BC/1032/P